Unlocking the Prison Muse
The inspirations and effects of prisoners' writing in Britain

Julian Broadhead was the co-founder and editor of *Prison Writing* journal from 1992-2002. A probation officer for almost twenty-five years, he has been a regular contributor to the *New Law Journal* since 1992 and has also written for *The Times*. In 2002 he was awarded a Cropwood Fellowship at the Institute of Criminology, Cambridge University, where he began the research that led to *Unlocking The Prison Muse*.

Cover image by Tony Bashforth

Unlocking the Prison Muse

The inspirations and effects of prisoners' writing in Britain

Julian Broadhead

Cambridge Academic

Imprints include:
Liverpool Academic Press
Liverpool Business Publishing
Tudor Educational

© 2006 Julian Broadhead

First edition published by Cambridge Academic, The Studio, High Green, Gt. Shelford, Cambridge CB2 5EG.

The rights of Julian Broadhead to be identified as the author of this work have been asserted by him in accordance with the Copyright, Designs and Patents Act 1988.

All rights reserved. No part of this publication may be reproduced, stored in a retrieval system, or transmitted in any form or by any means, electronic, mechanical, photocopying, recording, or otherwise without prior permission of Cambridge Academic at:
The Studio, High Green, Gt. Shelford, Cambridge. CB2 5EG

ISBN 1-903-499-267

The contents of this publication are provided in good faith and neither The Author nor The Publisher can be held responsible for any errors or omissions contained herein. Any person relying upon the information must independently satisfy himself or herself as to the safety or any other implications of acting upon such information and no liability shall be accepted either by The Author or The Publisher in the event of reliance upon such information nor for any damage or injury arising from any interpretation of its contents. This publication may not be used in any process of risk assessment.

Contents

Prologue	i
1] The Governor Was Strong upon the Regulations Act	1
2] Life Stories	21
3] Facts, Fictions, Poems and Plays	55
4] Inner Forces	85
5] Time and Opportunity	113
6] Inhibitions	136
7] Effects	152
8] Those Who Oppose	180
9] Epilogue	191
Bibliography	196
Footnote Reference	201
Index	232

Prologue

"My own drug of choice had now become the written word. Once I discovered that people in the outside world were actually interested in reading what I had to say, there was no stopping me. I began to write every day ...."
Razor Smith
A Few Kind Words and a Loaded Gun, 2004

"The cage is not an idyllic place to live, but it is ideal to write. The keeper becomes a patron of the arts, so to speak, and there are no neon lights to distract. After all, what self-respecting sociopath could sit down outside for two years and write a book?"
Edward Bunker
Scribbling in the Cage, Prison Writing 8, 1996

"I have a new stimulus to sustain me. I labour away with a pen, and enjoy it all as much as the old power-play of the convict-criminal world."
John McVicar
McVicar by Himself, 1974

"You can imprison a man bodily but I don't think you should imprison his soul or his pen."
Jonathan Aitken
Interview with author, 2002

Unlocking The Prison Muse

Prologue

What is it about imprisonment that inspires men and women to write? Is it about having the time, the solitude, being away from the demands and distractions of the outside world? Do the anxieties and tensions of prison life stimulate creativity, raise the adrenaline and cause prisoners of all types to lay out their souls onto the printed page? Or is the practice of writing in prison merely what inmates call a 'bird-killer'- a way of getting through a sentence, of channelling energy and emotion, of combating the relentless grind and stultifying routine of incarceration? Is it a quest for redemption, for recognition, for self-esteem, an attempt to make something positive out of a negative situation?

Nelson Mandela, speaking of the constructive ways he passed his time in captivity, said "Nothing was as encouraging to a prisoner as to know his life was not being wasted." [1] The American crime novelist Edward Bunker, who spent many years in reform schools and penitentiaries, has stated that he would never have written if he had not gone to prison. His quest for publication, which would take seventeen years and six rejected novels, began in San Quentin when he read a magazine extract of a book written by Caryl Chessman, a Death Row inmate: "It blew my mind! I'd never imagined that a convict could write something – and get it published in a magazine. I was a reader but I wasn't well-read at that time … And I said man, if this guy can do it, why can't I? Then as I read more and more, I found out that, historically, many writers had been in prison." [2]

Indeed, some of the classic works of literature were created by writers incarcerated as criminals. The 6th Century philosopher Boethus, awaiting execution in Rome, wrote *De Consolatione Philosophiae*, which would become one of the most influential books of the Middle Ages. In England, Sir Thomas Malory, accused of rape, is believed to have completed the manuscript of *Morte D'Arthur* in prison, where he died soon afterwards. John Bunyan, arrested for preaching following the Restoration of Charles II, spent twelve years in Bedford Gaol where he wrote his spiritual autobiography *Grace Abounding to the Chief of Sinners* and, locked up again for a shorter period, began *The Pilgrim's Progress*.

Prologue

In Spain, Cervantes wrote parts of *Don Quixote* behind the bars of a debtors' jail and Frenchmen Voltaire, Verlaine and the Marquis de Sade did not let spells of imprisonment deter them from literary endeavour. More recently, Dostoevsky, Genet and Solzhenitsyn discovered their subject matter in prison and, as a result, began to write with distinction.

Although convict life was of great fascination to earlier novelists such as Daniel Defoe, Henry Fielding and Charles Dickens, in modern British fiction the prison has been largely ignored. It is more than twenty years since G.F. Newman's *Law And Order* trilogy and in the intervening period no other writer has come close to capturing the atmosphere or dynamics that Newman achieved in *The Prisoner's Tale*. No British prisoner or ex-prisoner to date has published a significant novel based in a custodial setting, in the way that Edward Bunker and Chester Himes have done in the USA.[3] Here, the only ex-convicts to have made a comparable impression in print have been John McVicar and Jimmy Boyle, both in the genre of autobiography. [4]

But if prison is the crucible that fires the imagination, stirs the soul and draws forth the creativity of the imprisoned, what becomes of the words they write? Is anything actually achieved by the publication of prisoners' work? Can dedication to writing improve prisoners, assist them to come to terms with their crimes and lead to positive changes in behaviour? Can prisoners' writing influence public or political awareness of prisons, and lead to penal reform?

Opportunities for prisoners to see their prose or poetry in print, or to have their plays performed outside the walls, are limited unless, as in a small number of cases, they are already established writers . Nonetheless, over the past fifty or so years a surprising number of people who first took up the pen in prison have gone on to enjoy success in varying degrees. My aim in this book has been to gain insight into the creative process that leads from prison to the printed page, to consider the inspirations and motivations, the facilitating and disabling factors and, perhaps most importantly, the effects of prisoners' writing on themselves and on wider society.

Apart from passing reference to Edward Bunker and the exception of Brendan Behan, I have focused exclusively on the work of British prisoners convicted under the criminal law, in particular the ones for whom writing has brought opportunity to change. Thus, those who consider themselves political prisoners have not been included. Ion Davies wrote in *Writers in Prison*, "Most writing out of prison is necessarily by privileged prisoners – not only are they literate but in a large number of cases they are there for political, religious or other ideological reasons which set them apart from the everyday criminal."[5] Davies concentrates on writers such as Solzhenitsyn, Wole Soyinka and Dostoevsky. He mentions the Americans Chester Himes and Jack Henry Abbott, also Oscar Wilde, but ignores all modern contributors to British prison literature. Those who comprise that group are the subject of *Unlocking the Prison Muse*.

The publication of books by convicted criminals can create controversy. The tabloid press is often inconsistent in its attitude, provoking outrage and protest while at the same time paying for serialisation or extract rights. Moral issues that relate to profiting from crime, to victims' rights and to what constitutes public interest are as topical as they are difficult to determine unequivocally. In the 1990s there was a glut of ghost-written autobiographies published under the names of notorious criminals, many associated with the London gangs of the 1960s. Some attracted a lot of coverage in the tabloid and magazine press and brought demands for a change in the law to prevent criminals profiting by writing about their crimes. While ghost-written books do not come within the scope of this study, victim considerations and personal benefits most certainly do.

The seed of an idea for this book began during the ten years I edited *Prison Writing*, a journal published on a non-profit-making basis and aimed at encouraging prisoners to write for publication. In 2002, a Cropwood Fellowship at the Cambridge University Institute of Criminology allowed me to develop the idea further.

There have been two main areas of research, the first being the published work of prisoners and ex-prisoners; the second, what they and others have said about their writing in interviews, essays, letters, press articles, reviews and interviews.

I am grateful to nineteen men and one woman who were serving prison sentences in 2002 for answering a series of questions about their interest in writing, in correspondence and interview. All had been published, although their experiences were varied. Some were avid contributors to prison magazines; some had won awards in the annual Koestler or Prison Reform Trust writing competitions. Two had written occasional articles for national newspapers and stories for outside magazines; one had had a play performed at the Edinburgh Fringe. Some of this group are identified by name within the text; others have chosen anonymity. As well as the works and opinions of prisoners past and present, I have drawn on numerous other sources for the benefit of their experiences and opinions. My thanks are due to the following either for their specific help with this book or earlier contributions to *Prison Writing* that helped to inspire it:

Paul Agutter, Jonathan Aitken, Martin Amis, Clare Barstow, Rachel Billington, Alex Broadhead, Edward Bunker, Duncan Campbell, Hugh Collins, Steve France, Carlo Gébler and his students in HMP Maghaberry, Bryan Gibson, Heather Harker, Albert Hattersley, George Hayes, Tony Hoare, Ian Kentzer, Laura Kerr, Peter J. Lewis, Professor Alison Liebling, Paul Lumsden, Dr. Shadd Maruna, John McVicar, James Morton, Judge Michael Murphy QC, Professor Mike Nellis, Michael Pavlovic, Gill Platt-Hopkin, Anna Reynolds, Bruce Reynolds, Diana Ruthven, Will Self, Dr Stephen Shaw, Noel 'Razor' Smith, Jane Spikings, Clive Stafford-Smith, Simon Tasker, Sir Stephen Tumim, Valerio Viccei, Jimmy Walker, Malcolm Watson, Tim Wickham, Professor Brian Williams, Matthew Williams, Reg Wilson, John Wrigglesworth, and the staff of the Radzinowicz Library at the Institute of Criminology, Cambridge University.

Julian Broadhead
Sheffield, 2006

1] The Governor was strong upon the Regulations Act

De Profundis

Oscar Wilde's name is synonymous with prison literature. The playwright, poet, novelist and wit was one of the most famous men of the late Victorian era and at the peak of his fame when he was sentenced to two years hard labour in 1895, for gross indecency. He never recovered from the experience and died in 1900, aged only forty six, but while in prison he wrote what some critics consider to be his most important work - *De Profundis*, a 30,000 word expurgatory letter to his *homme fatale*, Lord Alfred Douglas. Soon after his release, living in voluntary exile in France, Wilde penned *The Ballad of Reading Gaol*, a poem which, more than a century later, is probably the most widely known work of prison writing, at least from the British Isles.

De Profundis, written in Reading between January and March 1897, was intended as an attempt to explain the conduct that had led to his downfall. It might never have come about had Wilde not been visited in Pentonville, soon after he was sentenced, by an acquaintance, Robert Burdon Haldane MP. Haldane, who happened to be a member of a Home Office committee investigating prison conditions, was Wilde's first visitor. He saw him in his cell, but when he entered Wilde was so embarrassed by his situation and so depressed by the privations and brutalities of prison that he could not bring himself to speak. Haldane got to the point. He told him that he had failed to use his literary gift to its true potential and that he had been too keen on a life of pleasure to make any subject his own. In the circumstances he now found himself he had the opportunity to do that and his fall could be a blessing to his literary vocation, if he could only realise it.[1]

Wilde burst into tears and told his visitor that during his time in prison – a period of only weeks at that stage - he had realised the folly of his earlier life and he would now try to make amends in the only way he knew how. He asked Haldane if he could use his influence to get him books to read and pen and ink so that he could write. The only books he had were the Bible and *Pilgrim's*

1

Progress - the latter allowed by the authorities because of its Christian message, rather than its genesis in Bedford Gaol.

Richard Burdon Haldane's representations led to Wilde being allowed to receive books, sent in by another friend, but it would be some time before he summoned enough energy to use the pen and ink to begin his letter to Lord Alfred Douglas. Had Haldane, later to be Lord Chancellor and Secretary of State for War, not visited Oscar Wilde in the depths of his misery and had he not urged him to use his talent to its potential, the canon of prison literature might be all the poorer.

The letter to Douglas, later published as *De Profundis*, which begins "Dear Bosie, After long and fruitless waiting I have decided to write to you …"[2] was written on twenty folio sheets, each of four pages, on blue, ruled prison paper stamped with the Royal Arms. He was allowed only one sheet at a time and when it was full it was removed and replaced by a new one. After difficulties earlier in his sentence, when he was forced to work the treadmill and punished for petty transgressions of the rules, Wilde had found a sympathiser in the governor of Reading Gaol, Major J.O. Nelson.

Wilde's intention was to send the letter by post to his friend and literary executor, Robert Ross. He told Ross, "… you will see the psychological explanation of a course of conduct that from the outside seems a combination of absolute idiocy with vulgar bravado. Some day the truth will have to be known – not necessarily in my lifetime … but I am not prepared to sit in the grotesque gallery they put me into for all time … I do not defend my conduct; I explain it."[3]

For all his compassion, the Reading governor was not prepared to let the eighty-page letter out of his gaol without the agreement of the Prison Commission. He sought advice and was told it could be handed to Wilde immediately prior to his release, to do with as he wished – an unusual privilege for the times. On the day, Wilde collected the letter and when he arrived in Dieppe the following morning he gave it to his friend Ross. Extracts of *De Profundis* were published by Robert Ross in 1905, but the first unabridged edition did not appear until 1949, mainly because of objections from Lord Alfred Douglas, who described it as a "filthy and blasphemous screed … which consisted largely of virulent abuse of myself and others then living, and which contained an apology for every kind of vice and abomination."[4]

Oscar Wilde's descent from the salons of London and New York to a prison cell began when he sued for libel against Douglas's father, the Marquess of Queensberry. He lost and as a result of evidence given during the hearing he was prosecuted under the criminal law. The vehemence of Alfred Douglas's opposition to *De Profundis* was not surprising because Wilde, while going some way towards accepting his own failings, although not his guilt, was at pains to point out those of his equally narcissistic but intellectually inferior lover. He wrote: "I blame myself for having allowed you to bring me to utter and discreditable financial ruin … Most of all I blame myself for the entire ethical degradation I allowed you to bring on me."[5]

De Profundis has been described as "a conundrum of conflicting emotions, a sweet and sour compound of bitter reproachfulness and spiritual serenity … It is a confession of wrongs, both inflicted and suffered, which was intended in its candour to purge the guilt from his anguished soul… Parallel with the pain is the serenity of a spiritual awakening, a serenity born of sorrow."[6]

Sorrow looms throughout the work. Wilde wrote:

> *Sorrow, then, and all it teaches one, is my new world. … Sorrow is holy ground …For us there is only one season, the season of sorrow. The very sun and moon seem taken from us. Outside the day may be blue and gold, but the light that creeps down through the thickly muffled glass of the small iron-barred window beneath which one sits is grey and niggard. It is always twilight in one's cell, as it is always twilight in one's heart.*[7]

There was no sparing of pathos:

> *We who live in prison, and in whose lives there is no event but sorrow, have to measure time by throbs of pain, and the record of bitter moments. We have nothing else to think of. Suffering – curious as it may sound to you – is the means by which we exist…*[8]

But this shared experience with his fellow convicts is only temporary. His own burden is, he feels, harder to bear than theirs.

> *The poor are wiser, more charitable, more kind, more sensitive than we are. In their eyes prison is a tragedy in a man's life, a misfortune, a casualty, something that calls for sympathy in others. They speak of one who is prison as one who is 'in trouble' simply … With people of our own rank it is different. With us, prison makes a man a pariah.*[9]

During his sentence, Wilde had been obliged to appear in the Bankruptcy Court to answer proceedings brought about by Douglas's father. These days out of prison brought him no respite, only added trauma. On one occasion he had been subject to public ridicule and humiliation during a delay on the platform at Clapham Junction station, while being transferred from Wandsworth Prison to Reading. To compound his troubles, his mother died and his wife divorced him. He wrote:

> *Other miserable men, when they are thrown into prison, if they are robbed of the beauty of the world, are at least safe in some measure from the world's most deadly slings, most awful arrows ... With me it has been different. Sorrow after sorrow has come beating at the prison doors in search of me; they have opened the gates wide and let them in.*[10]

Wilde was not one to indulge in false modesty and his letter to Douglas serves as a lament not only to their doomed relationship, but also, and in no small part, to his own fame and position in society. "Elegy generates eulogy" is the way his biographer Richard Ellmann[5] described such assertions as:

> *I was a man who stood in symbolic relations to the art and culture of my age... Few men hold such a position in their own lifetime, and have it so acknowledged . . . The gods had given me almost everything. I had genius, a distinguished name, high social position, brilliancy, intellectual daring; I made art a philosophy and philosophy an art; I altered the minds of men and the colours of things; there was nothing I said or did that did not make people wonder.*[11]

Setting aside his crushed pride, Wilde did recognise that his time in prison could be a watershed for him as a writer. He cited the two great turning points in his life as being when his father sent him to Oxford "and Society sent me to prison." He could see now the supreme emotion of sorrow as being the test of all great art and had experienced a spiritual awakening. "I see a far more intimate and immediate connection between the true life of Christ and the true life of the artist," he wrote. "I hope to live long enough and to produce work of such a character that I shall be able at the end of my days to say 'Yes! This is just where the artistic life leads a man!'"

He said that two of the "most perfect" lives he had come across in his own experience had been those of Paul Verlaine, the French poet and Prince Kropotkin, the Russian geographer and revolutionary, both of whom who had spent years in prison."

First and foremost, *De Profundis* is a love letter, but Wilde, as a professional writer and a man of deep emotions, was able to describe the trauma of incarceration in a way that many prisoners would recognise even a century later. There is no evidence that he wrote his letter with publication in mind, but three years later, as he lay dying in a cheap Paris hotel, he urged Robert Ross to get the work published, in the hope that it would go some way towards restoring his reputation.

The Ballad of Reading Gaol

Publication was certainly in Oscar Wilde's mind when he wrote *The Ballad of Reading Gaol*. Living in France and desperate for money, he had high hopes that the *New York Journal* would pay him between £200 and £300 to serialise it, while his London publisher could bring it out simultaneously.[13] To his disappointment, there was little newspaper interest in the USA and although the book, published under the nom de plume C.3.3,[14] the number of Wilde's cell in Reading, sold better than any poem had for many years, it did not make the sort of money that he had earned only a few years earlier from his plays.

The Ballad of Reading Gaol was inspired by an execution in the prison, during Wilde's time there. Charles Thomas Wooldridge, a thirty-year-old trooper in the Royal Horse Guards, was hanged for the murder of his wife, whose throat he had slit in a bout of jealousy. It was the first execution in Reading for eighteen years and the poignancy of inhumane punishment for a human crime was not lost on Wilde, who considered that he had been treated in a similarly inhumane, if less extreme, manner. Thus, while he focused on the fate of the doomed, but unnamed soldier,[15] he juxtaposed his own treatment at the hands of society:

> A prison wall around us both,
> Two outcast men we were:
> The world had thrust us from its heart,
> And God from out His care:
> And the iron gin that waits for Sin
> Had caught us in its snare.[16]

The popularity of Wilde's *Ballad* is not due to his solidarity with one condemned man. In an age where judicial hangings were regular occurrences, the trooper Wooldridge's execution was in no way out of the ordinary. It caused no stir among press or public. *The Ballad* symbolises capital punishment as a whole and exposes the reality of the ritual taking of a human life – a subject that remains contentious long after capital punishment was abolished in Britain.

Wilde described the despair of his fellow prisoners as "the secret deed" was done: "We were as men who through a fen / Of filthy darkness grope." He was contemptuous of the warders who "strutted up and down", who "stripped the dead man of his clothes and gave him to the flies/ who mocked the swollen purple throat and the stark and staring eyes" and he condemned the clinical coldness of the prison authorities:

> The Governor was strong upon
> The Regulations Act:
> The Doctor said that Death was but
> A scientific fact:
> And twice a day the Chaplain called,
> And left a little tract.[17]

In his earlier letter, that became *De Profundis*, Wilde said: "People point to Reading Gaol and say, 'That is where the artistic life leads a man.' Well, it might lead to worse places."

Not according to the *Ballad*, written only a few months later, where the images are of sheer desolation:

> The vilest deeds like poison weeds,
> Bloom well in prison air;
> It is only what is good in Man
> That wastes and withers there:
> Pale Anguish keeps the heavy gate,
> And the Warder is Despair.[18]

Before his release, Wilde told friends in his letters that when he got out he intended to write about the horrors of imprisonment. He kept to his word and barely a week after his release a long letter about cruelty to imprisoned children was published in the *Daily Chronicle*.[19] It has been claimed by some of Wilde's biographers that *The Ballad of Reading Gaol* brought about improved conditions for prisoners; whether or not it did will be considered later, but the poem certainly brought prison conditions to wider attention:

> Each narrow cell in which we dwell
> Is a foul and dark latrine,
> And the fetid breath of living Death
> Chokes up each grated screen,
> And all, but Lust, is turned to dust
> In Humanity's machine.[20]

While ever prisons exist, *The Ballad of Reading Gaol* will strike a chord with prisoners. In Britain, hangings are no more, but the iniquities of the modern system – overcrowding, deaths in custody, riots and widespread drug misuse - have seen Wilde's imagery much quoted by penal pressure groups and individuals working for reform. The poem received mixed reviews when it was published in 1898,[21] but almost 5,000 copies were printed in seven separate editions over the next four months. The seventh edition, besides bearing Oscar Wilde's name as author for the first time, was notable for also bearing the name of the printer, who had hitherto remained anonymous through fear of the libel laws.

In 1992, the bank robber-turned journalist John McVicar, reviewing two books by ex-prisoners in *The Sunday Times*, referred to what he called "the Oscar Wilde legacy":

> *It is a distressing penological fact that every book by a British prisoner published in the last 50 years – and there has been a library of them – either has a quote from* The Ballad of Reading Gaol *or includes the author's own Wildean doggerel. This practice has neither enriched our literary heritage nor reduced the crime rate, so on two counts there is a case for its being discouraged. Perhaps the Poetry Society could prevail on the Prison Department to insert into the prisoners' rule book a note to the effect that Wilde did not write* The Ballad of Reading Gaol *in prison, but after he was released. The work he produced in prison was* De Profundis *which, I would suggest, is a rather more edifying read than the* Ballad *for a prisoner agonising about the pains of imprisonment.*[22]

McVicar, who many years earlier had forsaken the gun for the typewriter, was well-placed to criticise this tendency towards cliché. But the *Ballad* had not always been such an influence on prisoners. Decades would pass following its publication before it could be obtained from prison libraries, where the emphasis was on devotional, reference and technical books and even light fiction was sparse.

A poem from the pen of an ex-prisoner, describing an execution and attacking everyone from the governor down was not the sort of literature the authorities would allow prisoners to read. Outside, it was available in bookshops, but Wilde's market was largely confined to the London literary circle. Ordinary convicts, even those who could read, were unlikely to be inspired by a poem written by a fallen toff convicted of gross indecency.

Wilde sent a copy of the first edition of the *Ballad* to the governor of Reading Gaol, Major Nelson, whose generosity in allowing him to write the letter to Alfred Douglas, and in providing him with the materials, cannot be underestimated. The importance of *De Profundis* to prison literature in Britain does not rest on its style and content; it was the first published book of modern times to have been written in prison and would remain the only one for many decades to come.

Other broad-arrow men

In the meantime, those who published first-hand accounts of prison life were obliged to wait until they gained their liberty. In 1906, Jabez Spencer Balfour was released from Parkhurst Prison on the Isle of Wight, where he had served a fourteen year sentence with hard labour, for fraud. Balfour, like Oscar Wilde, was no ordinary criminal. A former M.P. and the first Mayor of Croydon, his crimes had left a trail of financial ruin among thousands of ordinary people. He had only been brought to trial after a Scotland Yard detective kidnapped him in Argentina, where he had escaped to evade the law. On his release from prison, Balfour was supported by the press baron Lord Northcliffe, to whom he dedicated *My Prison Life*,[23] serialised over twenty-six weeks in his mentor's newspaper, the *Weekly Dispatch*.

Balfour wrote of the separate system and the rule of silence whereby men were held in single cells and prohibited from speaking to each other. On Saturdays work stopped at 11a.m. and they were confined to their cells until 9 a.m the next morning. The governor, Lieutenant Colonel Plummer, recognised the hardships of the regime and allowed "well-conducted" prisoners to have writing materials:

> *... a few sheets of foolscap paper and pen and ink, the paper being folded into a kind of note or copy-book, in which they could record their impressions of what they read, make notes as to what they should write about to their friends, or attempt some literary work which with many convicts was an unfailing source of not unprofitable amusement. . . No kindlier privilege more truly benevolent or more highly appreciated, was ever bestowed and I never heard of its serious abuse.*
>
> *In fact, it could not well be abused, for the notebooks were collected late in the afternoon, and their contents carefully and properly scrutinised by the schoolmasters. Any one accustomed to writing, who has been deprived of pen and ink and paper for a whole week, will realise what this boon meant to those among us who were educated men.. So soon as it was granted to a few, it was eagerly sought by scores...*[24]

Soon, however, a new governor arrived and the privilege was withdrawn. Balfour petitioned the Home Secretary on behalf of himself and other prisoners, pointing out that "we owed two of the noblest books in the world, *Don Quixote* and *The Pilgrim's Progress* to the fact that their authors, when languishing in prison, in other and much less merciful days, were still permitted to enjoy what was denied to us, free access to pen and ink."[25] The petition was stopped from going out of the prison.

In 1924, *Among The Broad-Arrow Men - A Plain Account of English Prison Life* was published anonymously, its author named only as B.2.15.[16] This reticence could have been influenced by a wish to emulate Wilde's C.3.3, alternatively he could have been promoting a mysterious image. If the cell number was indeed his old one, it seems unlikely that his anonymity had been instigated by fear of official retribution, as it would have been easily identifiable by the authorities.

Whoever he was, B.2.15 did not belong to same social class as Wilde or even Balfour and for this reason alone his book, dedicated to "To the tramps, the outcasts, the "wrong uns and the wronged – the world over", is an important milestone in prison literature. Stating at the outset "It is my intention to give, as briefly as possible, a straightforward account of prison life in this country as I experienced it in Leicester Gaol within the last few years,"[27] the author made it clear that he was no stranger to prison, but "it was Leicester that was destined to make its indelible impression on my mind."

Hard labour in Leicester, according to B.2.15, was little different to Balfour's experience in Parkhurst twenty years earlier. There was the rule of silence, punishments for the most trivial misdeeds, mailbags to sew and unrelenting loneliness. Eventually, he managed to get to the library:

> *The first prison library book I ever had was 'The Alps from End to End' by W. Martin Conway. This was of course an educational book and could not be changed for four weeks.*[28]

The passage of time has not placed *Among The Broad-Arrow Men* among prison classics but when it was published it offered a rare insight into what went on behind the walls. The world of prisons was a secret and largely silent one. An inmate was allowed visitors, but only for thirty minutes once a month and then under strict conditions.

He could not write a letter until eight weeks had been served whereupon he had to apply to the landing officer at six o'clock in the morning. Before the lunch hour, when the letter was to be written, note paper together with pen and ink was taken to his cell. On the front page was printed a summary of the regulations with regard to letters. No reference could be made to prison conditions, or to "slang or improper expressions". But difficulties of letter-writing paled beside the author's task in keeping notes for the book he later hoped to write:

> *Throughout my whole three years imprisonment I was able to make notes and thus keep some sort of a diary, else the material for this narrative could not have been retained ... For many weeks I had to be content with the use of a slate. Then, when a letter was allowed to be received, spaces between the lines were filled with shorthand notes, made by the impression of a needle.*
>
> *These needle-made notes continued for a long period, until I decided to take the risk of inking them in, for the impressions had a tendency to wear if the paper was not of the best. Thence forward I got my notes up-to-date in ink every time the pen and ink was allowed for letter-writing, and all of them came safely out of prison as part of personal property – prisoner's letters. Only at one gaol were they scrutinised on discharge and there, to my great surprise and relief, they were allowed to pass without comment.*[29]

The need for such dedication to the cause, as well as a capacity for cunning and subterfuge, explains the dearth of prison literature that lasted until well after the Second World War. To be caught with any unauthorised item was to risk loss of remission as well as the work being confiscated. Later, such oppression would be useful in publicising at least one book.

The dust wrapper of *The Truth About Dartmoor* tells how George Dendrickson and Frederick Thomas wrote the notes on which it was based on scraps of paper, in their cells:

> ... and every day – for discovery would of course have meant destruction – they found a new hiding place. Then, after their release, they returned to Dartmoor and dug up this material, which they had buried in canisters on a working site outside the prison walls.[30]

The 1930s – Wilfred Macartney

The most insightful and well-written prison book published between the two world wars was *Walls Have Mouths*, an account of life in Parkhurst, published in 1936 by W.F.R. Macartney.[31] A former army officer who had served an earlier nine month sentence for breaking a jeweller's shop window, Wilfred Macartney had embraced Communism and written articles for the *Sunday Worker*. After becoming involved with Russian agents, in 1928 at the Old Bailey he was sent down for ten years penal servitude. His prison memoir was published soon after he was released.

The four hundred and forty pages of *Walls Have Mouths* begin in Wandsworth but focus mostly on his time in Parkhurst. The style is not personally reflective - while he describes how certain events affected him, Macartney does not bemoan his fate or look back as to how things might be different. His former commanding officer in the army, the popular novelist Compton Mackenzie, who also contributed a prologue and chapter commentary, said he was "continually struck by the resemblance between prison and a kind of nightmare public school." Macartney admitted his book was "about convicts and has been written by a convict, and maybe idealises them, or sentimentalises them."

There was nothing sentimental about the way Macartney described the layout of Parkhurst, in such detail that the prison authorities must have seethed in their powerlessness to take action. Likewise, his accounts of the atmosphere in Wandsworth, at the time of an execution, of the flogging and half-starving of prisoners, of the interaction between them and their keepers - and all the other aspects of life within the walls - were written without hint of compromise and in a brisk, colourful style that still reads well today.

Nor did he shy from naming many of his fellow prisoners, especially the more notorious ones. The camaraderie of prison life shines forth in vignettes of jewel thief Ruby Sparks and his fellow bandit Jimmy Turner, forger Henry Smith, blackmailer George Taylor and Billy Brain from Birmingham.

Macartney's attitude to "jailors" was ambivalent. There were good ones, some of whose generosity extended to putting up the wives and mothers of convicts who had travelled hundred of miles to see their husband or son who was dying in the prison hospital. But as a group charged with guarding prisoners, they were the enemy, and a contemptible enemy at that:

> *The great majority of screws hate the brutality of the system, and yet become brutes themselves ... Never in any body of men have I witnessed such a lack of solidarity as exists among screws ... The only time they ever stuck together and went the same way home was when, at the beginning of the Dartmoor mutiny, they fled in a terrified bunch through the prison gates to safety.*[32]

He was under no illusion about the attitude of governors and prison officials towards himself and his fellows:

> *That the convict belongs to another biological species is the characteristic belief of the official. And to strengthen this conviction the convict is treated unnaturally: he is fed with strange food, must wear weird clothes, must not speak, must go to bed at a ridiculous hour and is treated like an animate tool. The distance that separates the governor of a gaol from a convict is fathomless.*[33]

Prison food was a bitter grievance and convicts were "broken-winded, round-shouldered, pot-bellied and spindle-shanked, and this really what the system in its hatred of the convict demands, for fear that if the man be decently fed he will rebel." No likelihood of that, even if the menus did list meals such as savoury bacon, beef-steak pudding or sea pie:

> *The vile concoctions masquerading under these honest names might make a hungry pig vomit with disgust. 'Sea pie' is a mess in a filthy tin, defying analysis. The top is a livid scum, patterned with a pallid tracery of cooling grey grease, and just below this fearsome surface rests a lump of grey matter like an incised tumour.*[34]

But it was as an avid reader that Macartney faced his greatest annoyance, through the restriction on books. He wrote:

> *I suffered many hardships in prison but without doubt that which frightened and shocked me most was the gradual realisation that there was a definite official bias against reading ... the official view that reading by convicts is not to be encouraged ... If there is anything – if there can be anything – to look back on with pride in a sentence of ten years' penal servitude, I look to my fight, waged without ceasing from the week I entered the prison to the week I came out, for the right to read what was published by reputable English publishers.*[35]

For criminologists and penal historians, *Walls Have Mouths* is a seminal reference work on the English prison between the wars. Macartney's story, possibly enhanced in presentation by his editor Compton Mackenzie, is told in a way that makes it accessible without dilution of content. Just as Oscar Wilde's imagery still chimes with the feelings of modern prisoners, so too will some of the situations that Macartney encountered in his battles against officialdom.

Jim Phelan – a convict writer by profession

Wilfred Macartney never published another book, leaving another Parkhurst man, his friend Jim Phelan, to take up the mantle. The year after *Walls Have Mouths* appeared, Phelan was released from Parkhurst after serving fourteen years of a life sentence for the murder of a man during a post office robbery in Liverpool.

An Irishman born in Tipperary, he had led a transient existence as a blacksmith, docker and deckhand. At his trial he claimed to have committed the robbery to raise funds for the I.R.A. He refused to name his associates and was sentenced to hang, commuted to life imprisonment after a month in the condemned cell. Before the murder he had written occasional pieces, a couple of which were published. In prison he found a wealth of material that would feed his literary intentions.

His potential had already been advanced by Macartney in *Walls Have Mouths*:

> *James Phelan, an Irishman doing a life sentence for killing in a post office hold up, has written during the twelve years he has been in gaol some poetry, among a lot of fine stuff, which to my mind has seldom been equalled in England since the beginning of the nineteenth century... It will be worse than a shame if Phelan's poetry is burnt by a gaol-house searcher when he has completed his life sentence.*[36]

The prison authorities never found Phelan's poetry, nor the fragments of a novel and other notes that would later form part of his books. In Maidstone Prison at the beginning of his sentence he had begun a correspondence course in literature, until the governor stopped it. Moving to Dartmoor he managed to resume his studies and was helped by an outside tutor in adult education.

When he finally gained his release, Phelan had only one aim - to become a published writer. In a bed-sit in Camden Town he quickly wrote his first novel, *Lifer*, and followed that up with two more, *Green Volcano* and *Ten-a-Penny People*. All three were published in 1938, by Victor Gollancz.

After this hectic announcement of his arrival, Phelan wrote an autobiographical account of his thirteen years in prison, *Jail Journey*, published in 1940.[37] In the preface he acknowledged the influence of his nineteenth century countryman John Mitchell, whose *Jail Journal* he had read before going to prison.

He also emphasised that his book was not an apology for the behaviour that took him to prison, saying it had become almost accepted that a prison writer should be innocently punished: "I was not anything like that. An ordinary intelligent man of peasant origins, I shot a man and I went to jail. I might quite easily and legally have been hanged."

Phelan had an antipathy towards those whom he called "scientifically inclined penologists" and believed that his own research carried much greater credibility:

> *I realised that I had an advantage over the orthodox penologists and commentators on jail-psychology. They dealt with reports, statistics, departmental accounts. I had first-hand information, or I was going to have it. The penologist got little printed forms, or uninformed statements on bits of official stamped paper. I had the men themselves, their chuckles and groans, their blood and sweat and excrement, the animal-growl of the jail voices, the sniffing one another from afar, the lip-licking saliva-drooling jungle technique of homosexual love-making, the fantasy-hiss, the small sadism, the neuroses.*

> *The penologists had nothing except cold dry dead reports, mostly about money, wherefore their books were likewise lifeless. I, pioneering against my will, had a world to put on paper.*[38]

If any penologists dismissed his assertions, others, notably Hermann Mannhein, praised *Jail Journey*. Mannheim accepted Phelan's book as an accurate picture of the English prison situation, comparing it favourably with the study of a U.S. penitentiary by sociologist Donald Clemmer and describing Phelan as an "intelligent observer".[39]

Jail Journey described many aspects of prison life that had not previously been written about in any detail, especially the experience of serving a life sentence. Phelan explained the workings of prison slang, the pecking order of "wide men" and "mugs". He researched diligently, if writing in a style that occasionally pre-dated tabloid journalism. In the convict prisons he had been shocked to discover the large number of inmates sentenced for sex and cruelty offences:

> *People chop off babies' legs, excrete in churches or offices, skin mice, lash little girls, burn cats, use knives in unmentionable ways on little boys, slash women with razors, use red-hot pokers, rape six-month babies, stick skewers in living rabbits, hack, chop, stab, slash, scald and bludgeon their relatives or lovers, run through all the gibbering, fantastic, bedlam gamut of pain-making, then find their way to Maidstone or Parkhurst or Dartmoor.*[40]

Jim Phelan was the first ex-convict to make a living from writing, the first to be accepted as a professional writer. Those who preceded him – B.2.15, Balfour and even Phelan's friend Macartney - were one-book autobiographers who, having said their piece, had nothing more to write about. Phelan, as his three novels within a year of release had shown, was different. He went on to publish six more books and numerous articles, drawing on his life amongst criminals and gypsies. He never had a fixed abode and usually lived in caravans or tents, having his mail forwarded to post offices around the country.

His work, if not his tendency to scrounge money, brought him many admirers, among them Victor Gollancz and the prominent Quaker, Reginald Reynolds. Much later, Mike Nelliss, in his appreciation of Phelan, said:

> *He wrote many kinds of story: some realist, some picaresque, a handful that were mythic, unified only by the outcast status – and stoic resourcefulness – of*

their central characters. Certain themes recur – the importance of self-reliance and physical strength, the working of fate, the impossibility of forgiveness, the inevitably of vengeance – but there is no consistent formula in Phelan's stories. He depicts a mostly masculine world, man living, of necessity, by older and more violent codes than civilisation permits, beyond the protection of conventional legal authority; his characters invariably get poetic justice, if not justice of any other kind.[41]

Moving on - Frank Norman and Brendan Behan

By the late 1950s, Jim Phelan's time had passed. Not only the world that he lived in had changed, the book market had too. His tales had become tired and bore the stamp of re-worked material. They – and he - belonged to the past. No one cared about the villains, tramps or travelling people of yesteryear - they wanted to read about the present. The publishing world had found a new ex-convict to promote – a man fresh from three years corrective detention, served in Wandsworth, Chelmsford and an unspecified prison on the Isle of Wight, referred to only as "The Island".

Frank Norman's *Bang To Rights*,[42] was written in a lively style that sprang from the page as if Norman himself was speaking the words in his native Cockney. He had no pretensions towards academic recognition, nor aspirations towards prison reform, and his book was published complete with many uncorrected spelling mistakes. If that deterred prospective readers, they could not ignore the testimonial from crime writer Raymond Chandler, who contributed a foreword. A plain-and-simple anecdotal account of a villain in prison, *Bang To Rights* had an immediate affinity with the popular culture of the time – teddy boys, rock 'n' roll and kitchen-sink drama.

Norman followed *Bang To Rights* with more books in the same vein but he never recaptured the same degree of success – although his ear for dialogue brought him fame and fortune in the 60s as co-author, with Lionel Bart, of the hit musical *Fings Ain't Wot They Used To Be*. The breezy, good-humoured, wide boy character of his books – those who knew him say it was a realistic representation of his true self - is reputed to have been a major influence on the television character Norman Stanley Fletcher, as played by Ronnie Barker in the 1970s BBC series, *Porridge*.

Frank Norman broke away from the traditional style of prison autobiography.

His priority was entertainment, not reform. Brendan Behan, whose memoir *Borstal Boy* was published in the same year as Norman came to notice, achieved both ends, albeit indirectly. Nor was Behan's book any fresh-from-jail first offering – seventeen years had elapsed since his time at Hollesley Bay Borstal in Norfolk and in the previous two years he had enjoyed huge acclaim for his prison-inspired stage plays, *The Quare Fellow* and *The Hostage*.

Brendan Behan's reputation has always rested as much on his behaviour as a stereotypical hard-drinking, roistering Irishman as on his plays and books. Notwithstanding Behan's turbulent life, *Borstal Boy*[43] is a major work, described by one reviewer as "The most important book of its kind to be published this century".[44]

Two years earlier, Behan's play *The Quare Fellow* – an indictment of capital punishment which was inspired by an execution while Behan was confined in Mountjoy Jail, Dublin - had received similarly enthusiastic plaudits from the London press, with Kenneth Tynan prophesying in *The Observer* that it would become part of theatrical history.

The opening of the play, which ran for six months in the West End, coincided with a House of Commons debate on capital punishment and gave added ammunition to abolitionist campaigners like Sidney Silverman M.P., who attended the first night. Behan was disappointed that the recently retired hangman Albert Pierrepoint, who had also been invited, did not turn up.

The Hostage, Brendan Behan's second stage play, opened in London in October 1958. By now Behan was the toast of the town; his work was compared favourably to the greats of Irish literature, the esteemed theatre critic of *The Sunday Times*, Harold Hobson, commenting "It made the impression on me of a masterpiece". Brimming with jokes, songs and eccentric characters, the play is fundamentally serious, a story of a young British soldier held captive as a reprisal against the imminent hanging of an I.R.A. man. Behan's future as a writer was assured but six years later, driven by a self-destructive personality, he was dead at the age of forty-one.

The autobiographical *Borstal Boy* is Brendan Behan's finest work. It begins in late 1939 with him aged sixteen, fresh off the boat from Dublin and arrested by Liverpool Police in possession of "a suitcase, containing Pot. Chlor, Sulph Ac, gelignite, detonators, electrical and ignition, and the rest of my Sinn Fein conjuror's outfit".

It is an uplifting, optimistic account of a young prisoner's travels from the dark despair and uncertainty of Walton Prison to the relative freedom of Hollesley

Bay, an open borstal. Behan, an idealistic youth from a staunch Republican background, was different from his fellow inmates by race and culture and was not a criminal by habit, but his lively personality meant that he was quickly accepted:

> *I had the same rearing as most of them, Dublin, Liverpool, Manchester, Glasgow, London. All our mothers had done the pawn – pledging on Monday, releasing on Saturday. We all knew the chip shop and the picture house and the four-penny rush of a Saturday afternoon, and the summer swimming in the canal and being chased along the railway by the cops.*[45]

He had been encouraged from birth to hate England, but the friendships he made among his peers and the kindness he received from some of the staff at Hollesley Bay, in particular the governor, made a lasting impression on him.

Borstal Boy is a complete work, conclusive in its account and devoid of loose ends. In the last chapter Behan returns to Dublin by ferry, in his hands an order excluding him from Britain. *Borstal Boy* was published in October 1958, only four days after *The Hostage* opened in London. Reviewed widely in Britain and Ireland, the first run of 15,000 sold out almost immediately. When it was published in the USA it sold 20,000 within the first month, in New York alone.

No concessions

Of all the prison literature published in or around the first half of the 20th Century, only *De Profundis*, *The Ballad of Reading Gaol* and *Borstal Boy* remain in print today. The autobiographies of Jabez Spencer Balfour, "B.2.15", W.R.F. Macartney and Jim Phelan were significant in their time for revealing what went on behind the walls, but the importance of their work today is sociological, rather than literary. Their relevance lies in depicting the roots of the modern prison service and as a means of tracing the attitudes and behaviour of criminals. Phelan had aspirations to be considered a literary man, but his work does not have the merit of Oscar Wilde or Brendan Behan.

What all of these ex-prisoners had in common is that their best-known prison work was written after release. Wilde was the only one allowed to write while inside and the uniqueness of that privilege – obtained through his social contacts and pre-prison reputation - is evident from the way other prison writers would be treated for the next sixty years or more.

The rule preventing inmates taking out notebooks on release remained in force until the 1960s – and the notebooks continued to bear the printed warning of what could not be written in them. In 1948, following the report of the Prison Commissioners, *The Times* printed a letter from Earl Haig, a surprising champion for prison writers. He said there was evidence of a conflict, "haunted by the ghosts of John Bunyan and Oscar Wilde … between the principle that a prisoner was not allowed to use his leisure to work for personal gain and the fear that some great work might be entirely strangled by red tape".

A prisoner should be allowed to engage in creative self-expression which could relieve some of the frustration of imprisonment, he said, adding "I was a prisoner-of-war for three years and I know." He quoted from *De Profundis*, "For us there is only the season of sorrow" and concluded that red tape would strangle the creative process when a prisoner was given a notebook but it was then taken away.[46]

Earl Haig's letter led to no further correspondence in *The Times*, and the matter received no more press coverage for over two years. Then, on 25 January 1951 in the House of Commons, home secretary, James Chuter Ede, was asked by the Conservative MP for Twickenham, a Mr Keeling, if he had made a decision about allowing prisoners to take their notebooks with them on release. Ede replied that "under certain conditions" this would be allowed.

> Keeling: "*Is the Home Secretary satisfied that if another* Pilgrim's Progress *is written in gaol it will not be destroyed?*"
> Ede: "*I think it would be a rather big notebook to contain* Pilgrim's Progress *but I certainly hope that any great works of literature that may be composed in prison will not be lost to mankind.*"

At this point, good intentions might have been imperilled when the Labour member for Bilston asked the home secretary to bear in mind that a large part of Hitler's *Mein Kampf* had also been written in prison. The debate rumbled on until Chuter Ede was asked for clarification on the "certain conditions" under which notebooks could be taken out. He replied that the prisoner "should have written nothing about his own life, the lives of other prisoners or ex-prisoners, his own offences or sentences or those of other ex-prisoners, prison conditions or methods of committing crime".

To the incarcerated writer, this was no concession at all, but neither James Chuter Ede nor any later home secretary has been noted for recognising the value of prison literature.

2] Life stories

Banned

In December 2003, the High Court ruled that the manuscript of serial killer Denis Nilsen's autobiography, confiscated by staff at HMP Full Sutton, should not be returned to him. Nilsen, it was claimed, intended to publish his work. In ruling against him, Mr Justice Maurice Kay said that the home secretary, who had refused to allow the return of the manuscript, was "entitled to have regard to the likely effect of publication on members of the public, including survivors and the families of victims."[1] Times had changed since the publication eighteen years earlier of *Killing For Company*, a best-selling book about the life and crimes of Denis Nilsen. Back then, the prison authorities allowed the serial killer to co-operate with the author Brian Masters and a television crew was allowed into HMP Albany to interview him.

One "likely effect" of the publication of Nilsen's autobiography on members of the public was that some of them might wish to read it. Besides any macabre curiosity about serial killers, of all the genres of prison writing, it has always been autobiography and memoir that attract the most interest. In recent years, society's attitude towards criminals has hardened, the tabloid press has become more condemnatory and there is a greater focus on victims, but criminals in captivity remain the object of public fascination and academic study.

The Inside Men

John McVicar, dubbed by the media 'Britain's Most Wanted Man' and 'Public Enemy Number One', faced no opposition from the High Court, the home secretary or even the prison authorities when, in 1974, he became the first prisoner to publish an autobiography from behind bars. In 1968, while serving twenty-three years for armed robbery, he escaped from maximum security at Durham Prison. Recaptured after two years on the run and remanded in Brixton on further charges, awaiting what he knew could be a life sentence, he wrote the story of his escape, what would become the first section of *McVicar by Himself*.[2]

The manuscript was smuggled out of Brixton and sold to a newspaper, McVicar's objective being to provide money for his then partner and their child. The second part of the book was driven by a different motivation; McVicar wrote it as a document to aid his defence and to explain his family background, the influences and beliefs that shaped his criminality - and his resolution, once recaptured, to turn his back on crime for good.

When *McVicar by Himself* was published it gained good reviews and quickly found a wide readership. There were several reasons for this, the first undoubtedly that the author's escape, re-arrest and his attendant media coverage were still fresh in the public's memory. McVicar was, in criminal parlance, a 'face'. Serialisation in two national newspapers - the *Sun* and *Sunday Times* – also helped, but an important factor was the part McVicar's exploits and book played in the *zeitgeist* of the 1960s.

Public fascination with criminals did not begin in 1963 with the Great Train Robbery, nor six years later with the arrest and trial of the Kray brothers and other members of their gang. It was, however, fuelled by both events, especially media coverage of the Kray twins' apparently glamorous lifestyles, their disregard for authority and the swingeing sentences they received. The Krays were now locked up in maximum security but the success of a book about them, *The Profession of Violence*,[3] had generated a keen demand for criminal biography. What better than one by another London villain, a bank robber doing twenty-six years, who had gone one better than the Krays and actually escaped from maximum security?

For the general reader, *McVicar by Himself* provided a first-hand account of the daily lives of top-security prisoners. The author's counterparts on E Wing in Durham prison included some of the most notorious criminals of the 20th Century: the gang-leader Charles Richardson, child-killers Ian Brady and John Straffen, Walter 'Angel Face' Probyn, who co-planned McVicar's escape, and many other names familiar to readers of the newspapers.

To criminologists, the book was an equally insightful text. It was the first personal account of life in maximum security – a relatively new concept at the time - and McVicar had gone about the task with an honesty rare, if not unique, for a man in his position. Besides the vivid descriptions, the strengths of *by*

Himself lie in McVicar's analysis of himself as a failed criminal and his belief in personal responsibility. He had been impressed by *De Profundis*, which he read on an earlier sentence and Wilde's influence is borne out in his book. Soon after he was paroled in 1980, John McVicar wrote the script for the feature film based on his escape.[4] He has worked as a journalist and broadcaster ever since.

Only one other British prison book from the 1970s stands alongside *McVicar by Himself*, in terms of lasting popular interest and sociological merit. *A Sense of Freedom*, the autobiography of Glasgow gangster and convicted murderer Jimmy Boyle, was published in 1977.[5] At the time Boyle was an inmate of the Barlinnie Special Unit and known as 'Scotland's most violent man', a label he had acquired after years of fighting the system.

There are inevitable similarities between the books of McVicar and Boyle. Both men were high profile prisoners whose notoriety in prison, as well as their original crimes, preceded publication. Both took on the prison authorities – Boyle through waging war on staff and McVicar by escaping from a supposedly inescapable prison. Both, as it would transpire, rejected their former lifestyles and became rehabilitated – McVicar through education and Boyle through art. Both were paroled within a few years of their books appearing and both books were made into films, in neither event doing them justice. For both, their autobiographies were starting points from which they launched careers, in Boyle's case primarily as a sculptor, although he subsequently published a volume of prison diaries and more recently has turned to fiction.

In structure, Boyle follows the traditional approach to autobiography, from his childhood in the rough-and-tumble, close-knit community of the Glasgow Gorbals. The son of a locally renowned criminal and fighting man, his account of his roots is one reason why *A Sense of Freedom* has been studied by subsequent generations of sociological students. Fundamental to the book is the way he describes his escalating involvement in crime and developing reputation for extreme violence which led, in 1967, to a sentence of life imprisonment for the murder of a rival gang member, Babs Rooney. In court he had pleaded not guilty to killing Rooney and in his book he maintains that stance, passing quickly over the event in a manner that leaves the reader unconvinced by his allusion to the culpability of another, unnamed person.

Murder apart – and it is of course possible that someone else was responsible – Boyle makes no attempt to depict himself, either before the life sentence or during the immediate post-sentence years, as anything other than a wild man who would stop at nothing in his war against prison staff, whom he despised. In Inverness, Porterfield and Peterhead prisons he spent years in punishment blocks that were little better than cages and was subject to repeated beatings by staff that would have finished off a lesser man. He wrote, "I was committed to fighting back. Death was all that would stop me."[6] The prison authorities were at a loss what to do with him and in a high risk experiment transferred him, along with a handful of other disruptive prisoners, to a new, experimental therapeutic unit at Barlinnie.

Against all expectations, Boyle responded positively. When, soon after he arrived, he discovered a talent for sculpting, he applied the energy he had previously put into fighting the system into art. Pieces of his work were exhibited and in time he decided to write his life story, "in a manner that expresses all the hatred and rage that I felt at the time of the experiences …" He did not seek to profit financially from the book, asking that the royalties be used to set up a trust fund to help children in socially deprived areas in Scotland.

Unusually for a book by a serving prisoner, the authorities were fully aware of the book. Although they did not attempt to stop its publication, Boyle knew that the contents were likely to do him no favours when the question of parole came round. By the time he was released, five years after the book came out, he had served fifteen years.

A Sense of Freedom is a violent book but not gratuitously so. Boyle does not have to sensationalise – his life on the streets and in prison needed no exaggeration. To people outside the closed world of Scottish prisons, it came as a shock to learn that such brutality existed in the name of the state. The book ends with Boyle still in prison, but in the enlightened atmosphere of the Barlinnie Special Unit, with definite hope for the future.

After his release, Boyle published a sequel, *The Pain of Confinement*,[7] the diary he had kept in the Unit from 1974 until he walked out of the gate for the last time in September 1982. Apart from occasional journalism, he concentrated on his career as a sculptor but in 1999 he revealed a considerable talent for fiction in his first novel, *Hero of the Underworld*.[8]

Boyle's autobiography came as no surprise to the prison authorities. In the therapeutic environment of the Special Unit he was able to write it without hindrance or concern that his manuscript would be confiscated. Before he began he informed a visiting official from the Scottish Office of his plans and was encouraged to continue.[9] John McVicar's situation, on remand and top security in Brixton, meant he had to negotiate a much more uncertain route – "I threw up the smokescreen that I was preparing my own defence, but I can't believe this washed even with prison warders."[10] When first the newspaper story and later the book appeared, the prison authorities showed no interest, although the publication of the book defied prison rules. McVicar's achievement should have served as an inspiration to other prisoners who felt they had a book in them, but if it did they failed to make it into print. It would be twenty years before another significant autobiography was published by a prisoner serving in an English jail.

In Scotland, the situation was no different. For fifteen years *A Sense of Freedom* stood as the only published account of what took place in the punishment blocks of Scottish prisons. It was, claimed the publishers, "a searing indictment of a society that uses prison bars to destroy a man's humanity". When, in 1992, John Steele, brought out *The Bird That Never Flew*,[11] what became apparent was that in the fifteen years since Boyle raised attention to the horrors of Porterfield, Peterhead and Inverness, the system had not improved.

Steele, like Boyle, was from a family entrenched in Glasgow's criminal community, but he was more petty criminal than gangster. He wrote, "I enjoyed stealing in the same way as my pals enjoyed football; it was becoming just like a sport." But the penalties for transgressing the rules were far more severe: throughout his childhood he had been humiliated and beaten by a cruel father, when he was sent to an approved school the sadistic treatment was continued by monks, then in borstal by prison officers. Given a twelve-year sentence for an inept robbery of a debt collector, an escape from Barlinnie meant that Steele's next stop was the Inverness segregation unit.

His story is one of a man so damaged by the mistreatment he suffered as a child and youth that he has little chance to live a normal life. His father's reputation follows him everywhere; while in Peterhead, he learns that his younger brother Joseph has been charged with the Glasgow Ice Cream Murders, where six members of a family were burned to death in their own home.[12]

As the years of riots, dirty protests, beatings, escape plots and suicide thoughts roll on, Steele is sustained by his passion for country music and by writing poetry. The title of his book is taken from a verse he learned in childhood, relating to Glasgow's coat of arms:

> The Bird That Never Flew,
> The tree that never grew
> The bell that never rang,
> The fish that never swam.

Some of Steele's poetic efforts are included within the text of his book, but one of the most powerful images is his description of using his own excreta to write verse on the walls of the Peterhead cages. Later on the Glasgow poet and author Freddie Anderson provided him with pen and paper. When the prison authorities learned of his book he was told that he would be punished if he tried to have it published without allowing them to read it first. But by the time *The Bird That Never Flew* did see the light of day John Steele had been released, after serving fourteen years.

The Barlinnie Special Unit[13] was the crucible in which damaged lives were repaired. It was an outpost of the Scottish prison system that brought change to men whose violence and anti-social behaviour had caused them to be written off as hopeless cases with no future, men who were so dangerous that they would otherwise have been likely to have remained in prison for the rest of their natural lives. Through role modelling, counselling and other therapeutic methods, they learned a new, responsible way of living. It was a place where emphasis was placed on art and writing, a way of channelling aggression and releasing frustrations that in many cases had built up since childhood.

Hugh Collins devoted almost half of his *Autobiography of a Murderer*[14] to his time in the Special Unit, and to the guidance he received there from fellow inmate, Jimmy Boyle. Collins, like his mentor, was convicted of killing a gangland rival in Glasgow and had followed a similarly rebellious route through the life sentence that ensued, culminating in him stabbing three prison officers in Perth Prison. But unlike Boyle, Collins does not deny his guilt – or much else that is negative in his life or psyche. He writes:

> *Most criminal autobiographies lean on black-outs, glossing over the facts. It's amazing how many murderers can't recall actually killing a person.*[15]

At an early stage, Collins emphasises that his book is different to other criminal autobiographies. The mid-1990s had brought a glut of books by gangsters, train robbers, cat burglars and, so it seemed, almost anyone who had ever nodded to either of the Kray twins on a prison landing. Most of these books were ghosted by journalists and aimed at an impressionable market that regarded certain criminals as folk-heroes who, if they were gangsters only killed their own, and if they were thieves robbed those who could afford it.

Collins, brought up to believe that his bank robber father was "the Robin Hood of Scotland", was well aware of this perverse mythology. Perhaps as a consequence, his book is devoid of gloss, as his rage, confusion, guilt and paranoia spills onto almost every page. His relationship with his parents casts long, troublesome shadows, but so too does the extent of his own violence. "What I'm describing here," he writes, "is the ugliness of gratuitous violence. Is there any other kind?"

In typical Glasgow gang style, he moves from fighting with knives, hatchets, meat cleavers and cut-throat razors to a sawn-off shotgun, which he announces by firing it in a crowded pub. He stabs William Mooney, a man who had assaulted him in his bed, years earlier in a young offenders prison, and embarks on his life sentence in the same spirit as that in which he had rampaged the streets. After an inevitable long spell in solitary following the stabbings in Perth, the authorities decided to take a chance on him in the Special Unit. Having gone so far down the same road as Jimmy Boyle, he now went the last furlong, immersing himself into sculpture and keeping a diary that formed the basis of his autobiography.

Collins' stark title, *Autobiography of a Murderer* is as uncompromising as the book itself. In a commanding style he goes much further than Boyle in describing the factors that contributed toward his behaviour, and the omnipresent feeling of guilt at taking a man's life. He offers explanations but not excuses, while his honesty verges on the reckless. Few lifers, out on licence would admit that, leaving prison for a few days home leave, they had taken out with them four grams of heroin. Collins writes, "I'm a murderer, but I'm not a liar."

Hugh Collins received much praise for what would be his first volume of autobiography, begun in prison but published three years after he was released. A sequel, *Walking Away*,[16] covers the immediate post-release years in Edinburgh as he struggles to come to terms with gaining his liberty, while still haunted by his past. By this time it was clear that Collins intended to make a career as a writer and two crime novels, *No Smoke*[17] and *The Licensee*,[18] both set in his familiar Glasgow milieu, soon followed. Collins' transformation, from homicidal hoodlum to author of fact and fiction so rare in its depth, intensity and authenticity, is remarkable.

At the other end of the spectrum is Valerio Viccei's *Knightsbridge – the Robbery of the Century*,[19] written and published while Viccei was serving twenty two years for stealing cash, jewellery and drugs estimated at up to £40 million from a safe deposit company. Viccei, born in northern Italy and the son of a wealthy lawyer, had always sought excitement. He gave up law studies to join a right-wing terrorist group, moved on to bank robberies and arrived in London in 1986 on the run from the Italian police. The following year he planned and carried out the Knightsbridge robbery, leaving behind a thumb-print that soon led to his arrest and conviction.

Viccei was extremely proud of his crime, even though he was caught. The robbery was reported as the biggest in history and his playboy lifestyle - fast cars, beautiful women and plenty of cocaine – was good copy for the media. Described by a detective who knew him as having an ego "the size of the Old Bailey",[21] he wanted to ensure the robbery – especially in his version - was enshrined in criminal history. He had spoken little English on arrival in Britain the year before the robbery; in Parkhurst he learned the language and then wrote his book in the Special Security Unit, using his own word processor. It was against prison rules, but he faced no opposition, nor did he experience difficulties in negotiating a publishing contract.

The authorities' compliance with *Knightsbridge* is not consistent with the experience of other prisoners and is difficult to understand, especially as Viccei presents crime as glamorous and himself in heroic light, expressing no remorse for his actions. An intelligent man who made a conscious choice to be a criminal, Valerio Viccei had a personality brimming with contradictions. His book ends with his arrest, without any reference to his sentence or time in prison.

Shortly before publication he explained:

> *I will not speak about prison at all. What's good about it? That would make the establishment smile too much; they endure our suffering and the misery we have to endure in these poxy places. On the contrary I want them to gnaw their knuckles and curse my disrespect and my pride.*[22]

In the book, however, he goes to great lengths to acknowledge not only the Parkhurst governor, John Marriott – "The man has earned my respect and my appreciation" – and other staff, but also the detective who arrested him and the judge who sentenced him to twenty-two years. He sent them all signed copies. Viccei planned to continue writing and was working on a novel with himself as a fictionalised main character[23] when he was repatriated to Italy in 1992, to continue his sentence and face further charges. He tried to start a prison magazine but nothing more was heard of his novel. In 2000, while out on day release, he was shot dead in a confrontation with Italian police.

When major publishers consider prisoners' autobiographies they inevitably favour those whose names are known to the public, be that through the notoriety of their crimes or their conduct inside. Although Mark Leech had been a disruptive prisoner and the publication of his life story, *A Product of the System*,[24] was delayed for him to face a crown court trial, he was no gangster like Boyle or Collins, no headline-hitter like McVicar or Viccei.

Leech was a small-time conman whose criminal path had begun at the age of eight when his mother died, his father fell into alcoholism and he was taken into care and sent to a boarding school. There he was sexually abused by a housemaster before running away and winding up in borstal and then prison.

A therapeutic prison – Grendon Underwood, in Buckinghamshire – was the turning point for Leech. He began to write, won Koestler Awards, had a play performed on Radio 4 and, when he moved on to Leyhill open prison, wrote his autobiography. At Leyhill he was given leave to interview a judge, James Pickles, for *The Guardian* but while out of prison he discovered that he was HIV-positive. He returned to Leyhill but absconded two days later and travelled to Scotland, where he was convicted of an armed robbery at a restaurant and sentenced to seven years. He denied the offence.

A Product of the System is the story of an ordinary individual from a non-criminal background who was abused, went off the rails and spent years in and out of prison until he finally found a focus to get his life back together. Grendon Underwood provided the foundation, but Leech's writing and his self-acquired knowledge of prison law, which he used to challenge the authorities in court, sustained him. His book, with a Foreword by Judge James Pickles, reveals his development in both fields. Mark Leech was released in 1995, and has since broadcast widely on penal matters, worked as a consultant to solicitors on prison law and edited *The Prisons Handbook*.[25]

Neither Valerio Viccei nor Mark Leech was charged with breaching prison rules for writing and publishing their autobiographies. Nor were other high profile serving prisoners like Reginald Kray, Charles Bronson or Archibald Hall, under whose names 'ghosted' autobiographies appeared around this time. But when the Tory peer and novelist Jeffrey Archer, serving four years for perjury, published a diary of the first three weeks of his sentence, spent in the maximum security Belmarsh Prison, the authorities reacted with astonishment and alarm.

A Prison Diary by FF 8282 [26] - Archer's name was not printed on the cover - should have surprised no one. Was it really unexpected that that a man who wrote for a living intended to capitalise on his experiences? Since going to prison he had been able to sign a new publishing contract worth millions of pounds and more than a year earlier it had been widely reported that he was working on a book about prison life, writing in longhand for two hours on and one hour off. Later, his lawyers confirmed a newspaper story that someone had retrieved several discarded pages from a prison bin and offered them to a newspaper.

But in October 2002, when the *Daily Mail* serialised *A Prison Diary*, by FF 8282, there was uproar. As the paper's front page asked "How did shamed peer get away with writing memoirs in his cell?",[27] an angry Martin Narey, director-general of the Prison Service, said, "He can't make money while he is a serving prisoner from publications and I have a duty to protect the privacy of other prisoners and members of staff."[28] There was talk of applying for an injunction, of Archer being challenged to donate all his royalties to charity and of him jeopardising his chances of parole. After all the fuss, when the matter was resolved Archer lost two week's prison wages – about £24 – suspended for six months. His publisher commented that the book could earn up to £300,000 in royalties.

Media coverage of *A Prison Diary* was vast, in excess of any previous book by a prisoner. The *Daily Mail* boasted the diary was "sensational" and "unprecedented", as though Archer's account was the first any inmate had ever written about life in prison. Elsewhere and without suggestion of irony, Archer was compared to Alfred Dreyfus, John Bunyan and, inevitably, Oscar Wilde, with whom he identifies himself in his book. He asks if, when he gets out he will have to follow the same path as Wilde and live a secluded life abroad, unable to enjoy the society that was so much a part of his existence: "Will I be able to visit old haunts – the National Theatre, Lord's, Le Caprice, the Tate Gallery…?"[29]

Formerly one of the most powerful men in the land, Archer now saw himself as a writer persecuted by the establishment. His diary contains no recognition that he has committed any crime, while his rhetoric is matched by his sense of melodrama. Wilde left the country penniless and abandoned; even during his sentence the multi-millionaire Archer was able to attend a cocktail party, while on home leave from North Sea Camp open prison.

A Prison Diary is a day-by-day account of three weeks in Belmarsh, written by a man who might never have dreamed in his worst nightmare that he would end up in such a place. Once inside, Archer takes on the unlikely mantle of penal reformer, hectoring the home secretary on the poor conditions, the cramped dimensions of his cell, young people whom he believes should not be in prison, and drugs. He is not the first prisoner to be dismayed by the standard of the food, but few could say "I've eaten shepherd's pie at the Ivy, the Savoy and even Club 21 in New York but I have never seen anything like Belmarsh's version."[30]

Nor does he want readers to forget for one moment that he is of a higher order than mere inmates and staff, as with this description of being searched on arrival:

> First, I take off my jacket, then my tie, followed by my shirt. 'Aquascutum, Hilditch and Key, and YSL' says the officer … I am then asked to slip off my shoes, socks, trousers and pants – 'Church's, Aquascutum and Calvin Klein."[31]

Such entries might have entertained Archer's friends and even other inmates, who are usually pleased when any prisoner manages to get one up on their keepers, but it is easy to see why the prison authorities were antagonised. Jeffrey Archer was one of the most newsworthy people in Britain and he was intent on trying to gain some form of revenge against those he saw as responsible for his downfall.

He rails against the trial judge, claims a fellow inmate has offered to deal with his former secretary who was a witness for the prosecution, and loudly bemoans his fate, while criticising prison conditions with lines like "This is not Turkey, not Nigeria, not Kosovo".

Anyone who writes an autobiography must be tempted to settle old scores. Prisoners and former prisoners invariably take such an opportunity and Archer dedicated his book "To Foul-Weather Friends". In the majority of cases there is little if any response from those criticised, but such was the controversy around *A Prison Diary* that the head of the Prison Service felt obliged to comment. In hindsight, the authorities could not ignore Archer's book, given the sensational nature of much of its content and the publicity machine that delivered it via every news medium in Britain.

So it was that a week after publication, director-general Martin Narey, questioning Archer's motives in publishing his diary, accused him of being self-centred, of exaggerating the state of prison conditions and of being destructive in his disregard for prison rules. Narey said: "He says blithely that every child sitting on a father's knee has drugs in their nappy, or some nonsense. What are we to do? Are we to say that no father in prison can ever have a child on his knee again?"[32]

A Prison Diary, the first volume of a trilogy of Jeffrey Archer's prison memoirs, was reported to have a first print-run of 50,000. It appeared in the top ten bestseller lists for two weeks and aroused a variety of responses within the criminal justice system. In the long run it is unlikely to be remembered as a serious prison memoir, although for a short time Archer did focus media attention on prison conditions.

From his cell in the maximum-security Whitemoor Prison, armed robber Noel Smith, better known as Razor Smith, watched with interest as Jeffrey Archer's book was published, while Dennis Nilsen's was banned. A casualty of the "two strikes and out" law introduced by the Crime (Sentences) Act 1997, Smith, was - still is - serving eight life sentences for armed robberies in London. Born in 1960, he had spent most of his adult life in prison. At the same time as his contemporaries were appearing before juvenile courts, the sixteen-year-old Smith was sentenced to three years detention at the Old Bailey, one incident in a chain of events that confirmed his identity of himself as a career criminal specialising in armed robbery.

In 1992, while serving a nineteen-year sentence, Razor Smith heard of the recently-founded *Prison Writing*. He sent two poems which were immediately accepted [33] and from that point on he was set for a new career as a writer. Over the next decade his short stories, poems and articles were regularly featured in the journal, which led to his work being published in more widely-circulated magazines, several national newspapers and broadcast on Radio 4. Paroled in 1997, he was out for only twelve months before he was arrested for more armed robberies and sentenced to life imprisonment.

In the short time he had been at liberty, through his connection with *Prison Writing* he met John McVicar, who introduced him to the novelist Will Self, who was interested in background information about Wandsworth Prison for a story he was writing. Smith took along to the meeting some work of his own. Will Self recalls, "I was impressed by its vivacity, humour and clear-sightedness. It reminded me a lot of the American writer and former bank robber Chester Himes' work, with a generous dash of Damon Runyon thrown in."[34] The next time Self met Smith, the London bank robber was back in prison, serving eight life sentences and mourning the death of his son: "Looking at the whole compass of his life and his very strong need to make a contribution to the costs of his son's funeral, I felt that the most saleable commodity he had as a writer was his autobiography."[35] As Will Self arranged a publishing deal, Razor Smith got down to writing. Although he was a Category A prisoner and in HMP Whitemoor, the same prison and at the same time as Denis Nilsen, whose legal challenge regarding his own autobiography was winding through the judicial system, he was able to write his book unimpeded, to send his manuscript to Will Self and to see it published in 2004.[36]

In *A Few Kind Words and a Loaded Gun*, Smith pulls no punches regarding the life he led prior to getting his life sentence.

> *Not once in my life had I questioned my criminality. I just accepted it as my lot. I embraced the life of crime and punishment as though it was my only friend. I loved the excitement and danger of living life on the edge, the vagaries of fate deciding whether I would be shot, stabbed or nicked. I craved the recognition of being a 'face' in, and out of, prison. I loved the respect I got from others in my world.*[37]

By the time he wrote these words he was forty-three years old and had fifty-eight convictions. If nothing else had brought home to him the futility of his criminal life, the suicide of his son at the age of nineteen, shortly after he was released from a sentence in youth custody, certainly did. In the 482 pages of *A Few Kind Words and a Loaded Gun*, Smith's long-suffering wife and three children do not get much of a look-in amidst the gang fights, shoot-outs, police chases and years behind bars, but the death of his son makes him seriously self-examine his earlier lifestyle and beliefs.

Smith's book is not one padded with the names of criminal 'faces'. Few of his contemporaries are notorious outside prison walls or their own localities. His story is one of a boy who grew up lacking in parental guidance, who fell foul of police malpractice at an early age and from then on believed he was totally justified in acting out the label that had been placed on him. He describes a life of crime as being "like a raging river at flood time; once you get into it you find it hard to get out again without a bit of help." Up to the age of fourteen, he says, he had merely dipped a toe in, but he then made a conscious decision to dive in and fully immerse himself. Soon he was "out in the middle where the waters raged most furiously, where struggling only makes you drown all the quicker".[38]

A Few Kind Words and a Loaded Gun is as comprehensive a guide to modern criminal and prison values as any reader will find, without living the life. In detail Razor Smith describes how it felt to rob, stab and handle firearms - "I can appreciate the weight and power of a decent shooter". There are harsh recollections of the dark, desperate years he spent in borstals, the many beatings he endured, the suicide attempt, the recurring vision of having years of imprisonment in front of him – as he explains why prison, rather than deterring young men from crime, in fact encourages them.

Smith explains his criminal actions, but does not apologise. While vehemently indicting the system, he accepts his own culpability. He concludes with the statement:

> *Like the ghost of Jacob Marley, I have spent my life carefully fashioning the chains that now bind me, link by link, and in mitigation, I offer only this: I never slashed a face that wasn't looking at me, and I never robbed a bank that wasn't insured.*[39]

These are bold words for a life-sentenced prisoner, whose eventual liberty lies in the hands of others.

Looking Back

Pablo Picasso, according to an apocryphal story, was asked to support a campaign to release writers imprisoned in Russia for their political beliefs. He declined, saying leave them inside, they write better in prison.[40] If the story is true then Picasso might have had a point, because in Britain the best prisoner autobiographies have certainly been those written while their authors were still inside. In those books, the tensions of prison life bring an immediacy to the prose; an urgency that sharpens powers of description and characterisation, while heightening the sense of drama and dialogue - a creative hothouse effect that often cools once the writer has walked out of the gate to freedom. The ex-prisoner who writes his or her memoirs will have filtered the experience, revised opinions for good or bad and placed their time in prison in a wider framework.

For the reader, knowing that the writer is still in prison can carry a greater impact. There is curiosity, an air of mystery – the author cannot be interviewed and the book has a tangible authenticity as coming from a hidden world, one that most readers never experience. Of course, many ex-prisoners write well and the experiences they describe are just as relevant, but evidence suggests that their autobiographies do not enjoy the same status or longevity of interest as the contemporaneous accounts published from prison.

There have been significant autobiographies published by ex-prisoners, some of which have made a mark at the time of publication and have enhanced the canon of prison literature. What is noteworthy is that in many of these cases – and especially the ones by writers jailed for the first time - they have taken the form of prison memoir, rather than the whole-life autobiography favoured by most inmates writing in prison. Perhaps this is to be expected - like Oscar Wilde in *De Profundis*, the incarcerated prisoner often looks back to his earlier life for explanations as to how he took the course he did. For most first-timers, prison is a life-changing experience and to write of that is a means of coming to terms with it.

One such first-timer was the pseudonymous Zeno,[41] whose book *Life* reveals how the serving of a life sentence in the 1960s was easier than it had been in Jim Phelan's time, twenty years earlier. The author took his name from the Stoic philosopher, Zeno of Citium, who retreated from the world for ten years to study. *Life* is a prison memoir that includes little information about the author or his crime, other than the publicity material on the cover.

We are told that he pleaded guilty to murder for a *crime passionel* and during the nine years he served in prison he won two Arthur Koestler Awards, with a collection of short stories and a novel. His novel, *The Cauldron*, published while he was in prison, was about the battle for Arnhem in World War II, where Zeno was said to have fought as an officer in the 1st Airborne Division. Released in his late forties, he wrote *Life*, published in 1968.[42]

Written in the first person, *Life* is paced and polished, if the message – principally that prisoners are subject to indignity and petty rules and that time inside is largely wasted – is somewhat hackneyed. When it was published, *The Times* declared it "a strange and unusually valuable document", saying of the author "He writes with the disdain of a man who expected at least integrity from authority and has found lies, deceit and funk."

Zeno is certainly disdainful of prison staff :

> *On the faces of some of the screws is an animal brutality, a shallow insensitivity that is hard to imagine as being wholly human.*[43]

Fellow inmates fare no better:

> *Most of the faces in this little local prison are like the crimes for which their owners have been convicted: petulant, mean, weakly vicious, and petty.*[44]

He even expresses irritation at avoiding the gallows. Convicted shortly after the 1957 Homicide Act, he avoided the possibility of capital punishment:

> *If they had hanged me, as I thought they would, I should have had only three or four more weeks to do, and then …oblivion. Now I must drag on, month after month, year after year, until I reach some undetermined date in the distant future.*[45]

Throughout *Life* there is a great deal of introspection, but no attempt to explain how a man who, according to his publishers, had previously been a sailor, farmer and timber merchant, came to commit the murder that put him in prison. Nor is there any hint of remorse for the victim. The closest the author gets is:

> *I killed a man. I may have thought that my action benefited a few people who were close to me but I took it upon myself to be both judge and executioner.*[46]

The majority of *Life* focuses on Wormwood Scrubs, where Zeno met and befriended George Blake, serving a forty-two year sentence for spying for the KGB. In Blake, who was reputed to have been responsible for the deaths of many British agents in the field, Zeno believed he had found a man of his own intellectual level and one possessed of many admirable qualities. George Blake escaped from Wormwood Scrubs the year before Zeno was released and wrote his book, a large part of which is devoted to time spent with the spy.

Life retains a penological importance as a rare account of a life sentence served in the 1950s and 60s. Then, Zeno, as what used to be termed a 'model' prisoner, was required to do little more than see out his time. He admits that after winning a Koestler Award five years into his sentence, he was virtually able to withdraw from ordinary prison life in the knowledge that he could expect release before he had served ten years.[47] Today, the starting point for a mandatory life tariff is fifteen years, and to be released the prisoner must satisfy stringent risk assessments, successfully complete cognitive behavioural courses and be tested in open conditions.

Pettifogging rules and policies frustrate all prisoners and can lead to the law courts or the punishment block, often both. The twelve months Rod Caird spent in Wormwood Scrubs and Coldingley prisons left him with a lasting impression on the need for reform of conditions and the overall treatment of inmates. On his release he wrote *A Good and Useful Life*,[48] the title used ironically and taken from the first of the rules he was given to read on arrival in Wormwood Scrubs in 1970:

> *The purpose of the training and treatment of convicted prisoners shall be to encourage and assist them to lead a good and useful life.*[49]

Caird was jailed in 1970 for his part in a political demonstration while a student in Arabic at Cambridge University. Like all first timers with no knowledge of prison, he had difficulty getting to grips with the conditions and anachronisms of the system. His book is a considered analysis of what he found during his sentence, set against official documents and other literature which defined prison ideology. Aware that the prisoner's word is often dismissed as unreliable, he wrote with the intention of avoiding "reference to bitterness or bias" and not to be limited by the constraints of personal narrative.

Much of *A Good and Useful Life* reads like a report, but a report in which the rigidity of prison life is revealed in all its absurdity:

> *If a prisoner wants to cut his toe-nails, it is necessary to make an official application in the morning, which is then processed by whatever bureaucracy grinds away in the depths of the wing, and results in an officer solemnly coming to your cell carrying one of the wing's pairs of scissors, which then has to be returned immediately after use. If nothing else, graduates from the Scrubs are masters of the complex art of finding a way through seemingly impenetrable regulations and procedures.*[50]

Rod Caird had written for student magazines before he went to prison. Better placed than most inmates through his background and education, in the last few weeks of his sentence he received commissions to write articles about prison for the *Sunday Times Magazine* and *New Society*. He went on to follow a career in journalism.

Twenty five years on from Caird, another recently released first-timer published a prison memoir. John Hoskison, a professional golfer, was sentenced to three years for causing the death of a cyclist while driving with excess alcohol. He accepted the sentence without complaint - but in prison he was dumbfounded by the manner in which petty rules were applied while the prison authorities chose to ignore widespread drug abuse, violence, bullying and extortion. Hoskison expected to be sent to an open prison, but he was disappointed. Throughout *Inside - One Man's Experience of Prison*,[51] his shock at going to Wandsworth - known to inmates for decades as "the hate factory" on account of staff attitudes - never leaves him and when he, like Caird, is transferred to Coldingley, he finds its official designation as a training prison a gross misrepresentation.

Hoskison contrasts the confined conditions of prison with flashbacks to his former life on the greens and faiways of the European golf circuit, an effective technique if one that had not been specifically available to earlier prison writers. He writes well and captures the feeling and fears of prison life through sharp description and strong dialogue, most of it written while he was still inside. His strictly personal indictment of the prison system in the 1990s received favourable reviews in the national press. Hoskison was invited to speak at training seminars for judges organised by the Judicial Studies Board and Mr Justice Hooper, the judge who sentenced him, declared *Inside* to be "a very, very interesting book".[52]

Jonathan Aitken was not the first former government minister to be jailed in recent times, but unlike his erstwhile colleague Jeffrey Archer, he made no claim to be wrongly convicted. He pleaded guilty and was sentenced to eighteen months for perjury.

He served only seven months before he was released on home detention curfew, but five years elapsed before he published *Porridge and Passion*,[53] his account of the time he spent in prison and the months that followed. Like so many first-timers in prison, Aitken registers continuing amazement at the quirks and pettiness of bureaucracy, but his dominant theme is his discovery of himself and his reliance on his new-found spiritualism.

Aitken relives comic moments, too. Going through the reception procedures at Belmarsh, he is asked by the prison psychiatrist if anyone other than his next of kin knows he is in prison. Thinking of the hordes of reporters and cameramen who had been outside the Old Bailey and the prison, and the result of their work in the evening media, he replies that perhaps ten or fifteen million people will probably know he is in prison. The psychiatrist, who has apparently not noticed the media interest, says "May I ask, have you ever suffered from delusions?"

Aitken fills his time with "journeys of the mind, pen and spirit". He apportions his days into four sections – Quiet Time, when he prays and reads the Bible; Greek Time, which he spends learning New Testament Greek; Reading Time – both for pleasure and spiritual study, and Letter-writing Time, replying to the large number of friends and strangers who had written to him after his sentence.

His story is an insight into how the media whip up anti-prisoner feeling through false reporting, and the influence they wield. His narrative is strong and colourful, as one might expect from a writer who had already published several books, including an award-winning biography of Richard Nixon, another politician who fell from grace.

For S.R. Krishnamma, writing *The Ballad of the Lazy L* brought mixed emotions. A man of restless temperament, he had emigrated from Bangalore, India and settled in Britain as a teenager. In subsequent years he was a restaurateur, casino manager, tennis coach and eating-out columnist for the *Costa Blanca Post* before he became tempted by the profits of the cannabis trade and found himself in Long Lartin serving ten years.

Divorced by his wife during the sentence, he lost his home and contact with his children. But in prison, Krishnamma saw colour all around where others might have seen only dullness - *The Ballad of the Lazy L* [54] is the result.

At the outset, Krishnamma tells how he began his book intending to write a story of the degradations of prison, a personal story of hardship and suffering, "a book full of rough, tough, mean, vicious, nasty people, some of whom were prisoners." While he was in prison, a draft version of the book won a Koestler Award but he made no progress towards getting a publisher. Time passed, he was released and met a man he had known on remand in Winchester Prison. They reminisced and Krishnamma realised his "heart-rending" book was perhaps not the correct approach:

> *In remembering those prison days, each memory nudging another one into life we became reflective, but mostly we laughed. Some of it was thankful laughter, for even though we had been scarred by the prison experience we were still standing. In enabled us to recall those times as grown-ups do their schooldays or ex-soldiers their war, with a nostalgic fondness that doesn't seem possible.*
> *After that I had to scrap all that I had written and start again.*[55]

Whether as a consequence of meeting his old acquaintance or not, Krishnamma looks back without bitterness, focusing on the interactions between prisoners, the fiddles, scams, feuds and the camaraderie between inmates. His account of the 1978 Long Lartin Christmas Padda-Tennis Championship, where he beat John McVicar in the final, is worthy of inclusion in any anthology of sports-writing.

But underlying the light-heartedness is a criticism of the prison system and all its perceived faults, which Krishnamma invites the reader to:

> *Imagine, if you can, a hospital where the sick are taken in and made worse; where legless men are admitted to have their arms amputated; where cases of cholera are infected with smallpox for good measure; and where men who once believed they are Napoleon come out thinking they are Caesar as well. Imagine too, the crazy panel of doctors, consultants and scientists, who formulate the policies of such a hospital; holding board meetings, attending conferences, issuing directives, pontificating theories to be passed on to the mindless lower echelons to be implemented. Could such a gruesome anomaly survive as a credible institution? It does, it thrives all over the world; and one of the most vigorous and self-aggrandizing of its affiliates is called the British penal system. A powerful, politically persuasive unit of society, that encourages the growth of crime while purporting to limit it.*[56]

S.R. Krishnamma's book was published by a small press in Wiltshire after two short stories were printed in *Prison Writing*[57] and, more significantly, he had appeared in *Underworld*, a BBC TV documentary series. *The Ballad of the Lazy L* never received the media attention that it might have done; it came at a time when the trend was for ghosted autobiographies by criminals seeking celebrity. The market was about sensationalism, not rational commentary on life in a maximum security prison. Christopher Hudson, author of *The Killing Fields*, described Krishnamma's account as "a book about doing time unlike any other I have read … it transforms the dull weave of prison life into a colourful tapestry of grotesques whom he observes with an angry humour which never descends into bitterness or spite".[58] But the time was not right and *The Ballad of the Lazy L* was destined to be a neglected prison memoir.

In 1984, after being arrested in possession of cocaine, Taki Theodoracopulos spent eleven weeks of a four month sentence in Pentonville Prison. Although prison memoirs are usually based on much longer periods behind bars, it was perhaps inevitable that a man who might have been described as a 'gentleman journalist' would write of his experiences in a world far removed from that in which he was familiar. Taki, as he was and is professionally known, had enjoyed the playboy lifestyle that came with being heir to a Greek shipping fortune. He had been a war correspondent in Vietnam and at the time of his incarceration wrote the *High Life* column for *The Spectator*, chronicling goings-on within the jet-set circuit of the capital cities and exclusive resorts of Europe.

Like Oscar Wilde before him and Jeffrey Archer some years later, Taki was a writer who became a prisoner rather than vice versa. As such, he had publishing contacts and a market for a prison book. While in prison, he kept a diary, which he began writing between the printed lines of the only book he had been allowed to take in with him, continuing between the lines of letters he received. Ever conscious of the risk that these notes, which he always intended to use for a book, could be confiscated, he arranged for an American lawyer friend to visit him and take them out the day before his release.

Nothing To Declare: Prison Memoirs[59] is a day-by-day account of a wealthy playboy's time among society's losers in a dirty, crumbling, Victorian jail. Taki spices the monotony of the present with tangential recollections of his life, loves and exploits in better times. There are humorous moments. Deployed to sew buttons he is told by an officer that he is the worst button-sewer he has ever seen. Taki asks if Oscar Wilde was any better. The officer replies, "If you think I keep records of who comes in here, you're mistaken."[60] In his epilogue he says that his eleven weeks in Pentonville were too short to qualify him as a "con" and admits that he found writing the book an irritant, which might explain why it was not published until six years after his release. *Nothing To Declare* is notable, too, for its omission of suggestions for penal reform. Taki, a man not lacking in opinions on other matters, concludes that while his prison experience led him to consider a number of questions, "not one of these questions has led me to a single answer I can stand on."

Taki's book was aimed at a popular, rather than sociological readership. Even more so was that of Norman Parker, whose *Parkhurst Tales* [61] appeared at the height of the criminal autobiography boom, sometimes referred to as 'gangster chic'.[62] But while books published in the names of the Kray twins, Frankie Fraser, Freddie Foreman, Charlie Richardson and others were written by professionals, Parker's came from his own hand. It was also, as the title suggests, a prison memoir rather than an autobiography.

Parker reveals little about himself or the offence that led to him serving twenty four years of a life sentence. Over a page and half he gives the briefest outline of the murder by shooting of a criminal accomplice and an earlier manslaughter conviction, where his girlfriend was the victim. *Parkhurst Tales* is an episodal account of life in the at-the-time maximum security jail on the Isle of Wight. Most of the book comprises stories of prisoners with whom he served, men Parker refers to by their nicknames - 'Top-cat', 'Shuffling Bob and the Slow Walkers', 'Scouse Roy', 'Dave the Rave'. The comic effect should not belie the fact that these men were some of the most violent, subversive and unstable inmates of any English jail at the time.

Parker presents himself as a man respected by his peers, with whom others tangle at their peril. His ego and a self-image of himself as a macho character figure largely in his writing, as he admits when describing how he avoided involvement in a plan to escape with another convict, David Martin, an avowed homosexual:

> *I was quite hung up about poofs generally. As their homosexuality was a major facet of their characters, it would certainly be mentioned in their records. In the event of my escaping with them, the press could well pick up this fact. I could imagine banner headlines about 'gay escapers'. As silly as it may sound, this was a major deterrent to me. I'm afraid I was still very much into image at this stage.*[63]

Parkhurst Tales was written in prison but Norman Parker waited until he was released in 1994 to publish. A few weeks later, three high security prisoners, all lifers, escaped from Parkhurst Prison, an event which led to the drastic upgrading of prison security in all closed prisons. Parker, who received a lot of media coverage for his book, claimed that the escape, following so closely on its publication, was not coincidental.

Three years later he published a second volume, *Parkhurst Tales 2*,[64] breathless in delivery, with a preface that begins "Dear Hollywood, Thank you for the murderous images that filled and fuelled my younger years", and with the names of many of his former fellow prisoners changed.

Here, Robert Mawdsley, a four-times killer, becomes Robert Wexler, although his real name has appeared in many press reports over the years and he has been the subject of television documentaries. Why Parker chose pseudonyms is unclear – he was not subject to prison rules and Mawdsley was in no position to sue for defamation of character, even if what was written about him had not been accurate.

Walter Probyn had a story that could have earned him a large sum from the Sunday newspapers. Put on probation when he was nine for stealing a tin of peas, over the next five years he absconded from six approved schools. At the age of fifteen, serving four years without remission in Wakefield Prison, for wounding a policeman, he was declared mentally defective and transferred to Rampton Hospital. He escaped, was returned and got out eventually only after threatening habeas corpus proceedings.

In 1974, when the idea of a book was suggested by his solicitor, Probyn had recently been released from a twelve year sentence. More than thirty of his forty-two years had been spent in custody of one sort or another. He had also escaped fifteen times and would have got out of Durham's E Wing in 1968 with John McVicar, had he not been recaptured on the way, leaving McVicar to go it alone.

Shortly before that event, Probyn attended a discussion group in Durham, where he met sociologist Stan Cohen. Probyn's intellect, never recognised by the formal education system, together with his troubled background, gave him an affinity with Cohen and his subject and when the book proposal came about, instead of taking the easy and probably more lucrative approach, he decided to write about his life from a sociological perspective. The result, exploiting the sobriquet given to him by the police and press when he was fourteen and about to appear at the Old Bailey, was *Angel Face – the Making of a Criminal*.[65]

Stan Cohen, who contributes an introduction, writes that Walter Probyn's story "has the dual characteristics of what for me has always constituted good sociology". He refers to "unmasking, debunking, reading between the lines" and to "the ability to make the connection between private troubles and public issues." As the sub-title implies, Probyn recalls - with barely suppressed anger and resentment - the factors that led him to a life of crime, his sentences and escapes and the way he fought bureaucracy on its own terms. He cites petitions to the Home Office, a letter to the Parole Board, press reports and questionnaires in an autobiography that is very different from that of his former wing-mate in Durham, McVicar, or indeed from any other British prisoner autobiography.

The uniqueness of the book, together with the testimonial of Stan Cohen, brought *Angel Face* considerable critical and academic recognition. Probyn, whom his mentor describes as "an amateur sociologist", deserves credit for adopting the approach he did and not simply cashing in on the sensational aspects of his criminal career.

The book, however, did nothing to divert Probyn from crime and he returned to prison before it was published. Three decades on it appears dated. In a period when great emphasis is given to the need for personal responsibility, his complaints read as the litany of one who blames others for his every predicament without recognising any culpability of his own.

One Black Prisoner

Published accounts of black prisoners' prison experience are rare in Britain. Ethnic minority groups comprised about twenty-two per cent of the male and twenty-nine percent of the female prison populations in 2002[66] but only one significant first-hand account of the black prisoner's experience has ever been published - *Labelled a Black Villain* by Trevor Hercules.[67] Hercules served a seven year sentence in the 1970s for armed robberies in London. His book is an angry, articulate account of the emotional turmoil he felt as a young man growing up in a predominantly white society, one that stereotypes black youth in negative ways and is surprised when they protest. Arriving in Wormwood Scrubs, almost immediately he is placed in the segregation unit after responding to racial insults from a prison officer. The threat of violence from dangerous inmates is constant. In Gartree he is caught up in a riot and in Parkhurst a fellow prisoner is murdered in cold blood.

As he did during his sentence, Hercules challenges prejudice in his book. He rails against the apathy of black people who are "wasting our lives away" and black professionals who have given up their identity, unlike his heroes, George Jackson, Mohamed Ali, Malcolm X, Marcus Garvey and Angela Davies. But Hercules is no separatist; he describes a moving scene where a group of white and black prisoners, their inhibitions and grudges relaxed by sharing some smuggled-in brandy, suddenly realise that in prison at least they are all in the same situation. *Labelled a Black Villain* is more than a prison memoir; it is one man's analysis of resentment, stereotyping and, especially, black consciousness.

Hercules was released in 1981 after serving the whole seven years of his sentence. Looking back some years later, he felt that prison had done him no good at all, that the effects had been just the opposite:

> Prison doesn't help you to understand your crime or why you did it, nor does it help prepare you to go out into the world you left behind, the same

world where you committed your crime. There was no form of reform, not even any attempt at it. If you were labelled a criminal and imprisoned, you would still be a criminal when you came out because there was nothing inside to dissuade you from criminality. When criminals are lumped together then criminality is accepted as quite normal and nothing to be ashamed of. Prison is for confinement; or for spite – you've done something to society, so society will do something to you: jail, tit for tat."

Labelled a Black Villain made only a low-key impression when it was published. It has long been out of print but the messages within are as strong as ever and it stands as the only serious memoir by a minority ethnic prisoner in Britain. In the early 1990s, Trevor Hercules was said to be writing another book. If he did so it has not yet been published.

The Women

As a former debutante, the cousin of an earl and a descendant of two prime ministers, Joan Henry was an unlikely inmate of Holloway Prison. But that is where she went in 1951, sentenced at the Old Bailey to twelve months imprisonment for passing fraudulent cheques. For many women - or men - from her background, prison would have meant ruin, but Henry was a writer with three romantic novels published and, just like other writers sent to prison, the experience proved to be an unsought opportunity.

Who Lie In Gaol,[68] a memoir based on her time in Holloway and Askham Grange open prison, was an immediate best-seller, and Henry's writing took a new direction. Her book was filmed as *The Weak and the Wicked*, and her 1954 novel, *Yield to the Night*,[69] centring on the moral iniquities of capital punishment, became instantly topical when, soon after it was published, the club hostess Ruth Ellis was hanged for shooting her lover.

Who Lie In Gaol sent shock waves through the criminal justice system. Joan Henry's writing style was light, her characters sharply described and dialogue lively, but her account of conditions in Holloway brought accusations of sensationalism from the Prison Service and the involvement of the home secretary, Sir David Maxwell Fyfe.

The Prison Officers' Association threatened libel proceedings, although they failed to materialise, and even the Howard League for Penal Reform distanced itself from Henry's book, the chairman writing to the Manchester *Guardian* alleging inaccuracies in it about Holloway and deploring what he claimed were unwarranted attacks on the staff.[70]

Henry described prisoners being treated with brutality that caused many to suffer "nerve storms" or "go off their heads". She wrote:

> *Discipline is not enforced by yelling at women as though they were pigs. I witnessed one woman, goaded beyond endurance by a particularly sadistic officer, empty her slop-pail over her, before being dragged off, screaming and cursing at her tormentor, by six other screws for punishment.*[71]

Henry's critics were alarmed at descriptions of sick prisoners being left to suffer unattended all night long, of pregnant women giving birth in their cells, while their babies sometimes died of neglect, and her claim that prison staff thought convicted women were "unfit for normal consideration". Such comments would have been bad enough for the Home Office and POA to stomach, but Henry went further, describing lesbian relationships in Holloway not only amongst prisoners but also involving predatory officers. She quotes one inmate, "My mum wouldn't believe the stories I could tell 'er and she's ever so broad-minded."

Who Lie In Gaol was the first account by a prisoner of life in a women's prison since the Suffragettes and those involved in the 1916 Easter Rising. The authorities protested but many reviewers, including Bertrand Russell who declared it "completely convincing", acclaimed the book, feeling that it was both timely and reliable.[72]

Going to prison shaped Joan Henry's subsequent career. Her novel *Yield to the Night*, a tale of the last fortnight in the life of a woman in the condemned cell for murdering a rival in love, was inspired by a prisoner she had met who had been sentenced to death but ultimately reprieved. Reviews for the book were excellent, some urging the home secretary – under pressure at the time from anti-hanging campaigners - to read it. Like *Who Lie In Gaol*, it was made into a movie, directed by Joan Henry's future husband, J. Lee Thompson. Henry went on to write a play on the theme of legalising homosexuality, which had a short run in the West End and two television dramas. She died in 2000, aged eighty-six.[73]

More than thirty years separated Joan Henry from previous prison memoirs by women,[74] and thirty more passed before another such book was published. This time, too, the author was no typical prisoner. Audrey Peckham was a deputy headmistress in Gloucestershire when she was arrested in 1982 for attempting to hire a private detective to murder her lover's wife. She served five months in Pucklechurch Remand Centre and three months in Styal and published *A Woman in Custody* in 1985.[75] Peckham protests her innocence of her conviction for incitement to murder in a book that is best summed up in the words of a journalist, who described the author, as "obviously unhappy about the inevitable exposure of her private life that goes with the publicity she so badly wants." [76]

Publicity was never likely to be lacking for Rosie Johnston's *Inside Out*.[77] In 1986 she was convicted of supplying heroin to her friend Olivia Channon, daughter of a Tory minister, at an end-of-finals party at Oxford University. Olivia Channon died and Johnston received a nine months prison sentence. In Holloway she resolved to write of her prison experiences, and her memoir was published three years later.

She does not discuss her crime, or the events leading up to it, but believes she should not have gone to prison. Channon takes a high-handed tone in her opinions on penal reform.

The Observer, reviewing *Inside Out*, commented:

> *Prisons are generally for the lower orders, but occasionally a middle class person gets sent there and discovers that the system does little except degrade and corrupt everyone involved ...Her book is perceptive on the squalor of prison life, unperceptive and self-pitying on her own predicament.*[76]

Anna Reynolds does write about her crime in her autobiography, *Tightrope – a Matter of Life and Death* [77], published four years after she had been given a life sentence at the age of eighteen for the murder of her mother. Reynolds appealed against the murder conviction on the grounds of pre-menstrual syndrome and in a ground-breaking case her murder conviction was quashed and she was released on probation. She then wrote the story of her life, without, initially, publication in mind. In her book, she does not describe the act, breaking off seconds beforehand and picking up immediately afterwards, but she gives a full account of the events that drove her to such an extreme.

Tightrope is a whole-life, albeit to the age of twenty-two, autobiography, rather than a prison memoir, although Reynolds unsurprisingly covers her time in Holloway and the maximum security women's wing at Durham. She writes of her troubled early life as the only child in a dysfunctional family, of her guilt at the age of eleven when her middle-aged father, an angina sufferer, died after she had kept him waiting in the cold while out shopping. In harrowing terms she describes suicide attempts, becoming pregnant while studying for her A-levels, giving up the baby for adoption and only then telling her mother. Terrible scenes ensued. Depressed and confused and after one too many rows, she picked up a hammer and killed her mother, as she lay in her bed.

Of her decision not to describe the killing, she writes:

> *I have thought and thought and I can see nothing good to be gleaned from the details of the act that happened. I killed my mother. The past cannot be whitewashed by reconstruction, and it is never far from my mind anyway, whatever I am doing, wherever I am, whoever I am with. It always haunts me and I pay for it every day with my heart's pain and memory that is too vivid for peace or comfort.*[78]

Her book won praise from *The Times*, whose reviewer said "Reynolds is a natural writer, and it is a tragedy that she should be introduced to her reading public under these conditions."[79]

But the reading public had little time to take in the fine detail of Anna Reynolds' life – the priest, after her father's funeral, getting drunk and setting his cassock on fire; meeting other mourners at her mother's funeral – "how do you commiserate with a murderess?"; waiting for the jury's verdict at her trial as a nurse and probation officers did their best to amuse her, and countless other vignettes of an unusual but tragic life – for soon after it was published, *Tightrope* was hastily withdrawn, following a claim that Anna Reynolds had libelled the trial judge.

Interviewed later for *Prison Writing*, she said "There was all sorts of kerfuffle went on with that. The libel was about something that happened with the jury and something that happened when the jury were in the room and were filing out."[80]

Anna Reynolds became the first editor of *Inside Time*, the national prisoners' newspaper, while simultaneously embarking on a writing career that has included a novel and plays for television and the theatre. Her work has been influenced by the time she spent in prison, although she is first and foremost a writer not a reformer. As such, and despite her own traumatic history, in the 1990s she went back into Holloway and Bedford as a writer-in-residence.

Prosecutions that become *causes celebré* can inspire *Prison Writing*. The Wintercomfort case of 1999, in which Ruth Wyner and her co-worker at a Cambridge day centre for the homeless were jailed for allowing the premises to be used for the supply of drugs, was no exception. Wyner, a woman with no previous criminal record, got five years and her colleague four, even though there was no suggestion that either of them had been involved. The case hung on the question of whether they had done enough to try to stop drugs being sold within the centre.

As the campaign to release them gained a high media profile, they were released on bail. The ensuing appeal did not quash their convictions but the sentences were reduced to allow them to remain at liberty.

In Highpoint, a women's closed prison in Suffolk, Ruth Wyner wrote an account of Christmas in jail, which was published in *Prison Writing*.[81] Following her release she wrote *From the Inside, Dispatches from a Women's Prison*,[82] a book that captures the distress, rage, pain and constant anxiety of being in prison.

She asks:

> *Did I really deserve this?*
> *I had been outspoken during my time working in homelessness, certainly more outspoken than most of my colleagues, speaking up on behalf of those I was entrusted to serve. That was my job. Was it also my crime? To speak up for the destitute and the dispossessed in our midst, people from all walks of life who had lost hope for the future. I had got to know these people, those who lived like shadows, seen by many as a stain on our communities, as lower and lesser, undeserving of our aid.*
> *Now, locked away, I had become one of those shadows myself.*[83]

From the Inside begins at Kings Lynn Crown Court, as Ruth Wyner and her co-accused are sentenced and the public gallery erupts, drowning out the judge's words. Like many memoirs by those to whom prison is a new experience, it describes the procedures in detail and the author's shock at what is happening to her and fear of what lies ahead. These feelings remain strong throughout, as she goes first to Holloway and then to Highpoint, where she gains some solace from the Kainos Community within the jail.

Wyner writes with an introspection brought about by her indignation at the pointlessness that pervades so much of prison life and the way she and her fellow inmates are treated by staff. She blends in the stories of those around her – drug mules, shoplifters and her cellmate who had stabbed her boyfriend - and readily falls in with the tenet of prison culture that says "The screws are our jailers. They are the common enemy. Only cowards cross the divide."[84]

First-hand accounts of life in women's prisons are not plentiful. Those that have been published commercially are mostly by ex-prisoners whose sentences were relatively short. Joan Henry and Audrey Peckham each did twelve months less remission, Rosie Johnston nine months. Phoebe Willetts published a book on the strength of a six month sentence for CND activities in the 1960s[85] and a few years later another campaigner Pat Arrowsmith, who had served eight short sentences, lightly disguised her prison experiences as fiction.[86]

It is ironic that most of these books received more media coverage than the memoir of a woman who served eighteen years of a life sentence, almost all of it as a Category A prisoner in the only maximum security wing for women in the country, and was then found to have been wrongfully convicted. In 1974 Judith Ward was given twelve life sentences after being found guilty of planting a bomb which exploded on a coach, killing twelve people.

Quashing her sentence in the Court of Appeal, Lord Justice Glidewell condemned forensic scientists, prosecution lawyers, police officers and a prison doctor for concealing evidence that could have pointed to her innocence. "Our law does not tolerate a conviction to be secured by ambush, he said" - words that stayed with Judith Ward when she published her book, *Ambushed – My Story*.[87]

Brought up in Stockport, she had drifted between Britain and Ireland, working on a farm, as a chambermaid and even in a circus, besides a short spell in the British Army. Her aimless lifestyle led her to Liverpool, where, sheltering in a shop doorway, she was picked up by police officers on alert following the coach bombing which had occurred ten days earlier on the M62. Her Irish connections aroused suspicion and media outrage led police and prosecution to jump to false conclusions which were confirmed by scientific opinion that would eventually be proved valueless.

Placed in segregation for her own protection at Risley Remand Centre, the isolation made her retreat into herself:

> *My moods swayed between high hysteria, when I would sing for hours and laugh at nothing, and times when I wouldn't utter a word all day as I read book after book, retaining nothing. Then there were depressions, black foul, soul-destroying. I wanted to lie down and die, never wake up. I cried at nothing and everything: prisoners talking to each other through the bars at night, a bird singing in the early dawn, disturbed prisoners crying in the cells below.*[88]

Durham's H Wing – now holding women but only six years before known as E Wing and the scene of John McVicar's high profile escape - was to be Judith Ward's location for the next fourteen years. She had the company of other women serving life sentences but as a Category A prisoner her visitors and correspondents were vetted.

She estimates that in all she spent 150,000 hours alone:

> *My mental state was such that if I had been left locked in my cell for ever more, I don't think I would have objected... It's very hard to describe such an emptiness of feeling. A draining of the soul, a state of total apathy and abjectness to the nth degree, where physically one functions but mentally one is totally indifferent.*[89]

Ambushed tells how it felt to be a woman in maximum security, to be innocent of a horrendous crime with little hope that the truth would ever emerge. Unlike the Birmingham Six, the Guildford Four and other victims of miscarriages of justice, Judith Ward had no campaign or pressure group supporting her. She was eventually vindicated only through the efforts of a solicitor who believed in her, after the forensic scientist whose evidence had been crucial to the prosecution case had been discredited. Her story rises from a pit of the darkest despair to her eventual freedom and desire to write for a living. Although published after her release, much of the material in her book was worked on while inside. *Ambushed* was a solid start but it has not found the position in prison literature that it deserves.

The impact of life stories

The early prison memoirs by Balfour, Macartney and Phelan were written by men who had served long sentences in what were known at that time as convict prisons. They reflected the closed, secret worlds of Parkhurst and Dartmoor, the brutality and oppression of regimes that punished men for trivial transgressions of the rules and totally suppressed any form of *Prison Writing*. Changes in British society following the end of the Second World War led to improvements in prison conditions and the works of Frank Norman and Brendan Behan's in the 1950s had an entertaining and idiosyncratic approach.

The style and content of Behan's work was so powerful that *Borstal Boy* and *The Quare Fellow* retain their currency five decades on.

Not until the 1970s was a prisoner's autobiography published while the author was still inside. The books of John McVicar and Jimmy Boyle differed in approach but both gave insights into maximum security that appealed to a general and academic readership and both authors emphasised their rejection of crime. In more recent times the emphasis for many prison writers, as well as telling their own stories, has been to highlight deteriorating conditions whereby overcrowding and drug abuse have become norms, and to call for reform.

All life stories are inevitably unique and there is no typical prison writer, but among those who have published autobiographies and memoirs some links can be made. John McVicar, Valerio Viccei and Razor Smith were all bank robbers. Walter Probyn was in Durham's E Wing with McVicar and organised his escape. Jimmy Boyle, the first of what could be called the 'Scottish School' of *Prison Writing* to be published from the Barlinnie Special Unit, was followed by Larry Winters, John Steele and Hugh Collins, while other former inmates have published life stories co-authored by journalists.

Oscar Wilde's *De Profundis* was a major influence on John McVicar, while established writers Taki and Jeffrey Archer, who were sent to prison claimed identification with Wilde. Of the women, with the exception of Judith Ward and Anna Reynolds, both of whom had life sentences quashed, all who have published were in custody less than twelve months – and all believed that they should not have been sent to prison. Clearly, the prison memoir by a woman to compare with seminal works such as those by McVicar, Boyle or Collins has yet to be published.

3] Facts, Fictions, Poems & Plays

Correspondents and Columnists

When Jimmy O'Connor was released from a life sentence in 1952, his one priority was to fight the murder conviction that had caused him to serve ten years in prison. A petty thief found guilty of murder on doubtful evidence, O'Connor spent two months in the condemned cell and was reprieved only two days before his execution date. Many people with knowledge of his case believed that he was innocent, including the news editor of the *Sunday Empire News*, Jack Fishman, who, once O'Connor was out of prison, gave him a job as crime reporter.

O'Connor had no background in journalism. His value to a newspaper editor lay in his contacts and inside knowledge of the London underworld. Later, he wrote: "I negotiated series, thought of ideas and sold them. Most of these were involved with crime but that is what I knew best… Doors were opened to me all over the place and I used to get first hand information."[1]

As a reporter, he covered many of the major cases of the 1950s, besides ghost-writing several autobiographies for infamous criminals of the period. His obituary in *The Independent* would say, "For Fishman and other Fleet Street editors, Jimmy was like a foreign correspondent reporting from the underworld, someone who could interpret for them news and even language they could not understand themselves."[2]

Three decades later, John McVicar took a similar route from prison, albeit as a freelance rather than a staff journalist. Unlike O'Connor and other ex-prisoners who began writing for the press and went on to publish autobiographies, McVicar's book had already been published and his name was known in media circles:

> *Because I came out with a little bit of publicity it enabled me to get some offers for articles. I just started to hack it, I suppose … My first hit was* The Sunday Times. *I always remember that, they paid me a lot more than they needed to and Will Ellsworth-Jones worked with me and he just let me run… Then I got some work with the* New Statesman *and gradually I started to tick over.*[3]

McVicar's column in the *New Statesman* detailed aspects of his life on parole, with references to old acquaintances in the underworld, new friends, and day-to-day events like meeting with his probation officer and sparring with a champion boxer. His descriptions of the fast, picaresque world in which he moved entertained the left-wing, liberal readership and the discipline of a weekly column proved valuable experience to him as a journalist.

Over the next couple of decades John McVicar wrote for most of the national newspapers and many magazines, moving easily between commentary on criminal justice issues to feature articles on sport, lifestyle and popular culture. In 1998 he was required to defend a high-profile libel case brought by the athlete Linford Christie. McVicar had written the offending article for a small circulation, underground magazine that was no longer in existence by the time the case reached the High Court. Unable to get legal aid, he represented himself and lost the case, but only after putting in an impressive performance as his own advocate.

From 1997 until 2000 McVicar was a mainstay of *Punch* magazine, where he regularly exposed contentious issues that mainstream journalists could not or would not touch. Drugs in sport or show-business, miscarriages of justice and the Russian Mafia were typical subjects that interested him. When the television presenter Jill Dando was shot dead in London in April 1999, McVicar's investigative reporting of the murder went from campaign to crusade, which he later published as a book, *Dead On Time*.[4] Soon afterwards he embarked on a new venture as a publisher, setting up Artnik Media with his wife.

O'Connor and McVicar found their respective niches in journalism by writing about the worlds they knew, after their release. Other ex-prisoners, notably Jim Phelan and Brendan Behan,[5] had done the same. Mark Leech, in Blundeston, serving a sentence for arson, took a more confrontational line.

Already a seasoned litigant through cases he had brought against the prison authorities, in May 1990 Leech began writing articles for *The Guardian*, while still in prison. Critical in tone and content, his first piece 'Watchdogs on a Tightrope', looked at the inadequacies of prison disciplinary procedures and was pertinent in the aftermath of the riots at Strangeways Prison, Manchester.

Two years earlier, he had won a House of Lords judgement against the deputy governor of Parkhurst Prison, regarding the non-independence of adjudications.[6] Now he was concerned that "many of the Strangeways rioters will never face charges in open court but will be disciplined behind closed doors by prisons boards of visitors."[7]

After this journalistic debut, *The Guardian* began to publish articles by Mark Leech each month. In October 1990 he tackled the failings of the system and the unwillingness of those responsible to be accountable:

> *The publication of the latest rapidly escalating crime figures shows the uselessness of our penal system as a place of reform; the buck has been passed with the speed of a dud cheque.*[8]

In his autobiography, *A Product of the System*, Leech claimed that he had received seven hundred letters following the publication of this article.[9] He remains a prolific writer and broadcaster, his focus rarely wavering from penal matters.

A thirteen-year sentence for armed robbery was the grounding for Peter Wayne's journalistic career. By the time he was released he was a full member of the National Union of Journalists, had a regular column in *Prospect* magazine and was about to sign a book deal. Wayne's route to publication was unusual: the well-educated, adopted son of a wealthy businessman, he took to crime as a more exciting option than conventional life.

While in prison he became recognised as an expert on the baroque architect Thomas Archer, designer of churches and country houses, and in 1993 Wayne was the subject of a *Within These Walls* television documentary, in which he was allowed out of Long Lartin, a maximum security prison, to film in a London church, among other locations. The press were interested in him – but he was more interested in them. As he would later write:

> *I began my "career" as a writer because I was sick and fed up of journalists writing about me. They got a fat pay packet at the end of it and I got a few fan letters from cranks and religious maniacs. As I have always kept a journal I was in a position to turn back the pages and reconstruct in a journalistic and (I hope) literary way.*[10]

He sent some articles to Matthew Parris at *The Times*, who was enthusiastic and spread the word to other editors, notably Auberon Waugh and Dominic Lawson. Wayne began reviewing books, initially for the *Literary Review* and *The Spectator*, later *The Economist* and *Times Literary Supplement* and then *The New Yorker*, where he reviewed *The Oxford History of Prisons*.

His work was well-crafted, with an air of erudition, and it was inevitable that he would not be content to remain a reviewer. He had contacts in literary London and when the monthly magazine *Prospect* was launched in 1994 he was invited to write a piece about cuts in prison education. This led to his column, 'The Prisoner', which continued until after his release, when his chaotic lifestyle eventually brought it to a close.

Wayne's monthly *Prospect* pieces, each of them around a thousand words, were despatches from a closed world. They were atmospheric, colourful and humorous, none more so than when he wrote of New Labour winning the 1997 General Election, and the widespread rumour within the prison system that an amnesty was imminent and all inmates were to be released early on parole.[11]

In another he described the joys of seeing the countryside while being transferred between two prisons seventy miles apart – a journey that took three days and two overnight stops. When he left Lindholme, "my winter retreat … somewhere out in the windy flat wilderness of South Yorkshire", he condemned the prison officers as "offhand, abrupt, distant and monosyllabic", while the prisoners, "with their strong brews and flat vowels, for the most part unloved, undernourished, uneducated boys from the badlands…were warm, welcoming, winsome types."[12]

Wayne's homosexuality and the heroin addiction he had acquired in prison frequently pervaded his column, as he wrote from Channings Wood, where he went for drug treatment:

> *The good news is that, despite several relapses, I finally appear to have expunged the devil's dandruff from my system.*[13]

Peter Wayne was released in 1998. His architectural studies had brought him to the attention of, amongst others, Lord Richard Rogers and the Earl of Plymouth, who supported his parole. He was awarded a scholarship to the Courtauld Institute in London to take a degree in history of art. However, the temptations of what he called the "newly cool Brittanic kingdom"[14] proved more attractive and within weeks he was back in prison serving twenty-seven months for theft and fraud.

Once again he was writing for *Prospect*, where on occasion he hit the topical button, as with a piece on the recently convicted murderer Michael Stone, whose path he had crossed fifteen years earlier in Albany.[15] With this sort of anecdote and his own history, the national media were more interested in Peter Wayne than ever, and several journalists visited him. Soon he had a literary agent, a handsome advance and a contract with a leading publisher for a novel and a book based on his journals. To date, neither has been published.

Most journalists yearn for a 'scoop', to be first to report on an exclusive story. Not too many would consider a spell on remand in Belmarsh Prison a price worth paying to get such a story, especially with the prospect of a life sentence to follow. This was Razor Smith's situation when his big opportunity came along – in the shape of Jonathan Aitken, the former Tory minister who perjured himself while suing *The Guardian* for an alleged libel and ended up in Belmarsh, two cells away from the armed robber Smith.

'Jonathan Come Lately' by Noel 'Razor' Smith appeared in *Punch* magazine on 3 July, 1999 The article told how Aitken had arrived in Belmarsh and as he stood among other prisoners "he looked like a ham-strung lamb surrounded by hungry wolves". At first meeting, Smith had harangued the disgraced politician for his friendship with Michael Howard, the former Home Secretary, but Aitken stood his ground and the two men, from opposite extremes of the social spectrum, spent some time together. Smith contacted John McVicar, crime correspondent on *Punch*, the article was sent out of Belmarsh and Smith was paid £800. [16]

At the time, Jonathan Aitken was hot news in the British press. Wealthy, debonair and a high-flying politician, he had once been romantically linked with Margaret Thatcher's daughter. He sued *The Guardian*, he said "with the simple sword of truth and the trusty shield of fair play", in his fight to "cut out the cancer of bent and twisted journalism" - terms that would return to haunt him and lead to the eighteen-month sentence he was now serving. Until this time Razor Smith's writing had been mainly restricted to *Prison Writing*, with a handful of articles in *New Law Journal* and, ironically, *The Guardian*.

After the *Punch* article appeared, Aitken agreed to an exclusive interview with Smith, which was duly published in the next issue. By now the Belmarsh authorities were alert to this breach of the prison rules but Smith was undeterred, dictating his piece to John McVicar by telephone. Shortly afterwards, he smuggled out an article about Barry George, on remand at the time for the murder of television personality Jill Dando, but he was unable to find a taker as the case was *sub judice*.[17]

The Guardian might not have been Jonathan Aitken's newspaper of choice, but a regular column by serving prisoner Erwin James became so popular that a collection of the articles was published in book form.[18] James was thirteen years into a life sentence for murder when his first piece, a comment on the effect of prison suicides on other inmates, appeared in January 1998.[19] Two years later, an account of how prisoners celebrated the dawn of the new millennium informed readers:

> *At ten to midnight every prisoner in the country must have been standing by his door, blunt instrument in hand. I clutched a coffee tin. Then, at midnight: bedlam.*[20]

These early articles led to Erwin James's column, 'A Life Inside', which initially appeared once a fortnight but soon became weekly.[21] Written almost as a diary, each episode a snapshot of prison life, James's column provided a window into what for most *Guardian* readers was a closed world reported on from a distance. He avoided all real names and established a cast of fellow prisoners – friends and foes, presumably based on real prisoners - whose identities he disguised. Names like Big Rinty, The Celtic Poet, Felix the Gambler, Japes the Joyrider, Felton Leaky, Weevo, Yodle, Cody and Sid Fearlittle, created perhaps to circumvent the rule that prohibited writing about other prisoners, at times gave 'A Life Inside' a comic effect.

From the pen of a lesser writer, this could have detracted from the authenticity of the work, but despite their Runyonesque sobriquets, these were strong characters and James's eye and ear for dialogue and situation meant that the 'message' intended in many of his columns usually got home.

Like the characters in *'A Life Inside'*, Erwin James operated under a cloak of disguise. He never revealed his real name, nor the circumstances that took him to prison. He referred to being in a London prison after receiving his life sentence, in a closed prison in the Midlands and eventually in open conditions, but as for his offence or offences, he gave no details.

In an introduction to the published collection, he refers to his trial, explaining that this is intended only to put the columns into a context. Writing the columns, he states, "A Life Inside is not and never has been about me … my only motivation was to try to shed some light on the dark world that is prison."

James's style was understated and laconic, humour often arising out of situations as he detailed the minutiae of daily life among men who in some cases had been inside even longer than himself. Each column had an expository sub-title, often containing the essence of the piece: "You learn to live with the knock-backs by taking it one day at a time – and not hoping too much. Till it's your turn."[22] In another he reveals: "My recurring nightmare is all about tasting freedom and then losing it again – but that is Big Rinty's reality."[23]

'A Life Inside' was not all about James and his fellow inmates or the issues around them. He tackled topical issues, providing readers with inside opinions on such subjects as the 'Does prison work?' debate,[24] the House of Lords judgement on tariff-setting for life-sentenced prisoners,[25] the return of the ailing train robber Ronnie Biggs[26] and the publication of Jeffrey Archer's diaries.

The latter produced a rare diversion from James's otherwise tolerant and uncritical tone, when he castigated Archer for:

> ...writing about some of his fellow prisoners in a way in which they could be identified. Not only is this against prison rules but, for the high-profile prisoners he names, it is grossly unfair and amounts to the abuse of powerless men already enduring wretched lives.[27]

Few would have described Jeffrey Archer as powerless, even while he was in prison, but he was certainly a high-profile prisoner. James was now writing about him as he had earlier about Ronnie Biggs, who was a powerless and wretched case by any standard.

What did this say about the prisoners he featured in his *Guardian* columns? In his condemnation of Archer's prison diary, James raised the question of whether 'A Life Inside' might have included a greater ratio of fiction to fact than had hitherto have been apparent. But even if that were so, it took nothing away from the columns' appeal to readers.

Opportunities for prisoners to write for national newspapers are not plentiful. Erwin James got his opening through a writer friend who heard that *The Guardian* was looking for a prisoner to write occasional articles. The friend put James's name forward and he was invited to send in some sample pieces. Until then, his published writing had amounted to letters in local newspapers and bits and pieces in prison magazines, plus a first prize in the prose section of the Koestler awards.

The Guardian has a history of using freelance writers and it was in keeping with that ethos that Erwin James was encouraged. In 2003 the paper advertised for a "Prison Correspondent" to cover "all aspects of prisons from day-to-day stories of life inside to broader areas of penal policy". The advertisement stated that the post, for twelve months, would suit "a recent former prisoner".²⁸

The successful applicant was Eric Allison, aged sixty, who began work in October 2003. Allison was well-versed in his subject, having served a total of fifteen years in Strangeways, Brixton, Wormwood Scrubs, Wandsworth among many other prisons. Along the way he had written occasional letters to newspapers and magazines and co-authored a book on the Strangeways riots.²⁹

The editor of *The Guardian*, Alan Rusbridger, had a simple explanation for the decision to hire his new correspondent. He said: "We don't know enough about what goes on inside our prisons."

Of life, reality and beyond

Edward Bunker, who began writing in San Quentin, the U.S. penitentiary, had five novels rejected before *No Beast So Fierce* was published in 1973, while he was still in prison. His book, the story of a released prisoner who is driven back to crime was made into a film and Bunker quickly gained cult status as an author.

His success had been a long time coming and not without many hurdles:

> *I wrote six novels before getting one published. I tried to write short stories … I wrote a hundred short stories and I never sold one of those. I had written from 1953 to 1972 and I never sold a word … I used to have to sell my blood to get postage.*³⁰

The eighteen years of rejection slips and letters were not wasted. Bunker read widely and developed his writing craft. He published another two novels before taking up acting, a career that peaked with his appearance in the Tarantino film *Pulp Fiction*. By the late 1990s Bunker had achieved a degree of cult status in Britain and France, sealed by a new novel, *Dog Eat Dog* and a first volume of autobiography, *Mr Blue*.

The United Kingdom has no novelist to compare with Edward Bunker, whose crime and prison-based novels have been championed in the USA by literary luminaries such as William Styron and James Ellroy. Indeed, on this side of the Atlantic, while no novel of any significance has ever been published by a serving prisoner, there have been only a handful by others who have been released.

But even in America, as a prison writer Bunker has no peers. His years of rejection, re-writes and struggles to pay for postage would have deterred most would-be authors. Bunker used the hardships to develop the skills to become a writer. Here, prison writers have mostly taken the autobiographical route – and in many cases, publishers have seen that as easier to market, given the British media's hunger for crime stories. Only a handful, including Jimmy Boyle, Hugh Collins and Anna Reynolds, have branched out and published novels.

Hero of the Underworld, published almost two decades after Jimmy Boyle's release from a life sentence, begins with a passage suggestive of the author's own experience in segregation units:

> *A forethought . . .*
> *In trying to describe the vacuum of my solitude, I can only compare its monotony to the constant drip of tap-water from the nearby sink. Thereafter, being a totally subjective experience, it defied description.*[31]

This could be Boyle recalling the years he spent segregated from other prisoners in the notorious cages of the Scottish system, had such places not been without any facilities whatsoever, least of all sinks. Here, the speaker is main character, John Alexander Ferguson, who insists on being addressed only as Hero and has just been released from The Institution. For years Hero has suffered violence as well as medical and sexual abuse, following a gross miscarriage of justice. When he gets out, life is little better as he is bullied by his "supervisor", exploited by his two landlords and terrorised by the workers in the abattoir where he is sent to work for a pittance.

Boyle's novel is dark country, but not the sort of book the title might suggest and far from the mainstream crime novel. Hero becomes the leader of a collection of misfits with similar histories to his own – the midget Bonecrusher, the fearsome Lockjaw, and Sligo, who speaks with an Irish accent despite never having been to Ireland.

The characters are as picaresque a collection as ever appeared in print – Pig Thompson from the abattoir, a prostitute The Widow, soon to become Hero's first ever lover, Morty the mortician who teaches him the funeral trade, once he manages to get away from the abattoir, Morty's necrophiliac assistant Shuffles and the rat-eating tramps, Warthog and Skelly.

When Hero and Bonecrusher rescue a prize bull from slaughter, the fight-back begins. As their foes fall out among themselves, after Hero and company rob their evil landlords' money, the nightmare scenario, if it comes to light who is responsible, is too horrific for anyone to contemplate.

Hero of the Underworld is a powerful allegory. The suggestion of autobiography at the start is deceptive, but the final sentence of the novel – Hero saying "This has taught us that the ultimate revenge lies in making the positive decision" – does reflect Boyle's own road to redemption.

The two volumes of autobiography that Hugh Collins published, one covering his criminal lifestyle before going to prison and the second the difficulties he faced on release, confirmed his talent as a writer. When he then moved into crime fiction he was able to delve into a lifetime's experience in the Scottish underworld. His debut *No Smoke*, in 2001, was set in Glasgow twenty-five years earlier, shortly before Collins committed the murder that led to his life sentence. Both this and its immediate follow-up *The Licensee*, set in the early 80s, are fast, pacy tales from the nether world: violent but comic and, like his autobiographical work, written in dialect that is not always totally intelligible to a non-Scots reader.

Collins's novels have no heroes. They brim with corrupt police officers, psychopathic gangsters and eccentric petty criminals. The references to his own past are evident, if distorted. The title, *The Licensee*, was the sobriquet of a real-life gang leader, albeit of an era later than the period of the story. In the novel a family is murdered by the burning of their home, as were in reality six members of the Doyle family in what became known as the Glasgow Ice Cream Wars.

The father of one of the main characters was murdered by a man who turned to sculpture while in the Barlinnie Special Unit – as did Collins. Mischievously, perhaps, a corrupt detective is known as 'The Hammer', a nickname the press gave to a chief constable of Glasgow in the 1970s, although there is no suggestion of a link.

Collins writes fiction with the confidence that comes from hard-earned experience. In *No Smoke*, he understates situations that a "straight-peg", as he calls non-criminals, might exploit, but when he describes a prisoner on hunger strike it is clear that he is portraying an experience in a way that only one who has been there could. Almost without exception his characters are devoid of any semblance of morality, while Collins, through their words and actions, makes no concession to political correctness.

Mainstream crime fiction they may be, but Hugh Collins's work is a far cry from the middle-of-the-road crime novels written by middle-class authors for a middle England readership. Time and output will tell but his first novels suggest Collins is the most likely candidate to claim UK rights to Edward Bunker's mantle.

Boyle's novel is influenced by experience, enhanced with a great creative flair. Collins deals with raw reality, building on stories and characters he met in and out of prison. Another Scotsman, Howard Wilson, who published a novel while still serving a life sentence, also wrote a crime story, but one set in New York, a place he had never visited.

Angels of Death[32] concerns a private eye, Brent Grant, who stumbles upon a religious cult while he is investigating the disappearance of a teenager. Grant is called upon to help his old friends in Homicide and when he starts to probe, the cult, who call themselves the Angels, are not happy. Prostitutes are murdered, the private-eye mixes violence with tenderness and the action trundles on over seven hundred pages.

In Scotland, the publication of *Angels of Death* received a lot of press coverage, but interest centred on the author rather than the book. Twenty-five years earlier, ex-detective Howard Wilson had shot dead two of his former colleagues in the Glasgow force after committing a bungled armed robbery.

In prison he was involved with Jimmy Boyle in the riots at Peterhead and Porterfield, receiving a six year sentence in addition to his life term, for attempting to murder prison officers. The Scottish media had not forgotten, nor had the victims' friends and families. The book made little impact and although a follow-up was said to be in progress, it was not published. In 2002, at the age of sixty-four, Howard Wilson was released on life licence.

Autobiography provided Anna Reynolds with her publishing debut, although libel laws meant the experience was short-lived. From the outset she showed indications of being a dedicated, rather than opportunist, writer and it was no surprise that when she came to publish a novel the basis of the story bore echoes of her own life. *Insanity*[33] is the bleak and oppressive tale of teenager Rosa Raine's attempts to escape from a dull suburban existence and a detached mother.

Like Reynolds, Rosa gives birth to a baby from whom she is soon separated. When asked what she will call the child, she replies "Insanity". Obsessive love becomes mental illness as Rosa becomes entwined with two art students and is eventually admitted to a mental hospital. When the book appeared, Anna Reynolds's history guaranteed media interest, although reviews were mixed.

For a short time in the mid-1990s, The Mount, a medium-security prison in Hemel Hempstead, seemed a hotbed of prison-based fiction. Journalists from national newspapers visited, writers-in-residence were photographed beside their protégés and prison writing received a definite boost. While novels by prisoners are rare, in 1994, from The Mount, Phillip Baker published *Blood Posse*, and two years later Rocky Carr who had just been released, brought out *Brixton Bwoy*. Unusual as it was to see a prisoner's novel in print, it was even more so to see two, and both by black prisoners from the same prison.

Philip Baker received the most coverage, perhaps, like others before him, helped by publicity that played up the fact that he had been in prison.

According to the *Daily Telegraph*:

> *Philip Baker uses words like a sawn-off shotgun. The point-blank blast of his prose rips through the reader, leaving a dazed impression of overwhelming damage. His first novel,* Blood Posse *, is an account of American gang-warfare and prison life ...Blood, guts and sweat splatter on every page.*[34]

Baker was serving fifteen years for drug offences and had begun writing his novel in Parkhurst, encouraged by an education officer. He had grown up in Brooklyn, got involved in the drugs and gun culture and, it was claimed, had a murder charge dropped. His novel features a young Jamaican in New York at a time when West Indian immigrants are threatening the established order on the streets. One reviewer commented: "You won't learn much about street gangs but you can surmise a fair amount about the author, his anxieties and his compensatory myths."[35]

Rocky Carr also went back to his roots for his novel, *Brixton Bwoy*. He had taught himself to read in prison and was encouraged to express himself on paper by Jeremy Gavron, writer-in-residence in the prison. Seeing an early story he had written on the pages of a prison magazine gave Carr the impetus to write more and by the time he was paroled in 1994 he had completed five chapters. Six months of freedom produced only another one-and-a-half pages, when he was convicted of robbery and returned to prison for another four years.

Back behind bars, Carr resumed writing and the novel was published shortly after he was once again released. *Brixton Bwoy* is, by the author's admission, a fictionalised autobiography. At the age of nine, the main character, Pupatee, is sent to England from Jamaica, to live with his brother, Joe. Pupatee discovers electricity and snow for the first time, but his brother beats him unmercifully and to survive the boy turns to crime.

Carr's tale is uncomplicated and simply told, but it attracted several features in the national newspapers, helped by the fact that Carr had moved from London to live in the seaside town Lowestoft, hoping to get away from his former life and make a living from writing.

Neither *Blood Posse* nor *Brixton Bwoy* were commercially successful. For Carr, certainly, writing was not to be his saviour and after a short time he was at odds with the law once again and back in prison.

Prison Writing, during its ten year existence, printed numerous short stories. Some, like those by Razor Smith, were based on personal experience, in his case firmly planted within prison walls or the streets of south London. Smith's were gritty tales. In his first, 'Johnny makes a Comeback',[36] Johnny the Jug, once a proud armed robber, is released from seventeen years in prison to a shabby bed-sit, where he contemplates his bleak future – and the shotgun that lies in a suitcase on top of the wardrobe. Johnny knows the dangers, but he needs money.

In 'Love Letters', which won first prize for fiction in a *Prison Writing* competition, a prisoner is told by his wife during a visit that their marriage is over. Distraught, he goes back to his cell, switches on his radio and slashes his wrists. As he fades into oblivion he hears Elvis Presley singing 'Love Letters' and in his mind he is nineteen and dancing with his wife-to-be.

In his stories Razor Smith used humour to good effect, in dialogue and in situation, but he was never afraid to highlight the iniquities of prison. In the uncompromising 'No Tears For Eddie', a prison officer is killed during a riot and his colleagues avenge him by hanging one of the rioters in the segregation unit and making it look like suicide. Eddie is a lifer with no friends or family outside to ask questions. Another story, 'The Reluctant Counter-Puncher', at the time unpublished, was read by novelist Will Self and led directly to the publication of *A Few Kind Words and a Loaded Gun*, Smith's autobiography.

Stories about daily life on prison landings or yards appeared regularly in *Prison Writing*. Sometimes just a snippet of dialogue or a basic situation produced a full story. John Wrigglesworth, a lifer with many years in jail behind him, was probably the first person to fictionalise the procedure and problems of mandatory drug testing in his story, 'Extracting The Urine'.[38]

When a prisoner is called upon to provide a urine sample he has great difficulty. Eventually he succeeds, but the next day he is told the sample has been lost and he must give another. He assaults the officer who issues the order and, in an ending perhaps not unanticipated by the reader, explains to the governor at his adjudication, "I thought he was taking the piss."

Jimmy Walker had no first-hand experience of heroin. He had seen the desperation of those dependant on the drug before he went to prison, and then realised that inside it could be even worse. In 'The Visit',[39] he draws on his observation in visiting rooms, conversations he had heard and the skills he had learned on a creative writing degree course to produce a story of an inmate who wants to overcome addiction but cannot, of his girlfriend who works as a prostitute to feed both their habits, and their ultimate tragedy.

Of lighter hue is 'Bogart's Coming Out Party', by Ian Watson. He was encouraged by novelist Daphne Glazer, who ran classes in The Wolds, a Humberside prison. The welcome home party had long been a feature in film and television drama, less so in fiction. Here, when Bogart gets out, his motley pals gather in the Diamond pub. The night, the drinking and the revelry all wear on, and Bogart and his party-goers end up arrested.

Many prisoners who write fiction, just like other writers in the outside world, restrict the scope of their imagination to the world with which they are most familiar. 'Write about what you know' is the common tip to be found in teach-yourself books on creative writing. The more imaginative take this further into the area of what they do not know, of what could happen if …

Matthew Williams's stories, poems and plays have won him several awards during a discretionary life sentence that began at the age of nineteen in 1989 and was briefly interrupted by a high-profile escape from Parkhurst six years later.

A regular contributor to *Prison Writing*, his 'The Memoirs of the Inaudible Man' – "You won't have heard of me, of course"[40] was utterly surreal. So too was 'One Day From Matthew Williams' Parkhurst Diary', where he awakes to find a ladies golf team:

> *I saw them and pawed them and loudly implored them – You're gorgeous and sexy, oh please now undress me, and quiver quite naked on my lap. I think you will find I am lovely and kind and a rather erogenous chap!' The women – all six – obliged me quite nicely, I pleased them by ones, by twos and (once) thricely. They gasped and they giggled, "Saint Matty, you're amazing! You're cheaper than gas and much better than double glazing"*.[41]

With other stories, Williams picks up an idea of what could happen to a person sent to prison and lets loose his creative vision. In 'Lazarus, Come Forth',[42] the characters are inanimate objects in the home of a man who returns from a prison sentence for possession of explosives. The door greets him but the room complains "We're left here for twelve years without so much as a bye-your- leave." The shelves grumble, the crockery tells him "We missed you" and the electric fire gasps.

The focus of the story is that in all the years he has been away the man had refused to tell the authorities his address, so that they could not search it and find parcels – presumably more explosives - hidden in the attic. There, the wallpaper croons softly as he approaches as a muffled voice says "I always knew in my heart you'd be back."

In 'Animal Farm'[43] Williams contemplates a nightmare scenario whereby a prison is abandoned by all its staff, leaving the inmates locked in their cells. Realisation comes after four days. Before then, the fictional prisoner who is writing in diary form, "For my solicitor, assuming I see him again", had first thought that the reason no staff came to unlock him and the others was because they were attending a meeting, then maybe dealing with a riot elsewhere in the prison. When the power goes off and the water in his toilet runs dry he knows that the situation is extremely serious. How he and his fellows prisoners cope with the fear and desperation makes for an imaginative story.

In the mid-1990s, as the criminal justice system was contemplating such technological ideas as the electronic tag which allows offenders to be monitored outside prison, an inmate of HMP Garth, Geordie King, suggested that the Home Office were about to announce a new innovation to keep tabs on those who were in custody. Under 'The New Inmate Bar-Code Headswipe System',

> *All inmates will have their very own bar-code tattooed onto their foreheads. This will give the concerted prison officer more time to himself while inmates count themselves in or out of their of their respective locations. All that is required from the inmate is that as he exits or enters a building, he head-butts the entry exit door frame, which has the bar-code reader built into it, and at the same time makes a left to right sweeping motion with his head.* [44]

The system, according to King, would extend to visitors who would be required to "headswipe" the bar-code reader situated on every table in the visits room - anyone having difficulty would be assisted by prison staff.

Governors were advised that if inmates showed reluctance to move about they should be given an incentive – a free pardon going to the one with the most bar-code "headswipes". To date, Geordie King's humorous and fictional forecast has not been implemented - but not so long ago tagging offenders was considered too impossible to even contemplate, so maybe it should not be totally dismissed.

One situation described in *Prison Writing* that is not likely to happen in life, was 'Unexpected Delivery',[45] by Clare Barstow, a lifer who has won numerous awards for her poetry, prose and plays. In this bizarre story, zoology meets gynaecology as the heroine, Sadie Janson, gives birth to a hyena. Immediately after the birth, Sadie asks: "Is she normal, doctor? I know her body isn't, but what about her mind?"

The doctor replies: "She appears normal – although she doesn't cry, But laughing all the time must mean she's happy enough."

Sadie racks her brain, trying to work out what coupling could have produced such a phenomenon. Even though she has studied giraffes for her doctoral thesis, she is as puzzled as anyone by her baby:

> *Her biology alone has to rewrite most of Freud, Desmond Morris, Masters and Johnston, Kinsey and Sheer Hite ...Perhaps she was the new Wonder Woman.*[46]

The story concludes:

> *"Fascinating," said Dr Hopkins. "I think we must study Sadie more closely. But let's not give the game away. Fob her off with some story and who knows, this could be the making of us."*
> *The baby in the cot begins to laugh, a wicked grin on her face.*
> *But who would have the last laugh?*

No less surreal than Clare Barstow's 'Unexpected Delivery' was 'Scene Two Be Done', a fragmented tale by Paul Agutter,[48] at the time in HMP Glenochil, Scotland. Winston O'Rafferty Minotaur, 378, unemployed and of no fixed address, appears at Bow Street Magistrates Court charged with indecent behaviour and acting in a manner liable to cause a breach of the peace. Pleading not guilty, he explains that his actions were brought about by his head being cold and he attempts to demonstrate to the court. Detective Inspector Ham-Jones, "a big, red-nosed, sore-arsed man in plain-clothes uniform", has the task of solving the mysterious deaths of women found in the local river, students demonstrate against minotaur persecution and the aged Winston is remanded in custody, to share a cell with one of the students who has been charged with the murders.

A significant number of the short stories published in *Prison Writing* showed clear promise of a talent for fiction that might have been extended and developed in to form a novel. In correspondence and in interview for this book, many of the authors appeared keen to further their writing in such a way, but for whatever reason – lack of confidence or guidance, distractions elsewhere - none have so far made it to publication.

Rhymers and Versifiers

In the mid 1980s, the renowned poet Ken Smith spent two years in Wormwood Scrubs as writer-in-residence. His brief was to encourage inmates to express themselves. The experience had a profound effect on him and inspired a book *Inside Time*,[49] "about the imprisoned imagination, about prison, about the Scrubs" - in which he described those he met and recounted what they told him of their lives, their crimes, their thoughts and their feelings.

Smith found that in Wormwood Scrubs many prisoners wrote in some form, but more than he expected wrote poetry. He observed: "Writing poetry is not considered odd in here." Indeed not, for poetry is the most popular form of writing amongst inmates of British prisons. As the judges of the poetry category in the 2002 Koestler Awards Scheme commented:

> *Widely publicized and well-organised poetry competitions have always had the effect of making it appear that almost everyone writes poetry ... A competition with a restricted constituency like the Koestler Awards is no different... there is something of a parallel between the conditions of prison existence and one traditional, largely romantic view of the poet's role in relation to society.*[50]

The total number of poetry collections entered in the Koestler competition is not publicised, but in recent years around 120 each year have been successful, receiving modest sums as awards. A selection of the winning entries is published in a booklet by the Koestler Trust.[51]

Prison poets do not become known in the way that authors of autobiography do. Even outside prison, the publication and performance of poetry is a minority interest and as an art form it is unlikely to bring a writer either fame or fortune.

When Oscar Wilde wrote *The Ballad of Reading Gaol*, he hoped to shake public confidence in the penal system and to change what he considered intolerable.[52] In the ensuing century many prisoners have hoped to achieve similar ends, but few would have considered poetry the most suitable medium.

During his lifetime, Larry Winters published only a handful of poems, in an obscure, long-defunct magazine, *The Urbane Gorilla*. At the time he was in the Barlinnie Special Unit but Winters did not write specifically about prison or penal reform. In 1979, two years after he committed suicide in the Special Unit, twenty-two of his poems were published in a slim volume, *The Silent Scream*.[53] The introduction by Daphne Brooke, a regular visitor to Winters in his last two years, describes his work as "a cry from a situation of very complex suffering"… a "search for self-acceptance".[54]

Winters was a man who, all his life, seems to have been at odds with whatever situation he was in. Born in a Glasgow tenement, he was a sickly child, bullied by those around him. As time went on he fought back, driven by a dangerous combination of anger, guilt and superstition that haunted him. His happiest times were spent in the Highlands, where his father obtained work, but as he grew older Winters got in trouble and was sent to an approved school, run by monks who abused him. He joined the Parachute Regiment and in June 1964, while stationed at Aldershot, he went absent without leave and made his way to London, where he held up a barman in Soho, shooting him dead. Capital punishment had not yet been abolished but Winters was sentenced to life imprisonment. Transferred to the Scottish prison system, he was further convicted of rioting, with Jimmy Boyle and Howard Wilson, and, like them, he was sent to the Special Unit as a last resort.

The single prose piece which gives its title to Winters' collection, *The Silent Scream*,[55] is written in the style of the Beat Poets, whose influence is apparent in much of Winters' work. It opens with a character Frank being attacked and killed by a tentacled creature -"the brain-eater".

Cutting forward, Frank is the first-person narrator in the stream-of-consciousness nightmare-ish prose piece with images from Winters' life:

> *Yes, sir, three bags o' shit, sir. I'm a shovel, sir. ("Why did you join the Army, soldier?" To kill people, sir. "The man's a psychopath, sir") doom doom doom …*[56]

Throughout, in flashbacks he return to the Soho murder, he contemplates the hanging that he could have faced, the sexual abuse suffered at approved school, prison events from earlier in his sentence and, fleetingly, being ten years old in Carbisdale, "where mountains grew, and flowers. The air was sensual with a miracle of feminine odours."

A "shadowless cardboard cut-out, a king of spades" says to him:

> *"Let's go, my friend, your soul is lost anyway. Leave the dead to rot, the quick to talk, the lame to walk on water. Come home with me." The air is difficult to breathe and everything seems as if seen through a reversed telescope. A long white corridor opens before my eyes and irresistibly I am drawn down it, spinning like a leaf, faster and faster.*[57]

The first-person narration ends with Winters deciding to rob the barman – "the till chimed insistently. Where was I to get money?" – his mind wandering back to the tenement where he was born. In the final section, he writes in the third person to describe shooting the man and escaping into the Soho night. Soon after finishing the story, Winters died in his cell from a drug overdose, his last line in *The Silent Scream*: "your life is measured in pain, the supreme quality of existence."

Desolation, isolation and mental turmoil are predominant themes in Larry Winters' poems. In 'The Summing Up', which opens the collection, he begins:

> My life is but a bitter black
> Fantasy spun from an obsolete
> dream machine whose malfunctioning
> circuit is beyond repair.[58]

In other poems he writes of his confusion – "The falling rain it's in my mind/ My mind is in the falling rain";[59] of drugs, in 'Electric Dreams' – for a long period in the Special Unit, Winters was dependent on barbiturates, and of childhood memories in the Highlands in 'Carbisdale' and 'A Dream of Two Eagles'.

'A Song of the Sixties' and 'Aces and Eights (Nirvana)' are in the style of the Beat Poets, but in 'The Onion' - inserted as an extra page rather than being bound in the volume, and sub-titled "A final offering" – he describes peeling his brain, discarding each layer as he looks for the essence. On reaching the core he finds "no essence, no spirit, no soul".[60]

Many small-scale collections of poetry by British prisoners have been published in recent years. Some were produced by writers-in-residence, others by outside organisations like The Burnbake Trust, who have done a lot to encourage art and writing in prisons. The Trust brought out an impressive selection in 1991,[61] featuring the work of inmates, among them Alex Alexandrowicz, who served twenty-two years for a murder he consistently denied.[62]

A booklet was published by Hampshire Probation Service following a request from a BBC radio producer for poems by prisoners. For *Prison Poets*,[63] the eminent poet and academic Professor Francis Berry wrote a Foreword in which he quoted Samuel Johnson as telling James Boswell that fine poetry could not be written on the island of St Kilda because of the "sad lack of variety" of images, scenes and events.

As Professor Berry made clear, many enclosed societies withstand this "sad lack of variety" by delving into their inner resources, none more so than the Hampshire prisoners whose work he had helped to select for the collection.

As for outstanding individual poems about prison, there have been few since *The Ballad of Reading Gaol*. Contemporary poets writing within the walls have tended, as Francis Berry suggested, to focus on past memories from before they went to prison, or future hopes for when they are free. Occasionally, a poem captures the imagery or atmosphere of landing or yard, a good example being Razor Smith's 'Old Lags', a duologue between two elderly villains who meet after a gap of many years:

> Hello there, John, how are you son?
> Who me? I'm doing fine;
> When did we last meet?
> Parkhurst '69!
>
> I saw old Jim in Pentonville, he's having it with Mugs,
> They nicked him down the Old Kent Road,
> With a joey full of drugs.
>
> Who? Tony? Ain't you heard, he's dead, shot down at
> Shooters Hill.
> It's getting very hard to tell the villains from the Bill.

> You hear about little Freddie? He's buggered off to Spain.
> Apparently he had a touch. Now he's on the gravy train!
>
> Old Charlie copped a seven, they caught him dealing Blow,
> Fifty-seven kilos in a lock-up near Heathrow.
>
> Who me? Yeah I been stitched right up, it's funny you should ask,
> I'm here for what I didn't do.
> I didn't wear a mask!
>
> Alright my son, be lucky, I'll see you on the yard,
> We'll chat about the good old days and how the Game is getting hard.
> Don't mention all the wasted years, the empty days and nights,
> The riots and the suicides, the murders and the fights.
>
> No, we'll just talk of robbing banks,
> flying lead and grassing slags,
> as we shuffle around the exercise yard,
> just a couple of tired Old Lags.[64]

'Old Lags' marked the first step in Razor Smith's writing career. He submitted it to *Prison Writing* in 1992, along with a letter saying he had taught himself to read and write in Borstal when he was sixteen and had written a few poems but had not felt able to show them to anyone. Smith's poem was as evocative a piece of writing as anything that ever appeared during the journal's existence. It was later read on a poetry programme on BBC Radio 4 and chosen for 'The 'Daily Poem' in *The Independent*.[65]

Another evocative example of prison verse to appear in *Prison Writing* was Mark D. Lawless's ode to Strangeways, 'The Warehouse of Years', which begins:

> Stacked, life upon life, year upon year,
> Rising upwards in four tiers,
> Landings and centre like a giant clock-wheel,
> Stands the warehouse of lost years.[66]

The poem, continues for nearly two hundred lines, with 'The Mouse', 'The

Nightman', 'The Cockroach' and 'The Man and the Woman' each taking roles. The influence of both Dylan Thomas and Oscar Wilde peeks through as Lawless captures the convict's loneliness and despair, describing the prison as a warehouse long before overcrowding made the term fashionable to journalists and pressure groups.

As competitions and prison magazines show, poetry is a popular form of creative writing for prisoners. It could be, however, that it holds more appeal for those who write than for intended readers, especially other inmates, past and present. Bruce Reynolds, sentenced to twenty-five years for his leading role in what became known as the Great Train Robbery, and who later wrote an autobiography,[67] says: "We always dwell on things we value most when we haven't got them – loved ones and liberty. For me, most prisoners' poetry has too much pathos. I realise it's a legitimate escape but if you feel like that why put yourself in the position in the first place?"[68]

Dramatic intent

Journalism provided a steady living for Jimmy O'Connor in the 1950s, after he was released from Dartmoor, Successful as he was in Fleet Street, he wanted to write something more substantial than crime reports for newspapers. In prison he had written plays and after ten years of trying he got a breakthrough with BBC television in 1963 in 'The Wednesday Play' series. O'Connor's play, *Three Clear Sundays*, was based on his experience in the death cell, awaiting execution in Pentonville – a very topical issue with abolition only two years away. Danny, an simple Irishman, is set up by two old lags to attack a prison officer. The officer dies and Danny is hanged. Eleven million viewers watched the play and O'Connor's name was made, along with that of the director, Ken Loach.

Tap on the Shoulder, broadcast in 1964, was about a gang of bullion robbers who strike lucky and go to live on the Riviera. As he wrote in his autobiography, "The Queen taps you on the shoulder when she knights you and Old Bill from the Yard taps you on the shoulder when he nicks you." [69]

In all, thirteen plays by Jimmy O'Connor were produced on television. *The Coming Out Party*, about a young man who finds out just before Christmas that his mother has been sent to prison, won awards for the director and *The Profile of Gentleman* featured a young actor, George Sewell, whose father, a London criminal, had been a prosecution witness in the case that led to O'Connor being convicted of murder. O'Connor's plays were heavily influenced by his experiences in prison and within the criminal fraternity but by the 1970s the individual play was in decline, replaced by series, and he could not adapt. His achievement, as described in an obituary, was that "in the new medium of television, Jimmy O'Connor became the first writer to open up the hermetic world of prison and the criminal underworld to general inspection." [70] O'Connor's legacy lay in the immediacy of his cinema verite style, with its slangy street dialogue, successfully appropriated only a few years later by *The Sweeney*.

As Jimmy O'Connor's career declined, that of another Cockney ex-prisoner was coming to the fore in television scriptwriting – and, ironically, it would be writing for *The Sweeney*, the Thames Television series about the Flying Squad, that made his name. Tony Hoare began to write in Hull Prison in the late 1960s, while serving six years for robbery with violence. Keen to make good use of his time, after several prison sentences he wanted to break away from the criminal lifestyle and a stint in the punishment block gave him the opportunity. He asked for a notebook and pencil and to his surprise was given them.

When he got out of the block he spent every evening writing and soon he had completed a hand-written a novel of 140,000 words. He persuaded the governor to allow him a typewriter to produce a prison magazine and on this he typed up his novel, which he showed to the television writer Alan Plater, who lived in Hull and visited the jail as a volunteer for a discussion group. The novel won a £25 Koestler Award, but that was only the beginning:

> *Alan read the novel and he said "It's interesting, but why don't you try writing a radio play?" So I asked him how it should be laid out, what it looked like on paper, and he brought me some scripts in, radio scripts and I wrote a radio play. I smuggled it out, cos you're not allowed to earn a living in the nick and Alan showed it to a producer who said he'd do it when I got out. Then six months later I got parole – and within a fortnight my radio play was on! A man called Alfred Bradley, wonderful man, said "Come up to a BBC meeting – we're doing it."*
>
> *It was called* It Must Be Better Than Doing Porridge. *So that was my first little chink in the wall and then while I was on parole I adapted the novel into a two-hour TV play and sent it off to Granada. They said it would have to be cut in half because of the time schedules. I said "Are you kidding, you can't*

cut it in half" - but I've discovered since that you can. It went out on Sunday Night Theatre which was a major programme then. It was called The Chaps, *as was the novel. I thought, this is better than doing bird, they give you money for it.*[71]

By his own admission, Tony Hoare was a failure as a criminal, but as a television writer he became a master of the craft. He wrote many episodes of *The Sweeney, Minder, London's Burning* and "all the cops and robbers shows – getting on for two hundred screenplays altogether". Scriptwriters tend not to receive the same degree of public recognition or high profile as do authors of books, but for thirty years he was one of the most prolific and successful writers in Britain, his work watched by millions of television viewers.

Jacqueline Holborough was not a complete outsider when she wrote her first play. A trained actress, sentenced to three years for an offence of extortion which she denied, she realised the dramatic possibilities of prison while in Durham's H Wing. She was not able to take her ideas forward until she got to Askham Grange, an open prison, with a sympathetic governor. On release, she founded Clean Break, a theatre company for women prisoners and ex-prisoners. It was the launch of Holborough's career as a writer and gave the opportunity for a career in the theatre for many women, some going on to become professional actresses.

The need for a play with an all female cast spurred Holborough into writing. Clean Break began in 1979 and two years later performed her play *Avenues* at the Edinburgh Festival. As the company developed, so did Holborough's writing. She has said that prison left her feeling angry for a many years, but with a tremendous source of material, not least as "People in prison tend to have bigger characters, just as they do in the theatre."[72]

In 1986 her first full-length play, *The Garden Girls*, was produced at the Bush Theatre. Set in an open prison, it follows the lives of five inmates, beginning as one is refused parole and ending as another is released. *The Times* reviewer commented: "Her knowledge of this world within the world is clearly comprehensive and one accepts the naturalistic detail without question."[73] When Holborough's play *The Way South* was put on at the Bush Theatre in 1989, the same paper described it as "an exploration of what prison can do to people".[74]

The same year the Bush staged *The One-sided Wall*, written by Janet Cresswell in Broadmooor Hospital. Cresswell, sectioned under the Mental Health Act after attacking a psychiatrist, spent more than twenty-five years in Broadmoor. Despite the stringent security of special hospitals and the prevailing regime of secrecy, two years earlier she had managed to write an article for *The Sunday Times* magazine, describing her life in Broadmoor. Her play was based on a mental health tribunal. In it, the main character has suffered abuse from a doctor, electro-convulsive therapy and, like Cresswell would, although she did not know it at the time, spent a quarter of a century in a mental hospital.

As Cresswell had too, the character stabbed her psychiatrist. *The Sunday Times* said the play made "an impassioned cry against a world obsessed with labels".[75] *The Independent* declared it "A harrowing indictment of the state machinery that defines and contains mental illness."[76]

Writing for the theatre was not high on Anna Reynolds's priorities until she became involved with Clean Break in the early 1990s:

> *I'd got this true story and I wanted to do something with it. I'd tried it as a novel and a screen play, nothing felt right. Then me and Moira (Moira Buffini, an actress) talked about it, got it together and she performed it… it started the ball rolling for me in drama because it got brilliant reviews which was a real surprise. And I kind of got the theatre bug …the business of going in a theatre and watching people watch your work, and respond to it."*[77]

In the spring of 1994, Anna Reynolds had three plays produced in London fringe theatres. Her first, *Jordan*, was a monologue exploring grief, about a young woman who has killed her baby and kills herself on the day she is released from prison. Based on someone Reynolds met in prison, it won awards from the Writers' Guild and *Time Out*.

Her second play, *Red*, was about two women in a holding cell who have murdered their husbands and the third came from her own experience after being charged with killing her mother. *Wild Things*, commissioned by the touring company Paines Plough, centred around two inmates in a mixed secure psychiatric hospital.

Anna Reynolds worked as a writer-in-residence with Paines Plough as well as Clean Break. In October 1994 her television play *Paradise*, was broadcast on BBC 2. Once again she touched base with her own history in a story of a dysfunctional family where a man who has been made redundant is too embarrassed to tell his children, so he persuades them and his wife to spend their holiday in the cellar, trying to convince them it is an adventure. After that was broadcast, Reynolds' career as dramatist seemed to go quiet.

One of the most prolific of latter-day prison writers, Clare Barstow had a play performed at the Edinburgh Festival in 1997. *Looking Towards a New Horizon* was written in Holloway and based on a short story she had published earlier in *Prison Writing*.[78] A troubled young woman, Cassandra, is sent to prison for stabbing a man who propositioned her. Haunted by being sexually and physically abused by her stepfather, she fights the system until she is befriended by an older inmate, Roxie, who convinces her that she has a future.

Clare Barstow, while serving her life sentence, and besides writing stories and poetry, wrote several plays that were performed by and for inmates at Holloway, Bullwood Hall and Cookham Wood women's prisons. Her work took a new turn when the London Shakespeare Workout, a project that visits prisons to encourage drama and writing, went into Cookham Wood.

Barstow showed two plays she had written to the director Bruce Wall, and some of her work was incorporated into *Voices*, a production that was performed in London and several provincial theatres, as well as the Lincoln Center, New York. Greatly encouraged, she wrote *Alba*, a re-working of Frederico Garcia Lorca's play *The House of Bernarda Alba*, in which a mother imprisons her five daughters. Clare Barstow's *Alba*, written around women in modern-day prison, was produced at the Criterion Theatre in London's West End in 2003, with a cast that included actress Gayle Hunnicut and inmates from Send open prison.

On the professional stage no prisoner or ex-prisoner has made an impression to compare with Brendan Behan since *The Quare Fellow* was first seen in London half a century ago. Behan's play carried a profound message and even so long after the abolition of capital punishment it still holds a dramatic relevance, as seen in 2004 when the Oxford Stage Company revived it for a national tour, twenty years after it had last been seen in mainland Britain. It is unlikely that a new prison-based play - written by someone who is, or has been, there – could have a similar impact in a theatre in the twenty-first century.

Letters

Letters to newspapers from serving prisoners are occasionally published in the national press. In most cases they are simply attempts to bring prison issues to public attention. Within prisoners' own world, the correspondence pages of

Inside Time provide a forum of lively and informative reading on a monthly basis, and, where policy or decisions are questioned, usually elicit a reply from Prison Service Headquarters.

The collected letters of Oscar Wilde and Brendan Behan were published after their deaths and included letters they wrote from prison, shedding light on their situations and their feelings while they were behind bars. Of course, had they not died famous writers, their letters – from prison or anywhere else would have been of little consequence, other than to family or recipients.

Correspondence between two pen-friends, one a convicted murderer from an unsettled background and the other a middle-class farmer, was an unusual basis for a book. The farmer, Christopher Morgan, wrote to Tom Shannon, serving life at Maidstone Prison in 1992, after joining a scheme run by the Prison Reform Trust to help prisoners maintain contact with the outside world. Their correspondence was published later under the title *Invisible Crying Tree*. [79]

Initially, Shannon was reluctant to be involved. As he explains, he had requested a female pen-friend, but as the correspondence unfolds he derives comfort and stimulation from Morgan's letters. A rebel, he appears to be at war with the system, its staff and many fellow inmates, but as he is shunted from prison to prison his pen-pal's letters with their tales of family life, the price of fat cattle for the farm and having his teeth out come as light relief to the humdrum of prison existence. For his part, Shannon enlightens the farmer on prisons and prisoners and to some extent into his own state of mind, saying "There's an awful shame and no forgetting in murder". He describes some splendid vignettes, notably on prison gangsters whom he considers "foul-mouthed parrots" and on the efforts of an inmate nicknamed Shortplanks to roast a captured pigeon.

Although we are told that the letters were not written with publication in mind, Morgan picks up on the possibility early on, and the book serves as a text book for anyone who wishes to write to a prisoner but is not sure what to say. Well-received by reviewers, all royalties went towards founding the Shannon Trust, aimed at helping lifers on release.

Curios

Not all works of prison writing are easily categorised. Brian Wilson's book about keeping birds in prison, *Nor Iron Bars a Cage*, is a Dartmoor memoir with a difference, telling the story of how, in his cell, he hatched sparrows, starlings, wagtails and blackbirds from deserted eggs he found around the prison.

A housebreaker who had spent fourteen years behind bars, he took advice from the prison doctor on tending the birds when they fell sick, as his own attitude changed from that of an embittered criminal to one of compassion. When he was transferred to Chelmsford and forbidden to keep birds he came close to a breakdown and was saved only by finding a sparrow egg which he hid and eventually hatched. In Chelmsford he began writing his book, which was completed and published on release.[80]

Written with the aim of providing an altogether different and less benign insight, Ian Brady's *The Gates of Janus* [81] is a pseudo-academic and self-deluded analysis of eleven serial killers, their psychology and crimes. Brady, subject to a whole-life tariff for the torture and murder of children in what became known as the Moors Murders case in 1966, claims special knowledge based not only on his crimes but on the years he has spent in maximum security prisons and special hospitals. Attempting to elevate the serial killer to superman status and ignoring the devastation caused to innocent people's lives, he writes:

> *Not even serial killers are entirely what you expect. Sometimes they can actually be the rope across the spiritual abyss, between man and his failed aspirations.*[81]

The subjects of his misanthropic attentions are mostly American and include Henry Lucas, John Wayne Gacy, Richard Ramirez and Ted Bundy, whose cases Brady studied from secondary sources. Two chapters, however, are dedicated to men he knew as fellow patients in Broadmoor. One was the St Albans poisoner, Graham Young, of whom he says, "His first and only ardent love was murder,"[83] the other Peter Sutcliffe, better known as the Yorkshire Ripper. Brady presents himself almost as a visiting professor as he describes their meeting:

> *I had the opportunity to interview Sutcliffe at length when I was passing through the south of England. He had a mild and pleasant mien, his tone of voice quiet and deferential throughout ... He spoke of the murders he committed in a matter-of-fact, humdrum manner, sometimes quite humorously.*[84]

The title of Brady's book, *The Gates of Janus*, alludes to Janus, the Roman god of gateways. Brady was encouraged by the author Colin Wilson, who advised him to seek publication only in the USA. When the book was imported for sale in Britain, Ashworth Hospital in Merseyside, where Brady was a patient and where he had written the book, took out an injunction.

That was lifted when it was established that he had made no mention of the hospital or other patients. Victims' organisations protested vehemently at the book being on sale and the novelist Ian Rankin said it was the only book he would gladly see burned.[85]

Dedicated to the task

Of all forms of prisoners' writing, memoirs and autobiographies receive the most attention, especially when the author is already notorious through his or her crimes or conduct in prison. Many prisoners have published books about their own lives and written nothing more. Those who have developed their craft and, by necessity branched out, are the dedicated writers: men and women who, having picked up the pen, did not want to put it down. In these cases, their life story was only the beginning, a catharsis and an introduction to a new discipline and often new lifestyle. John McVicar moved on to journalism, Jimmy Boyle and Hugh Collins to fiction, Anna Reynolds to plays, a novel, journalism and posts in prisons as writer-in-residence.

Some successful writers who began inside left their autobiographies until later. Jimmy O'Connor went from journalism to television drama before he published *The Eleventh Commandment*. Razor Smith had a varied if small scale output until *A Few Kind Words and a Loaded Gun* appeared, while he was still serving life. Others do not write in an autobiographical vein at all.

For them, prison or a previous criminal life has provided source material to be enhanced through imagination. The result is a body of work of great colour, insight and variety. It may not be factual, it could have been written primarily as entertainment, but its value cannot be under-estimated.

4] Inner forces

Inspirations

Imprisonment is an extraordinary experience. Forcibly removed from family, friends and normal surroundings, subject to stringent rules that would be considered outrageous if imposed in the outside world, obliged to keep their own company during long days and longer nights, prisoners have ample opportunity to consider their circumstances. Many of them also have the opportunity to engage in activities that they might not have done in normal life, including writing.

Extraordinary experience arouses varied emotions. Anger, resentment, bitterness, failure, a longing to escape, the resolve to change if or when one survives –it also inspires creative expression. Among literate prisoners, this can mean a wish to write something down, to have a personal record, to try to make sense of what is happening.

In elementary form that might be a diary, an attempt at autobiography, poetry or thinly-disguised fiction. Most prisoners go no further. Their scribblings may be therapeutic, may pass a few hours, may earn praise from a tutor in an education class or even a Koestler Award, but they are not published. To reach that level requires a talent to absorb stimuli and a will to create, which combine to become inspiration.

Essential too is some inner force to direct the will towards seeking publication or performance – motivation. The words on a page, as discussed in preceding chapters, are the 'what' of prison writing; inspiration and motivation are the 'how' and the 'why'.

Environment, inmates and events

If Oscar Wilde had not been sent to prison, *De Profundis* and *The Ballad of Reading Gaol* could never have been written. Only by being thrust into that lonely prison cell could Wilde gain the perspective to write as he did of his past life, his feelings and his attitudes. That his personal insight was at times flawed does not affect the power of the letter. *The Ballad of Reading Gaol*, a very different work and written post-release, concerns prison conditions, but was primarily influenced by Wilde's horror at the execution of a convicted murderer during his time in the prison.

An execution provided the inspiration for Brendan Behan's stage play, *The Quare Fellow*, but the event caused Behan more curiosity than repulsion. Following his deportation from Britain after being released from Hollesley Bay Borstal, Behan had only been back home five months when he was sentenced to fourteen years for the attempted murder of a detective.[1] Sent first to Mountjoy Jail, he was there in June 1943 when a pork butcher, Bernard Kirwan, was hanged for the murder of his brother, whom he had dismembered in an attempt to prevent the corpse being identified.

Behan met and spoke with the condemned man several times, including the night before his execution when Kirwan told him, "Tomorrow at ten past eight I'll be praying for you in heaven." Later in his sentence, after being transferred to The Curragh as a political prisoner, Behan wrote *The Quare Fellow*, originally titled *The Twisting of Another Rope*. It was based on Bernard Kirwan and the reaction of prisoners and warders to his execution.

Between the ages of sixteen and twenty-two, Brendan Behan spent all but a few months in custody. According to his biographer Michael O'Sullivan, "It shaped him completely and left an indelible mark … It gave him the leisure to write without distraction from his drinking or anything else to which he easily fell victim." He also met and learned from other Republican prisoners who were writers, as well as other prisoners who provided a great source of material for his later books.[2]

Edward Bunker, whose novels achieved popularity among British prisoners following the revival of his career by No Exit Press in the 1990s, found inspiration at the age of seventeen in San Quentin. There he met Caryl Chessman, a man who was writing a book, later published as *Cell 2455, Death Row*. Chessman offered him the loan of two paperbacks, saying "You like to read?" Bunker replied "I'd rather read than eat."

In his autobiography, *Mr Blue*, Bunker describes the effect of reading an extract of *Cell 2455 Death Row* in a copy of *Argosy* magazine, which Chessman had passed to him, clandestinely. The extract told of the eve of execution of a man who was to die in the gas chamber – as Chessman himself would do some years later:

> *I couldn't judge the writing but it was so real to me that my heartbeat increased. Of course I had the advantage as a reader of being where I was, not far from the reality. I read it again and although I had no critical judgement, it was impossible to be more astounded. A convict had written it, a convict I knew, and had published it in a huge national magazine, not the* San Quentin News.
>
> *A book was coming out soon. To write a book took a magician, or even a wizard, or an alchemist who took experience, real or imagined, and used words to bring it to life on a printed page. I have many flaws but envy is not one of them. Yet I was afire with envy that late afternoon in the hole of San Quentin.*[3]

Meeting charismatic, notorious or merely interesting fellow inmates provided the spark for several prison writers. Hugh Collins began in the Barlinnie Special Unit, where he found a role model in Jimmy Boyle:

> *I was really volatile when I went there... I couldny deal with it, the confrontational thing. I'd never used my brains in any way and then Jimmy took me up the stairs one day and he said 'Look, get one of these typewriters up, you're like an emotional time bomb,' he says. 'Just get all the stuff out of you'.*
>
> *So I went along doing my Harold Robbins, you know.* Sense of Freedom 2. *I kidded myself on in that way but I started to clean my act up. I hated writing, it made me very tense, it was repetitive sorta stuff.*[4]

The same year that Collins arrived in the Unit – 1978 - Jimmy Boyle's autobiography *A Sense of Freedom* had been published, to a very positive response. For several years Boyle had written a diary, its contents naturally influenced by the community and environment around him; after he was released he decided it should be published. In his introduction to *The Pain of Confinement*, he writes:

> *I began to write a diary of what was going on in the Unit. In the process I took copious notes of daily events. Publishing the diary seemed the best way of telling the story, since it is a record of my thoughts and reactions to each day, not judged with hindsight and distorted through time. All of this has shaped my past and present experience into a vision of what the penal system should be.*[5]

Forty years earlier, another lifer, Jim Phelan, found prison life in Maidstone to be an existence he had never envisaged.

> *No Martian city or savage jungle could have provided a stranger environment or personnel than this piece of unknown England. Curiosity began to grip me. I itched to ask a million questions, to have a note-book, to study and compare, that I might know the machine, might master its secrets as well as avoid its cogs and teeth.*[6]

Phelan satisfied his curiosity and became focused in his quest for information. By the time he was transferred to Parkhurst, to spend his days tin-clipping:

> *I was piling my note-books with legends, observations, scraps of jail-character. Things from the psychological text-books, previously regarded as million-to-one exceptions or cases of mal-observation, were here all around me. The intellectual starvation of tin-clipping was fast turning my thoughts inward. Wherefore the opportunity to do some real work was enthralling. But over and above that I had begun to understand that I was an explorer in a field of science that was almost virgin. Even the little I had already seen of the jails had convinced me that not one of the orthodox commentators knew anything whatever about the subject. Without at that time being at all clear about it, I could even then feel the job of jail-recording taking hold of me. Almost, but not quite, I began to think myself fortunate. I was a fairly intelligent observer with a profound, well-developed interest in people and a certain ability to put words on paper. Now I was dumped down in the finest psychological laboratory in the world, with a vast mass of the most interesting information ready to my hand.*[7]

Forty years on from Phelan's time in Parkhurst, the seeds of Peter Wayne's later writing were sewn in another Isle of Wight prison, Albany, where he spent two years without receiving a visit.

> *To stop the rot of insanity, I began to write a journal. I'd write down conversations I had with other prisoners; tell their stories; pen portraits of governors and screws. It was, and still is, a cathartic process.*[8]

The journals would be a valuable source of material for his *Prospect* column and other writing.

Ian Watson, whose humorous work was published in *Prison Writing* and won Koestler Awards, was another prisoner who did not write for publication until he was immersed into a world way beyond that which he had known before. After he was found guilty and sentenced, he looked round and the stimulus of what he saw and heard was too strong to ignore:

> *I was on remand in HMP Manchester for seven months. So much desperate effort went into defending myself and preparing my case that little time was left for anything else. Then I realised that I had an opportunity to gather characters for the future. I witnessed a particularly funny exchange between a black guy and a newly- imprisoned Harold Shipman and after that a notion certainly began to form that I might write something as I was surrounded by people who were making the headlines in the newspapers.*[9]

Clare Barstow had worked as a journalist and done some creative writing before going to prison. Sentenced to life, she spent most of her time working on poetry, plays and fiction, much of which has been published or performed. She found the environment often conducive to writing, if occasionally constraining:

> *Sometimes prison stimulates writing in that there is so much happening around you, there's always endless material to work with and you are living in an altered reality which can let you look at things from a different perspective. Also, you have the space to explore yourself and others. But it can deter you when there are other problems that you have no control over and cannot solve. You are reliant on others, which can be hard at times.*[10]

When Matthew Williams and two other prisoners escaped from Parkhurst in 1995, a massive police operation was mounted. Speculation was rife within the media as to where the fugitives might be, but they had never left the Isle of Wight. Williams had a long-held interest in the creative arts and when he was recaptured and confined to Special Secure Units within the dispersal system for years, he had plenty of time to paint and write. Much of his work is located beyond reality, but *Seascape*, a thirty-minute radio play that was produced by RTE in Ireland in September 2004, was different:

> *As I was heading north along Sandown pier I passed a row of neat terraces and I thought how nice it would be to be able to slip into one as a normal*

> *person – and the one I was walking past was called 'Seascape' which made me smile.*[11]

In his play, the main character, expecting to be arrested for a robbery, buys a boat and sails off to sea with his wife.

> *I was also taken with the idea of walking to the end of the country and just continuing. Initially I was going to set the play in northern England, but Ireland seemed better for the distances you could sail.*[12]

A single event inspired Razor Smith's first published work, the poem 'Old Lags':

> *I was just listening to the wing in Wandsworth one day and I suddenly realised how we all say the same things in greeting to each other. We always ask after other villains and laugh about our misfortunes because prison is such a macho world. I'd been having similar conversations for as long as I'd been inside yet now I was really only hearing them for the first time.*[13]

As a writer, Smith is a throwback to the likes of McVicar and Collins in that, unusually for a career criminal, he has remained dedicated to the task of writing and has been greatly influenced by criminal peer group and prison situations. Not all ex-prisoners who go on to write for publication get their inspiration while inside. Bruce Reynolds waited many years after his release before producing his life story, *Autobiography of a Thief*. Other priorities took precedence while he was serving the twenty-five year sentence imposed for his part in the Great Train Robbery:

> *I suppose four years on security wings should have been a great stimulus to write. I had all the time in the world and there was a definite drive to do something within the education system. But I never considered it - the priority was to get out as soon as I could. I was a career convict – from going in I did everything I could to get out. The priority was keeping my physical health, also I didn't know the "end" of the story like I did when I eventually wrote the book. And there was no demand for such books then, the social awareness wasn't there.*[14]

For the professional writer who is sent to prison, the experience inevitably provides inspiration. When Jeffrey Archer published the first volume of his prison diaries, the media and prison authorities caused a fuss, but it should have come as no surprise. As another novelist, Tony Parsons, wrote in *The Mirror*:

> *Expecting Jeffrey Archer to resist writing about his time inside is a lot like expecting a man with diarrhoea to resist going to the toilet. Not because Lord Jeff is an inveterate publicity seeker who is hungry for more headlines, but because he is a writer. Writing about their lives is what writers do. They are all cannibals. Expecting Archer to not write his prison memoirs is like expecting an alcoholic to resist that one for the road. Prison has to be an extreme experience for anyone. If you go from hanging out with lords, princes and politicians to being banged up with gypsies, tramps and thieves, then the experience is even more extreme. And the story even more worthy of the telling.*[15]

Taki, *The Spectator* columnist, was equally inspired while in prison, but afterwards, when it came to writing a book based on the diaries he had kept inside, he found the task difficult. As Jimmy Boyle sought to publish his diary entries from the Barlinnie Special Unit in order to preserve their contemporaneous immediacy, Taki observes the difficulty of writing with hindsight:

> *In reviewing horror stories, critics say that the more human the monster, the greater the character created. While I was in Pentonville, I was certain I would write a masterpiece once free. Needless to say this was not happening. While inside I dreamed of turning the dry facts of my diary into a lyrical tour-de-force, describing the 'monsters' well enough to make them unforgettable characters. I guess this is only human. Prison, as places of torment do, sharpens the image. Once outside, however, humility, reality and a sense of the ridiculous take over, and prison solipsism turns into embarrassment.*[16]

As soon as he was released, Taki resumed his column in *The Spectator*, but six years elapsed before the publication of *Nothing To Declare*.

Inspirational reading

With the exception of the Bible and Dante's *Divina Commedia*, Oscar Wilde drew little inspiration from books in the writing of what have become classic texts of modern prison literature. His stimulus to write of his experience arose from perception of his personal tragedy, both his own and that of the murderer hanged while Wilde was serving his sentence in Reading Gaol. At that time – and for many decades to come - the provision of books to prisoners was extremely limited and Wilde was only able to receive those he did through the intervention of his friend R.B.Haldane.[17] After reading *Divina Commedia*, in which Dante is visited by the poet Virgil and taken through Hell, Purgatory and eventually to Heaven, Wilde later told a friend that he had "tasted every word"[18] and it was only after he read Dante's masterpiece that he commenced *De Profundis*, his own quest for personal salvation. Of the literary influences that contributed to *The Ballad of Reading Gaol*, Wildean scholars have noted that the same ballad stanza occurs in Coleridge's *The Rime of the Ancient Mariner* and in Thomas Hood's *The Dream of Eugene Aram*, another poem about a murder.[19]

Seventy years after Wilde's prison sentence, John McVicar was in Brixton Prison, after being recaptured following his escape from Durham's maximum security wing. Already serving twenty-three years, he faced further charges and knew he could get a life sentence. He had written the first part of what became *McVicar by Himself* for financial gain, but the second part, titled 'McVicar's Defence' in the original book, was an attempt through the written word to convince his QC and the judge who would sentence him that he should be given a chance.

McVicar expanded on the influence of Wilde when he revised *by Himself* in 2002:

> *I decided to write my own* De Profundis…*I have read* De Profundis *more times than Osama bin Laden has the Koran … although it is only essay length it is the prison book. It is a rambling, disjointed, brilliant, lyrical but most of all profound piece. The truth it clarifies is intrinsic to the human condition. What lies at its heart is how Wilde as an artist tackled what humans have always done when they have become dissatisfied with their own lives. They put themselves under the microscope; they do a stock take of their character; they analyse themselves. They do it with a view to trying to change what is problematic. The reason why Wilde's account is so valuable is that it is true to the nature of what it is to be an ordinary human being. Wilde's approach has no ideological edge nor is it drawn from the perspective of a social scientist; it is that of a very intelligent, compassionate, discerning artist. As he describes in* De Profundis, *Wilde looked at himself when he was in prison; when I was on*

the run from my 23 year sentence, I did too, albeit in a rather more muddled, limited way than did Wilde. I described it in my defence document which is the second half of McVicar by Himself.[20]

De Profundis was not McVicar's sole influence. Interviewed in 1992, he recalled reading Zeno's *Life* and being impressed by the energy of Frank Norman's *Bang To Rights*. From a different field, he acknowledged the American author Tom Wolfe's anthology *The New Journalism*,[21] which he said he had found "very, very powerful". He said "That's a bit of a Bible for me - the *Rolling Stone* school of writers. Hunter Thompson - anyone my age would have been caught by that."[22]

John McVicar would himself be influential on the next generation of prison writers. To Hugh Collins he was "the only man I've ever really admired, simply because he was the first to turn his back on crime. Took a lot of courage".[23]

Razor Smith, like many prisoners, regarded McVicar as a prison legend, having read his book and seen the film based on it. When Smith was released from a nineteen-year sentence in 1997, McVicar promoted him in the pages of *Punch* and introduced him to Will Self, who put him in contact with the publishers of Smith's autobiography.

McVicar is only one writer to pay tribute to Oscar Wilde. Wilfred Macartney, describing the execution of a prisoner held only four cells from himself in Wandsworth, said *The Ballad of Reading Gaol* "will last longer than capital punishment". He was correct.

Jim Phelan, who experienced the death-cell at first-hand, writes:

> *No competent writer has left a record of a prolonged period in a death-cell… Strange that one who never knew it should have come nearer than any other writer to the pressure of the death-cell. Only Oscar Wilde, in* Reading Jail *(sic), approached the things I knew at first hand and had heard from scores of others.*[24]

At the beginning of *Who Lie In Gaol*,[25] Joan Henry quotes the stanza "I know not whether Laws be right …" She goes on to describe waking up on her first morning in Holloway with the thought of the months ahead and, recalling the line "And that each day is like a year, a year whose days are long", thinking "I wished that I had never read *The Ballad of Reading Gaol*." Later she recalls Wilde saying in *De Profundis* how "a day in prison on which one does not weep is a day on which one's heart is hard."

Long before Brendan Behan became successful he identified with Wilde as an Irishman as well as an ex-prisoner. He wrote a poem about his death, published in the Gaelic magazine *Comhar*[26] and, when living in Paris in the late 1940s, made regular visits to the Hotel d'Alsace, where Wilde had died.

Whereas Wilde was able, through his contacts, to receive a selection of books to read during his sentence, access to reading matter was greatly restricted for ordinary prisoners. In the 1930s Wilfred Macartney took up the challenge and in *Walls Have Mouths* he describes his battles with the Home Office and Prison Commission.

Of all the hardships Macartney endured during his sentence, the one that shocked him most was "the gradual realisation that there was a definite official bias against reading."[27] By various means, not all within the prison rules, he managed to get many of the books he sought and in *Walls Have Mouths* he reports on convict reading in the period, what was considered good and bad. The short-stories of American O Henry were very popular:

> *After all, he had done his time, he was one of us… Dostoevsky's* House of the Dead, *the only book yet written which gives a vivid and true picture of convict life, was, with a nuance of difference, looked at from the personal angle. "Well, he's done time; he knew what he was writing, and he had no shame for having been in prison." Therefore he could tell the truth and lags do like the technical details to be right.*[28]

Ex-lags do, too, as Jimmy O'Connor confirms in his autobiography, *The Eleventh Commandment*, but this alone does not always lead to them being impressed by another prisoner-turned-writer:

> *In Athens several years ago an American teacher told me about a writer called Genet. He described him as "one of the greatest contributors to literature". Had I read his works? As a result I read* The Thief's Journal. *Being an ex-thief, naturally I am always interested in other thieves, just as painters are interested in Rembrandts or Goyas. Because they have also been students and served an apprenticeship. One experience Genet wrote about was how he picked up a Police Chief Inspector in the back streets of Marseilles and buggered him. It always tickled my fancy and amused me, but I couldn't possibly see how this made him a great writer at the time.*[29]

O'Connor did not find Genet too convincing, but the mercurial columnist Peter Wayne certainly did. For him, reading *The Thief's Journal* made him realise time spent in prison need not be wasted. He told a journalist: "I've tried to use my eye as a camera and have always considered it an almost sacred duty to record everything I see in this *demi-monde*."[30]

Should crime writers have lived the criminal life and done time for their work to be accepted by prisoners? Wilfred Macartney praised O Henry and Dostoevsky and scathed the novelist Edgar Wallace for tripping up on detail and being "sublimely ignorant of the life or dealings of crooked people". This, said Macartney, "was enough to damn him in the lags' eyes".

Edward Bunker has said that only one who has been there can write a realistic novel about the underworld and imprisonment, an opinion that could be borne out by the depth of his work when compared to other writers in the U.S. crime genre. Razor Smith takes a less purist view. For him, reading *The Villain's Tale* by British writer and non-criminal G.F.Newman was a revelation:

> *I thought fuckin' hell. This geezer knows what it's all about. His books were 'floaters', banned by the borstal, but copies were smuggled in and from wing to wing. We used to rip the covers off them cos if you got caught with one it was seven days block. G.F.Newman gave me the idea that I might have some stories to put in writing...G.F. Newman wasn't afraid to say 'fuck' in print and that brought writing down to my level.*[31]

The criteria for Smith's approval extended beyond an enthusiasm for using expletives in dialogue. From Damon Runyon, the American short-story writer, he learned the effect of humour and he cites John Steinbeck as a great influence. But in the early days, before he found G.F. Newman and began to write, he was always on the lookout for anything that mentioned jail. In Wandsworth, around 1990, he discovered Oscar Wilde:

> *I'd started reading heavily and was always on the lookout for anything that mentioned jail. I used to go along the shelves in the library, looking at the spines. I suppose I was trying to find something to identify with. I saw a book, the complete works, in the library but* The Ballad of Reading Gaol *was the only part I read. I'd heard other prisoners quoting little bits of it for years – 'that little tent of blue they call the sky'.*[32]

One of the fundamental guidelines to anyone who wants to write is to read as widely as possible. Some writers who began in prison were already avid readers, others focused on the page only because they had the time. Most would recognise Matthew Williams' explanation of what inspired him to take up the pen:

> *I was always fascinated by how writers can build worlds from words. Mainly, I wanted to express some ideas, be creative, and have a go at 'world building'. I've read a lot in prison and so was inspired by other writers.*[33]

In her ill-fated autobiography, *Tightrope*, Anna Reynolds told how her mother encouraged her to read and to appreciate the value of words. She ruminates on her mother's awareness that a sensitive child would need some defence against the world and that books could be a salvation. Later, she said:

> *When I was about 12 or 13 I was bullied at school and I used to go to the library. Instead of reading Dickens and stuff like that, which I should have done, I read Kafka and Dostoevsky, Gunter Grass and Solzhenitsyn. I loved all the European stuff and read it avidly. Anything that was big and dramatic and about huge global subjects. That's why I tend to have an edge of melodrama that I always have to cut back on, in my work, because I didn't grow up on the sensitive delicate stuff.*"[34]

The doomed poet and prose writer Larry Winters read widely, according to Daphne Brooke, who visited him in the Barlinnie Special Unit. In her introduction to *The Silent Scream and Poems* she discussed Winters' taste in reading. He was familiar with the classics, Shakespeare's tragedies and the Old Testament and had studied Zen and Hindu scripture. Among his favourite writers were Edgar Allen Poe, Hermann Hesse and Tolkein. When Ms Brooke visited he read Nietzche's *Thus Spake Zarathustra* aloud to her, was influenced by the songs of Bob Dylan and the poetry of Thom Gunn, but identified most of all with the beat-writers, notably Jack Kerouac. Poignantly, given Winters own propensity for violence and his mental fragility, he had a keen interest in the legendary Irish hero Cuchullain, known as the Hound of Ulster, a warrior of superhuman strength and courage in single combat, but prone to fits of madness and depression.

The television writer Tony Hoare suggests that everything a writer reads, good or bad, influences him or her and remains in the conscious and subconscious:

> *Thinking back about it, if I have to be specific, the first writer who influenced and inspired me to start writing was Norman Mailer. Oddly enough, not so much his fiction but his anthology of essays/observations on life, covering most subjects from politics to porn and a critical look at creative writing. The two books I'm thinking of are* 'Cannibals & Christians' *and* 'Advertisements for Myself'. *He has an enormous ego does Norman and has an opinion about everything. These books were published in the sixties when he was at his peak. Nowadays he's a bit of a pretentious bore, but he was good stuff back then. Actually, I was doing four months solitary confinement in Dartmoor when I read these books. There's nothing like a bit of solitary to concentrate the mind.*[35]

Hoare was inspired by a serious writer's non-fiction, but he chose to ply his trade away from the didactic and even autobiographical, writing entertaining and hugely popular episodes of *The Sweeney*, *Minder* and other major series. Trevor Hercules, pioneering author of *Labelled a Black Villain*, found immediate inspiration at the age of seventeen when he discovered the work of American black writers:

> *They opened up a whole new world to me and within their pages I found my identity, I found myself and with it an understanding of my experiences in this country. Most of the black writers I had discovered were Americans but that didn't detract from the importance of what they had to say, in fact it enhanced it ... Nothing could compare with the joy of finding writers like James Baldwin with their black characters sharing their experiences with us, enduring the same things we went through. Then we had people like Eldridge Cleaver, Angela Davies, Rap Brown, Malcolm X; and then Bobby Seale with* Seize the Time, *the most influential book that I have ever read.*[36]

Through his reading, Hercules was driven to write his own story. Another young black man in prison who realised the possibilities of his talent was Benjamin Zephaniah. He cites the same influences:

> *Martin Luther King, Malcolm X, Michael X, Angela Davis, Marcus Garvey. They're all political people. I didn't read poetry at the time. I loved poetry but I couldn't identify with most of the poetry I saw. There was one artist who I really liked, a musician called Big Youth, sort of reggae DJ, a real Rasta kind*

> *of toaster. A few people do come up to me and say "You're influenced by Big Youth, I can hear it in your style".*[37]

Inspiration came to Mark Leech in Grendon when he randomly picked up a book *How To Write Radio Drama* in the prison library. He took it back to his cell, read it and five days later had written his first play.

> *I had found a legitimate outlet for my energies, which I enjoyed tremendously, which enabled me to achieve something good, and which, if others are to be believed, I'm not too bad at! I spent many hours typing up the play* The Facts Speak for Themselves *and after three re-writes sent it to the BBC as a 90 minute Saturday Night theatre – it was accepted! I also entered the play for the 1990 Koestler Awards . . .where it won a prize of £20; we all have to start somewhere!*[38]

Whatever books Jeffrey Archer had read before his sentence, they are less likely to have influenced his diaries than the experience of imprisonment. However, while he was in HMP Wayland, he appears to have done some spectacularly heavy reading. He claimed that during the sixty-seven days he was there - and at the same time he was starting to write the first volume of his prison trilogy - he read nine Shakespeare plays, three novels by Charles Dickens, including *Bleak House*, which runs to 1,072 pages, plus novels by Herman Hesse, Graham Greene and Evelyn Waugh - the 768 page *Sword of Honour* – and collections of short stories by H.E. Bates, Saki, Somerset Maugham, John Mortimer and O Henry, whose writing career began in an American prison.

Archer's reading programme was described as "fairly heroic going" by Professor John Sutherland of University College London. He commented, "I wonder whether he would be prepared to present himself for a *viva voce* examination on the books?"[39]

Oral tales

In *Borstal Boy*, Brendan Behan spices his prose with frequent snatches of verse. There are extracts from poems and hymns, songs from the Irish tradition and the English music hall - and one he had sung with fellow inmates as they were being transferred by coach from Feltham to Hollesley Bay:

> Oh, they say I ain't no good 'cause I'm a Borstal Boy,
> But a Borstal Boy is what I'll always be,
> I know it is a title, a title I bear with pride,
> To Borstal, to Borstal, and the beautiful countryside.
> I turn my back upon the 'ole society,
> And spend me life a-thievin' 'igh and low,
> I've got the funniest feelin' for 'alf-inchin' and stealin'
> I should 'ave been in Borstal years ago.[40]

Behan makes no mention of the origin of this song, but he refers to three other boys, "Ickey Baldock …Shaggy and Mac Stay" singing songs about Feltham, the borstal they had just left, and "we all joined in, whenever we could pick up the words". Later, he describes a concert in Hollesley Bay when a prison officer recited a long piece about Marshall Hall, "some big English lawyer, and though the blokes didn't seem to know any more about Marshall Hall than I did, the other screws and the visitors – especially the Colonel – went for it like fresh bread."[41]

Such songs, along with monologues and ballads learned by prisoners from other prisoners, belong to an oral tradition that once supported, maintained and enhanced the criminal and prison sub-culture in Britain. Jim Phelan, writing of convict prisons in the late 1920s and the 30s, described one form, the "balmy ballad, tooled and polished by generations of dwellers on C1 at Parkhurst, which narrates in some eighty-odd verses the downfall of The Bitches Basterd."[42]

This term refers to a prison officer, the butt of bitter convict humour, which as Phelan says, is always "very anti-screw". Composed by an anonymous prisoner, with parts no doubt added or changed along the way, it assumed an intimate knowledge of convict jargon that would have been incomprehensible to anyone outside prison. Phelan had heard the ballad in Parkhurst from a convict he calls Darky the Rat. This how it went:

> Down came the Bitches Basterd, to pipe a bitta stuff.
> He snooks a balmy Judas and sees him coppa duff;
> He snooks it working belty, and nuts the orly mug.
> - I want that bleeder chokied. Unauthorised. A plug.

Translated, by Phelan, this reads:

> *An extremely severe warder, prowling along C1 in the hope that he may catch some convict with contraband, uses the pin-hole at each cell instead of sliding the flap. Stealthily he watches at one cell, while the unsuspecting man within unwraps a piece of tobacco from a packet. He watches in bitches basterd glee until the man conceals it again, in the flap of his trousers, then hurries to the orderly office (to ask the orderly to unlock the man's cell door).*

The orderly officer is portrayed as a reasonable, good-humoured but lazy officer who does not want the trouble of putting the prisoner in "chokey" – a punishment cell - on slender evidence. He is dubious about the warder's motives and suggests that he may be mistaken. He underestimates the malevolence of the "Bitches Basterd", who has his eye on promotion. The latter believes he has had a stroke of luck when the governor passes on his rounds:

> The Basterd feels his cosh-poke. He pulls up Number One.
> He grins around the landing. The orly mug en.
> - Oh sir, my years of service, my braid and orky clock.
> This Principal is trafficking; he won't let me unlock.

In what Phelan describes as a "nice appreciation of bitches-basterd psychology", the "Basterd" curries favour with the governor by showing himself to be diligent, and at the same time incriminating his superior. The ballad is intended to make the worst type of warder look stupid as well as corrupt – and as such was an integral part of prison lore, passed on orally from convict to convict in Parkhurst. Undoubtedly there were similar ballads in other prisons but even by Jim Phelan's time they had mostly disappeared.

'Drummer Bill', a different type of monologue that celebrated the exploits of a burglar at liberty, survived to the 1950s. In his *Autobiography of a Thief*, Bruce Reynolds recalls being sent to Gaynes Hall Borstal, where he formed the impression that all the top thieves spoke in rhyming slang and he would have to do the same if he wanted to become one. While in borstal, he met a boy named Bowler, " a good story-teller and very fond of giving public recitals of the prison epic, 'Drummer Bill'". Reynolds sets out the first verse:

> Now I was in the pub, with my china Drummer Bill
> And as it was his nature he had one eye on the till

> Now things were very dodgy and funds were getting low
> We sips our mild and bitter and decide to have a go.[43]

Subsequent to the publication of Reynolds' autobiography, Albert Hattersley, once a northern safe-blower who had served long sentences between 1946 and 1970, dictated 'Drummer Bill' in its entirety, for publication in *Prison Writing*.[44]

Hattersley learned the monologue from a fellow prisoner in 1952 while walking round the exercise yard at Leicester. The language of his version is notable for its use of criminal slang – eyes are "lamps", a flat is a "letty", jemmy and torch are "stick" and "glim", a window is a "burnt", a safe is a "peter" and watches, rings and furs are "tickers, groins and pussies".

The narrator tells how he, Drummer Bill and Kate the Clocker –"Drummer's little judy" – steal a car from a lock-up garage and set out to burgle the home of a Lady Beech. They get the safe out of the house but the "bogies" arrive and in the melee that follows Bill slashes a policeman with his "chiv". At the Old Bailey the narrator gets seven years, Kate receives "a lagging" - three years - and Drummer Bill is sentenced to death.

He tells the jury:

> When they put the rope around me and ask what I've got to say
> I'll shout "Look out down there below, Drummer's on his way."

The monologue ends with Drummer getting "topped" and the narrator declaring that when the three of them meet up again "in the manor known as hell/ You can guarantee we'll go to graft and screw Satan's gaff as well." Although 'The Bitches Basterd' was recalled by Jim Phelan and 'Drummer Bill' by Bruce Reynolds when they came to write books, there is no evidence that ballads or monologues actually inspired prisoners towards writing, other than copying down the words, as Albert Hattersley did.

Oral tales served more as entertainment to prisoners who, through learning the rhymes, could feel more closely identified with their situation and fellows. But as Phelan wrote, it is regrettable that more examples have not survived, as they provide insight into the terminology and darker areas of prison life that have not been well chronicled.

Motivations to write

Why do writers write? George Bernard Shaw said he did because an author was never seen by his clients and so did not need not dress too respectably. Jorge Luis Borges claimed that writing eased the passing of time. The poet Robert Frost described his art as taking life by the throat. Vladimir Nabakov believed that the only importance of writing was to the individual. Samuel Johnson famously declared "no man but a blockhead ever wrote except for money".[45]

The factors that drive prisoners or ex-prisoners to write are not so different from those of non-criminal, even famously successful, writers. Those who are inspired to write by their experience of incarceration seek publication or professional performance for a variety of reasons. The hope of financial reward can be a motivation, but it is rarely that which makes them pick up a pen or sit at a keyboard in the first instance.

Setting the record straight

The sociologist Stan Cohen, in his introduction to Walter Probyn's *Angel Face, the Making of a Criminal*, comments on explanations offered by – or on behalf of - "society's deviants, rejects and outsiders" when they tell their own stories.

In most cases, states Cohen:

> *They are purging their guilt, expiating their sins, recording their self-pity, begging for mercy, hysterically justifying themselves to the world or even trying to show their superiority over the normals, the punters who have always played the system straight.*[46]

He goes on to say that *Angel Face* is quite different. While the tone may be "bitter, accusatory or even shrill", the main motivation of Probyn, whom he describes as an amateur sociologist, is:

> *...to put the record straight, to explain, to clarify. Not as an act of personal expiation, but as a testimony on behalf of others.*[47]

Thus Probyn, according to Cohen, was speaking out and describing past experiences within the prison system that were not unique to himself.

Jimmy Boyle, in *A Sense of Freedom*, also seeks to clarify, but his stated motivation is to prevent others from making the mistakes he made. Alarmed by criminals becoming younger when they begin to offend, and their crimes increasingly serious, Boyle writes:

> The book is a genuine attempt to warn young people that there is nothing glamorous about getting involved in crime and violence. I feel that the only way any real progress can be made in this direction is through having a better understanding of it and the only way this will be achieved is by putting our cards on the table, and this I've tried hard to do. I don't feel that sympathy or popularity contests have anything to do with it.[48]

Later, in *The Pain of Confinement*, he describes a more personal motivation for his writing:

> I need it as a testament to my experience. To reflect, in some small measure, what I feel. To help me see, like the sculpture, the natural development of me – the human being. Threads of life brought to the surface. Painful though it may be there has to be an understanding of what we are doing.[49]

Twenty years before Boyle's warning to young people, ex-debutante Joan Henry introduced her prison memoir as a salutary tale for readers to consider their own good fortune in avoiding imprisonment:

> This book is not written in defence of the criminal or to revile the prison system; neither is it designed for those to whom there is a great gulf between the law-abiding citizen and the wrong-doer. It is written for those people who are interested in human beings and their behaviour, in the evil and the good, who can watch, or read of, the man or woman convicted of any crime, from petty theft to murder, and say: 'There' – but for that little kink in the brain, the tiny twist in the mind, the shuffle of circumstance – 'but for the grace of God, go I'.[50]

As Oscar Wilde had done half a century earlier, Henry wanted to tell the outside world what it was like to be a prisoner. Many others have had the same need. Former professional golfer John Hoskison, jailed for causing death by driving:

> *It is with a great deal of anguish and uncertainty that I send this book off for publication. It is about an episode in my life that I am not proud of. As far as I and my family are concerned, the fewer people who know about the tragic event the better. However, there is hardly a day that passes without my reading or hearing that prison is a soft option. This may be so in some circumstances, It wasn't for me and it isn't for most. When people read this book I hope they understand why I could not simply turn my back and walk away.*[51]

As a first-time prisoner of middle class background, Hoskison's shock at what he found in Wandsworth and Coldingley is portrayed starkly and without equivocation in his book. John Steele, of a criminal family and with previous sentences behind him, was a different proposition, but in his introduction to *The Bird That Never Flew* his plea is for a better awareness of penal conditions:

> *It is time we opened our eyes. Our prison system is geared to torment its human stock, to lock us away in concrete tombs and cages, degrade us, strip us of our identity, punish us mentally and physically, and leave us to rot and die a thousand deaths. In the space of years or even months. With its constant misery, pain, deaths, psychiatric hospitals, and of course riots and escapes, the system has failed prisoners and society.*[52]

Similar sentiments are expressed by Reg Wilson, a lifer whose account of solitary confinement in the Close Supervision Centre at HMP Woodhill, 'Hope it Rains Again', was published in *Prison Writing*.[53] Asked what he hoped readers outside prison would gain from it, he said:

> *Insight into what's really happening beneath all the gloss and rhetoric of prison. Prison doesn't work. It never has and never will. The majority of prisoners walking through its gates to freedom are 'timebombs' ticking away. I'm sick of hearing people use the word rehabilitation when referring to prisons and prisoners. It's a politician's lie... I just wanted people reading 'Hope it Rains Again' to see how much of an animal man still is.*[54]

Razor Smith believes that writing can succeed where prisons, the courts and probation fail. For him, setting the record straight was as much a personal quest as an attempt to inform or influence the public:

> *I realize that writing my story will probably not discourage anybody who is hell-bent on a life of crime, but it will help me to see exactly where I went wrong and not repeat my mistakes. And when you consider that in thirty years the entire might of the British Criminal Justice System has failed to do that, you might say that writing has been an exercise in rehabilitation. I want people to know what goes into making a criminal like me: we are not assembled overnight but forged over many years in the unhallowed halls of juvenile jails and adult prisons.*[55]

Few prisoners have attempted to speak out for a whole community. One who did was Trevor Hercules in *Labelled a Black Villain*:

> *I wrote this book because I felt certain things needed to be said, and because those black people in a position to be a real voice for the black community have failed to speak out on our behalf. The black community still cry out for someone to put forward their real grievances about living in a white society; yet the few black people in a position of power have put across only a diluted version of our anger and frustrations, leaving the white community to go about their daily business without having to confront their conscience head on ...*[56]

For anyone who writes an autobiography, whatever their history, the wish to exculpate, explain or justify earlier actions is a normal motivation. As the novelist Martin Amis explained when he published a memoir:

> *I do it because I feel the same stirrings that everyone else feels. I want to set the record straight.*[57]

But the record is set straight only from the author's perspective. A book by a politician, a sportsperson or anyone who has had a "colourful" life, may be publicised as "warts and all", but few members of what might be termed "straight" society wish to convey a negative impression of themselves.

Conversely and by definition, career criminals do not always hold such conventional values and may go to the other extreme. When they have published books, especially those whose stories have been ghosted by professional writers, self-glorification has sometimes appeared to be the prime motive.

Valerio Viccei, having carried off what he claimed to be the biggest robbery in

British history – at the Knightsbridge Safe Deposit Company in 1987 – wanted to ensure his own legend, to preserve his notoriety. Viccei did not engage a ghost-writer. Such were the conditions in which he was held in Parkhurst Prison, he was able to obtain his own word processor and, once he had learned English, write his book himself.

Viccei was proud of his crime, it was the defining event of his life:

> *Once I was arrested, the extensive glamour of the case made me realise that someone at some stage would eventually write a book about it. I was approached by different characters connected with the media but I wasn't too sure about their real intentions – and I was very diffident of the press as a whole because the so-called tabloids had never shown a proper interest in the dynamics and motivation of the robbery itself.*
>
> *What I feared most was the possibility of the book treating the whole thing as a soap-opera, making me look like a cartoon character... If there was a story to be told I would tell it when the time was right.*[58]

Ian Brady did not need to write a book to ensure his notoriety. That had long been established. His stated motivation in *The Gates of Janus – Serial Killing and its Analysis* [59] was to produce a "a modest manual for helping to track and capture the greatest and most dangerous animal in existence: the human predator."

What comes across is an insight into his own distorted perceptions where, in the words of one journalist, "sodomising children and strangling women for pleasure is no more or less reprehensible than deriving a sense of fulfilment from curing lepers and aiding the needy."[60] The author Colin Wilson, who corresponded with Brady for ten years and encouraged him to write the book, thought he had done so because "he has nothing else, writing is the only thing he has left." He also speculated that Brady was settling scores with his co-accused and former lover Myra Hindley, while the opinion of Brady's solicitor, Benedict Birnberg was that he was "seeking to do something good, to provide some compensation for the crimes that he has committed ... He wants to give back to society something for the horrific things that he has done."[61] Society showed little gratitude for Brady's efforts. Amidst much scathing press coverage the general consensus was that the book was just one more in a long series of attempts by the child killer to gain publicity.

A need for expression

Within the environment that many prisoners live when not in prison, crime is often regarded as a means of expression. Through criminal skills or a capacity for violence, many career criminals have made their mark on a world that would have otherwise ignored their existence. As it was for Messrs Boyle, McVicar, Collins, Viccei and others, writing a book can be another form of expression.

Jimmy Boyle has described violence as "the cultural art" of the Glasgow criminal community in which he played a leading role prior to being sentenced to life imprisonment. He says: "In its own way this cultural art expression was appreciated as much as creative art is in so called respectable environments."[62]

When, in terms of energy and emotion, he replaced the violence with sculpture and writing, negative expression became positive. John McVicar writes of the danger, drama and exhilaration of crime and how it sustained him for eight years. Then, having begun to write in prison, he found:

> *I have a new stimulus to sustain me. I labour away with a pen, and enjoy it all as much as the old power-play of the convict-criminal world.*[63]

Razor Smith, while conceding that boredom and "the need to let the outside world know you still exist" is a motivation for many prisoners to write, explains why so many who make it to publication are of a certain type:

> *My theory is that most prison 'faces' are frustrated actors, glory-seekers and self-promoters. I include myself in that… We want people to know that we are not just ciphers, not part of the herd, and the more people that know that, the better. We want self-esteem, respect, fame – or infamy, and if there's a bit of fortune on offer as well, all the better… Some people become criminals not only for the loot, but because it's the only way for them to make a mark on the world. Writing gives the prisoner power – if you get published, especially in a widely-read publication, it makes the screws a bit more wary of you. Most of them have trouble filling in a nicking sheet… The pool of prison writers is relatively small – and the ones that make it into print are the ego-driven madmen who have interesting stories to tell and who have a modicum of writing talent.*[64]

Not all prison writers are underworld "faces", nor do they all seek to exploit their criminal pasts. Erwin James, whose column on prison life entertained and informed *Guardian* readers until he was released on life licence in 2004 wrote under a *nom de plume*. Being able to express himself in print opened up a new world:

> *I discovered that education, and writing in particular, freed my mind to the extent that being bound became my means of liberation – liberation from a past that was more constricting than any prison sentence could be.*[65]

The sense of liberation can be from the present, as well as the past. Ian Kentzer, a contributor to *Prison Writing*:

> *In an environment where it is difficult to express emotions and wherein survival often depends on 'putting up a front', writing affords prisoners the opportunity to set their emotions free, to be themselves, albeit through other characters, and to fulfil the creative urge.*[66]

Jimmy Walker had long wanted to write. His first time in prison and serving a long sentence, he found an unexpected opportunity:

> *I always felt, and still do, that I had a story to tell about the type of upbringing I had. It was as though something inside was urging me to prove myself. When I came to prison I thought, 'Well if you don't do it now, Jimmy, you never will.' That coincided with the opportunity to learn how to use a PC in prison. I always maintained a love of words and, as inarticulate as I am, I stood above my peers. I suppose it was or is an ego thing.*[67]

Transferred from the Barlinnie Special Unit, where he had spent part of most days writing repetitive diary entries, to Saughton Prison in Edinburgh, feelings of foreboding motivated Hugh Collins to attempt a narrative account of his experiences:

> *I had this constant anxiety that something was going to happen to me - a trapdoor would open and I was off. So I did a sort of a manuscript.*[68]

For many writers, when they begin, to simply see their words on paper is the first motivation. The effect, especially for those in an institution such as prison, is often described as therapeutic. While this study is concerned only with writing for publication, therapeutic considerations inevitably arise. Anna Reynolds:

> *Maybe at some stage there was something therapeutic about what I wrote, but it has gone well beyond that. It is a compulsion in its own right. Actually, at Holloway they did say write it all down and I thought, sod off. Writing as therapy is fine if you want to write for yourself and then put it away in a drawer. But don't expect other people to applaud it. I don't write for myself but for an audience, and I push myself harder and harder to be able to do that.*[69]

The last word on the need for a prisoner to express him or herself goes to Oscar Wilde:

> *If I can produce one only beautiful work of art I shall be able to rob malice of its venom, cowardice of its sneer to pluck out the tongue of scorn by the roots.*[70]

Money

If money was the only motivation to write, as Samuel Johnson famously implied, few prisoners would have ever felt emboldened enough to put pen to paper. Johnson, as a professional writer, earned his living from the pen. Had he been unfortunate enough to be sent to prison, like Wilde, Taki and Archer over two centuries later, he would probably have been paid to write about it later. Prisoners with a media-hyped story to tell may occasionally be offered publishing deals but for the great majority of ordinary prisoners who take up the pen or sit down at the keyboard, financial reward is not a realistic prospect.

Money was the motivation for Oscar Wilde when he completed *The Ballad of Reading Gaol*. Impoverished and exiled in France, he hoped the poem would be published by the *New York Journal* and he wrote to his friend Robert Ross, "I must have £300 at least – more if possible." He was disappointed; there was little initial interest for the poem in America.[71]

John McVicar's notoriety as a bank robber and prison escaper meant as soon as he was arrested and remanded to Brixton Prison, the tabloid press were interested in his story. He obliged them and wrote what became the first part of *McVicar by*

Himself to provide money for his then partner and their son:

> What drove my writing then was a wish to see her receive enough money together with what I had accumulated as a robber to give the boy a chance of a new life away from the environment that a generation before had been the crucible of my criminality.[72]

Financial considerations certainly motivated Joan Henry to write *Who Lie In Gaol*, her account of post-war Holloway and Askham Grange. Henry told sociologist Mike Nellis that she did not want to write a prison book. She had never written non-fiction and was not keen on the idea of notoriety. But when she got out of prison she was persuaded by her literary agent Spencer Curtis Brown, who told her it was a unique opportunity for a writer. She was short of money and the publisher Victor Gollancz advanced her a small sum of money.[73]

One of the most successful prisoner autobiographies made no money for the author. The royalties from Jimmy Boyle's book, *A Sense of Freedom*, were used to set up a trust fund to help young people in socially deprived areas in the west of Scotland. His motivation to write the book had been to warn of the issues they faced, by recounting how he had gone wrong. He felt it appropriate that anyone who bought the book would thus be helping the cause.

Trying to make sense of it all

The inspiration to write can arise from a single event, but more likely it is the accumulated result of being sentenced to a harrowing and life-changing experience. For some prison writers, especially those who publish memoirs after they are released, focusing on their time inside, the process of telling their story acts as a catharsis. This is especially noticeable in the work of first-time prisoners like Zeno, S.R. Krishnamma and John Hoskison. The prison-influenced autobiographies of career criminals - Boyle, McVicar, Collins, Razor Smith – tend more to examine the life as a whole, rather than just the prison sentence.

Inspiration through reading plays a big part in any writer's early and ongoing development. Surprisingly, there is no discernable body of work that prison writers have read. Of those who were interviewed or who completed questionnaires for the Cropwood Fellowship research that led to this book, only around half had read any work by their predecessors cited above.

As with inspiration, there can be more than one motivation. While the publication of Jeffrey Archer's prison diaries was a commercial arrangement, in them he shows great keenness to criticise the system that prosecuted and jailed him, as well as hitting back at his perceived enemies. Razor Smith, in his autobiography, offers the criminal's perspective, while his family have benefited from the advance paid by the publishers. Joan Henry needed the money and, when it was forthcoming, took the opportunity to tell the outside world what women's prisons were like.

But many prisoners who write, especially those whose words never get beyond the walls, are motivated by a need to try to clarify the past. Jeremy Gavron, writer-in-residence at The Mount, described them as men who have lost the thread of their lives. Prison, he said, with all its empty time, turns them to the past, to make sense of their stories.[74]

5] Time and Opportunity

Time

The long-term prisoner understands the meaning of time. From the moment sentence is passed, as long days and nights turn into weeks and months, all but the institutionalised, or those who know they are never likely to get out, start to look to the future, to their release. Held by the law against their will and better judgement, until relatively recent times denied any rights as citizens or even as prisoners[1], their lives are effectively suspended for the duration. They are 'doing time', but it is not their own time. That has been taken from them by way of punishment.

In his book about the two years he spent as writer-in-residence at Wormwood Scrubs, the poet Ken Smith recalls seeing one inmate's interpretation of the meaning of prison time, written on the corrugated cardboard table of a punishment-block cell:

> *Time* is what it is.
> Time *is* what it is.
> Time is *what* it is.
> Time is what *it* is.
> Time is what it *is*.
> Time *is* what it *is*.[2]

For many inmates, time is to be endured, wasted, even suffered. But to anyone keen to write, it can be a very different experience. As a contributor to *Prison Writing*, Paul Ruddock, comments:

> *It may seem ironic, absurd even, that prison might provide one with any kind of freedom, but, given the right attitude, it can be equally surprising just how conducive the prison routine can actually be to any new or even, I should imagine, experienced writer.*[3]

George Hayes, who had a short story published in a later edition of the same journal, explains what is enabling about the prison routine:

> *We have much more time to think, to feel and search our souls and inner beings, to listen to our minds and rationalise and reason inwardly more than we might outside. Our situation forces self-appraisal, but the writing could be about anything, jail or out of jail.*[4]

Time to think was one of the advantages of being in prison for former government minister Jonathan Aitken. A journalist and author, he published only one poem while inside, but the experience inspired his later books *Psalms for People Under Pressure* and *Prayers for People Under Pressure*.[5]

As to how prison can enable writers, he says:

> *Plenty of down time to fill, especially if you are in a single cell. Even if you're not, there's time and opportunity to write in prison. I found prison a good atmosphere to think in. I mean, solitude, even though there's a lot of noise going on, it does produce a reflective creativity. It is of course quite a shattering experience at the beginning, as you get used to the extraordinary ways of prison, but I don't think it need be a breaking experience. Once you've settled in to the prison way of life, I think you can find time and inclination to write.*[6]

The dub poet Benjamin Zephaniah has recalled how going to prison as a teenager was a creative turning point for him. Looking back, he considered himself a poet, although he did not actually write while he was there.

> *I didn't even write when I came out of prison. But I was a poet and a Rasta ... I developed the themes and thought about life more. Prison gave me time to do one thing which was to think. And what I realised while I was in prison was that not everybody who owns a car or owns a house is my enemy. I realised sometimes through other people, what I could do with my writing, and that there was another way of fighting the system.*[7]

John McVicar, on remand in Brixton and facing years of imprisonment, found writing to be an exercise that distracted him from his present surroundings and future prospects. He had already arrived at the realisation that as a criminal he was a failure and he knew he needed to find another way of life:

> *Writing up my escape story gave me not only a purpose in an environment in which the only purpose is either to escape or wait for release, but also the beginning of what turned out to be a career. One of the few things you can do in prison for your self is write. I had the composition skills to string a few words together and within a few days of recapture I had started to be a writer.*[8]

In John Hoskison's memoir he makes hardly any reference to the actual writing he did in prison, but towards the end he says:

> *Being able to write has saved me these last few months. Many things have happened, of course, but only the usual ones: a few stabbings, nothing much out of the ordinary. It's true what everyone says in here – once the initial shock of prison is overcome, it really is just a question of helping time pass as quickly as possible.*[9]

The pseudonymous Zeno, serving a life sentence in Wormwood Scrubs in the early 1960s, was aware that he was doing nothing constructive with the abundant time at his disposal. His decision to write, which resulted in a novel and his prison memoir, *Life*, was inspired by the example of a fellow prisoner, an Austrian financier, who won one of the first Koestler Awards for literature:

> *I shall try to follow Kurt's lead and write constructively for publication. I am ashamed that I alone of those I know and who are here with me in this room should be doing nothing constructive with the great wedges of time that I have at my disposal. I suspect sometimes that it is the sheer amount of time which defeats me: there is so much of it that I can always postpone any action on the grounds that there is no urgency – there is always tomorrow, next week or next year, and there are still years to fill.*[10]

In determining to use his time more productively, Zeno reveals how having too much time can induce lethargy. When Tony Hoare was sentenced to six years in the 1960s, he decided to write a novel. He found it difficult to concentrate in the local prison where he spent the first six months, but later realised that his procrastination was perhaps unnecessary:

> *I suppose if I'd been really determined to start writing at that point I'd have managed to overcome the obstacles somehow. The real destructive force in*

> *prison is the ease with which it seduces you into apathy.*[11]

As Zeno writes in the present tense for contemporaneous effect, so Anna Reynolds, in her autobiography *Tightrope*, conveys the atmosphere of a given time by referring to her diary entries. Thus, in Holloway, two months after she had been charged with the murder of her mother:

> *28 August 1986. 3pm. Time for contemplation. What else can you do in prison but think? Everything hurts. I want to get it all down, somehow contain the pain. Tears are no good any more. I can't yet go to the edge of the pain that I sense lies in waiting for me ... I feel blind, searching my way towards some kind of comprehension, but this evades me...*[12]

Serving terms of imprisonment, Peter Wayne wrote prolifically. Released, he preferred the hedonistic lifestyle to the discipline of writing. He told a journalist who interviewed him in prison that only when he was in prison did his literary creativity blossom. The structure of the regime and lack of distraction meant that in prison Wayne simply had time to write.[13]

Few would oppose the view that it is easier to engage in creative activity in prison today than it was in earlier, less liberalised times. But even in the harsh environment of Parkhurst in the 1920s, in a period when rules and regulations were rigidly enforced and writing about prison was prohibited, Jim Phelan was determined to make his life sentence work to his advantage:

> *What was a jail? For me, then and there, it was a place where I did the things I wanted to do. Let no one hastily call me normal, and judge thousands of poor devils by my standard. For no writer is normal, if he be worth reading...In 1927 I buried myself on the island and talked and wrote ... I was happy. For the jail could deprive me of nothing.*[14]

Removal from outside distractions and having time to reflect enables prisoners who wish to write. Some, as we have seen, get on with it there and then; others wait until they are released. In the latter examples, immediacy may be lost but that is not to underestimate the impact of time. A great deal of post-release prison writing, especially memoir, is about reclaiming the past, regaining periods of life dislocated by imprisonment.

Teachers and mentors

Education provision for prisoners varies according to establishment. The latter-day pre-occupation with key performance indicators – of questionable value to anyone but a bureaucrat – and the more laudable emphasis on basic literacy has meant that prison education departments give little time to those who wish to make their mark through writing for publication. Besides such practical issues, teachers working in prisons may well be cautious of being seen to assist inmates to break the rules, either by the content of the writing or by the prisoner making money from it.

Each year the Koestler Awards include poetry, prose and play-writing prizes. All entries must be submitted via prison education departments, but, paradoxically, many prison writers feel that official interest in their work is lukewarm, while encouragement in many prisons is non-existent. When education staff are supportive, it is usually an individual who has a personal interest in creativity and who sees promise in the work produced.

Such a man was Tom Sherrin, who taught English in Holloway for over twenty years. Clare Barstow found the creative writing class that he ran a great help. Prior to being sentenced to life imprisonment she had attended a course in London and had begun to write a play. After attending Sherrin's class she completed it and the play was subsequently performed in Holloway. Interviewed for a Sunday newspaper feature in prisoners' writing, Tom Sherrin said:

> *All that many of these prisoners have is their stories, and they should not be stolen and claimed by other writers. Some inmates have lived six lives in one by the time they are nineteen, more than enough material to make ten conventional novels.*[15]

Phillip Baker wrote his novel *Blood Posse* after encouragement from a teacher in Parkhurst during a low point in his sentence:

> *I was in a box with no way out. Then this lovely woman came along who was like an angel. She gave me my wings and now I can fly.*[16]

A few years earlier, the Knightsbridge robber, Valerio Viccei, generous in his praise for a number of staff members at Parkhurst, said he would not have been able to write his book without the education department. He went on to praise individuals who had given him technical support with the computer equipment he had arranged to be sent into the prison and the teachers who had assisted him in learning English.

Prison libraries can be havens for inmates who seek to learn about writing by reading. In the late 1920s and 30s Walter Macartney believed that the warder in charge of the Parkhurst library did his utmost – as he was directed to from above – to give prisoners as little to read as possible. A decade and more later, Jimmy O'Connor, already committed to a voracious reading programme, got himself a job in the Dartmoor library. Education facilities in convict prisons at that time were sparse, but for a fortunate few correspondence courses were available. Jim Phelan had managed to take one and so did O'Connor, who by that stage of his life sentence had listened to so many stories from "murderers, blackmailers and rapists" that he had decided to work on becoming a dramatist.

With help of the deputy governor he enrolled on a course with Ruskin College, Oxford. A tutor whom he never met sent him titles such as 'The Rehearsal' and 'The Sea' and he wrote thirty minute plays to fit the subject:

> *Then he told me that my plays were too violent. I wrote back and said what about the Greek tragedies. I also explained that I lived amongst violence in a very violent world. He told me that if I continued in this vein then I had no hopes whatsoever. The tutor was wrong.* Three Clear Sundays, *a play I wrote for television, has been shown nearly all round the world. Some newspapers said it contributed towards the abolition of the death penalty in this country.*[17]

A correspondence course arranged through the education department at High Down Prison gave Razor Smith the impetus to develop his writing skills. Serving nineteen years, he arrived at the prison in 1994 with a bad disciplinary record. But when he had not been fighting, subverting and escaping, he had been writing, with a few pieces in magazines and a Radio 4 interview to his name:

> *Stephen Pryor, who was the Number One Governor, came to my cell and told me that he'd heard my Radio 4 piece and was impressed. He made me a deal – he was willing to overlook my terrible prison record if I would keep out of trouble and start up a prison magazine. I jumped at the chance and as a result Mr Pryor and Eileen Jackman, the head of education, agreed to fund*

me for a diploma course in freelance feature writing at the London School of Journalism... The only prison that ever helped or encouraged me to write was High Down." [18]

Prison education was a saviour to Judith Ward, who served seventeen years of a life sentence before her conviction was quashed. In Durham's maximum security wing she exhausted all the facilities on offer. She did RSAs, O and A levels, a correspondence course in journalism and a degree in European history from the Open University. But when a writer began visiting the wing to help inmates who wanted to write, hitherto unrecognised horizons began to open up. She wrote short stories about life before her arrest and won a Koestler Award for one about working with horses. She acknowledged the writer, Tom Hadaway, a well-known stage and television dramatist, in her book, *Ambushed*:

> *He came once a week and a few of us went to his workshops. He told us of his writings, and read ours. He was a real help and encouraged me to put pen to paper about my experiences... Without Tom's encouragement in those years, I doubt I would be writing this book or have shared his enthusiasm for the written word. He visited other prisons in the area and in late 1987 wrote a play which was performed in the Live Theatre in Newcastle. Entitled* Yesterday's Children, *it is based on his experience of prison and those of the inmates he met.* [19]

Hadaway was not the first visiting mentor to Durham's top security wing who had encouraged a prisoner to write a book. A few years earlier, when the wing housed male prisoners who were considered serious escape risks, sociologist Stan Cohen had run a regular discussion group. His influence was evident when Walter Probyn wrote his autobiographical critique of the British criminal justice system, although Cohen stressed in his foreword that the writing of the book was all Probyn's work. In Parkhurst, Valerio Viccei took a different approach, but he received help from crime reporter James Nicholson, who had covered his trial at the Old Bailey and put him in contact with a publisher.

> *Every time James turned up I was more than eager to show him my work and he too helped with priceless advice and the kind of support that only a true friend could give.* [20]

Ward, Probyn and Viccei published only one book each, all autobiographies. Tony Hoare made a career out of writing, but believes he would never have got started without the man he describes as a "true mentor", the television dramatist Alan Plater, who visited him in Hull Prison in late 60s.

Whether Moors Murderer Ian Brady considered Colin Wilson, author of over a hundred books on crime and the supernatural, a mentor or not, he appears to have played a significant role in facilitating Brady's book on serial killers, *The Gates of Janus*. Brady had written to Wilson some years earlier and a correspondence developed. Wilson later said : "When people approach me with severe personal problems, I tell them to try writing a book. In Brady's case it seemed common sense. The obvious subject was serial killers such as himself, so he could bring to bear his special insights."[21]

But the help Wilson gave Brady did not spare him being lambasted in Brady's book for comments he had made many years before about Dostoevsky's *The Possessed*, in his own book, *The Outsider*. Brady was highly critical of Wilson, whom he said should feel guilty for making a lucrative living from writing about criminals and their crimes. Brady, a serial killer writing about serial killers was reported to be likely to earn £12,000 in royalties from *The Gates of Janus*. The proceeds were said to be going to his mother.

Writers in residence

Tom Hadaway, who was to have a notable influence on Judith Ward, took up the post of writer in residence in Durham in 1985. The three-month placement, the first of its kind in the UK, was jointly funded by the Women's Royal Voluntary Service, Northern Arts and the Arts Council.[22] With a brief to work with education staff to develop creative writing skills among inmates, Hadaway also spent a day a week in Frankland and Low Newton prisons. When his time was up he continued to run sessions on a voluntary basis with the women on Durham's H Wing.

An anthology of inmates work from all three establishments, *Prison Writers* was published by Iron Press in 1986 and quickly sold out. Hot on the heels of Hadaway, the poet Ken Smith began his residency in Wormwood Scrubs, one that lasted two years and was documented by his book *Inside Time*. Funded by Greater London Arts, Smith's one-to-one work resulted in one inmate having a pamphlet of poetry published, several others getting poems published in *She* magazine and interviews with Radio 4 and ITV.

Novelist and poet Alexis Lykiard's residency at Channings Wood was only of six months duration, in 1988, but he wasted no time. He persuaded writer friends including Kit Wright, Colin Wilson and Tim Page – a photo journalist famed for his work covering the Vietnam War - to give talks to the inmates. He also produced an anthology *Out of the Wood*, which led to a BBC2 programme on creative writing in the prison.

Many writers in residence have arranged publication of anthologies of prisoners' work, which serve as showcases of their own work as well as achievements of the contributors. *Words From Within*, edited by Jane Harris, provides a selection by male and female inmates of HMP Durham, where Harris worked in 1992-3. The most powerful writing comes from women, six of them lifers. Noeleen Hendry's 'The Widow's Tale' – a rather ironic title as the author had become a widow by murdering her husband - was reproduced in *The Guardian*.[23]

Since the first wave of writers in residence, the feeling has developed among many prisoners that their presence on prison wings is more about benefiting the writers than prisoners. Ian Kentzer, Koestler winner and published in small magazines:

> *Writers in residence have some merit but many prisoners suspect them of doing their own research and not being quite as altruistic as they suggest.*[24]

Anna Reynolds, who was 'in residence' as an inmate, before going back, into Bedford and Holloway as a writer on the Arts Council scheme, is critical of those who make money by writing about the work they have done with inmates:

> *The way I see it, if you go into prison as a writer in residence, the one thing you do not do under any circumstances is write about that stuff yourself. You're there to give – not to take… You need to be so fresh and so sharp and so full of that excitement. It's nothing to do with teaching – you're encouraging, saying 'You have got something worthwhile, do it.'*[25]

Many writers have written about their work with prisoners, some while they were there, others later. In 1999, after Jeremy Gavron left HMP The Mount, he wrote in *The Guardian* that he had found prisons to be "full of Ancient Mariners, men with stories they need to tell and which other prisoners don't want to hear." He compared the situation he had been in as a writer in residence to that of Nick

Carraway in F.Scott Fitzgerald's novel *The Great Gatsby* - "I found myself 'privy to the secret griefs of wild, unknown men'".[26]

Gavron felt that the most valuable work he had done was working with individuals, helping them make sense of their own narratives. He did the usual workshops, organised a poetry competition, set up a magazine and printed an anthology. Most significantly of all, he helped two inmates, Rocky Carr and Ron Piper, to get books published. Piper's *Take Him Away*[27] is a short memoir that begins at the age of seven and ends when he is fifteen, sentenced at the Old Bailey. He was sixty-two when it was published and had spent forty years in institutions.

Carr was the first prisoner Jeremy Gavron met when he arrived at The Mount:

> *He pulled me aside and thrust a prison notebook dense with scribbles into my hand. The stories were full of life but a mess, rather like Rocky, who in his late thirties was already on his sixth or seventh sentence. We worked on them together, and then Rocky was released. A few months later I got a letter. He was back inside. He had to do something. He was going to write a novel. I had to help him.*[28]

Gavron did help, typing up the words Carr sent him and arranging them into chapters. The book was *Brixton Bwoy*. Both hoped it would lead Carr out of crime and prison. Both were disappointed, but neither Carr nor Ron Piper were likely to complain about seeing their work championed in a national newspaper.

In his *Guardian* article, Jeremy Gavron described his experience as a writer-in-residence:

> *It was sometimes frightening, occasionally exhilarating, and always exhausting…By the end of two years, spending two and a half days a week in the prison, I was drained, glad to hand in my keys. How much of a difference I made is hard to say. Prison is a last resort, a place where men who haven't responded to help, who haven't been able to help themselves, end up.*[29]

The longest-serving writer in residence within a UK prison is not connected to the Arts Council scheme. Carlo Gébler has worked in Northern Ireland prisons since 1994, first at the Maze and latterly Maghaberry. Gébler is unusual among writers in residence; his curriculum vitae includes award winning novels, non-

Time and Opportunity

fiction books, stage plays and television documentaries. At any time he has work commissioned for months if not years ahead. The time he spends with prisoners comes from a sense of vocation, as many who have received advice and help testify.[30] He describes his working routine:

> *I'm in the prison one day a week. I do not teach a class. I work unescorted on the wings, in the Punishment and Segregation Unit or in the hospital or the kitchens or the workshops, or in fact anywhere. I see prisoners alone, usually in their cells, which is the best place to talk; it feels safe for them. Sometimes I'm locked in with them. I usually see in a day between eight and twelve people. They will read me what they've written or I'll have read what they've given me to read. Either way, I'll then go through the work with them rather as my publishers go through my work with me. Quite a bit of what's written concerns crime and/or the paramilitaries who are still a dominant feature of Northern Irish life despite the Belfast/Good Friday Agreement. Typically, we can't even agree on what to call the Agreement. However, there isn't one overriding theme that prisoners in Northern Ireland home in on.*
>
> *The work is diverse, it's as diverse as people are. One or two have been published in* Prison Writing *or in Northern Irish publications like* The Captive Voice. *A lot have submitted work to Koestler - and done well. A good number have gone on from writing for me to doing an OU degree. Some have just written for the sheer hell of writing. Some have left and gone out into the world and worked for community arts groups because of writing.*
>
> *Personally, I am not obsessed with publication and, though it's important, I don't see it as the be all and end all. Just write well, that's my motto.*[31]

Gébler is in no doubt about his role:

> *Everyone I work with wants in one way or another and for one reason and other to write. They've all got the bug. So I'm not really an inspiration. If anything, it's being in prison and alone with their churning thoughts that's their principal motivator. Prison, the fact of prison, solitude, quality time with the self, et cetera, more than anything else is what drives men and women to write. I don't. Mentoring, I would say, is what I do. One, I read what they write. Two, I give advice on how it might be improved. Three, I suggest books to read that might help them with what they're trying to write. Four, I'm a regular fixture of their lives on a Thursday. Most of the prisoners I deal*

> with have never had anything like this and probably in the chaos of their lives that is jail and the criminal lifestyle (forgive the term) that probably counts for more than any other single thing I do.[32]

All writers working in prisons quickly discover how important it is to gain the trust of inmates and to keep within definite boundaries. Prisoners who commit their thoughts and feelings to be published in any form, and a prison magazine can be as hazardous as a book or national newspaper, inevitably run the risk of providing information that could be used against them at a later stage. In such circumstances, the writer in residence might be seen as having worked against those he or she is there to help. Carlo Gébler:

> *In jail there is a fantastic level of anxiety regarding the sanctity or integrity of the self and psyche. Common to all prisoners is the fear that the state, or the prison authorities or whomever, want to get inside their brains and re-arrange the wiring, in prison parlance, 'fuck with their heads'. If, for a single second, I gave the impression that I was in any way connected with such a project, relations with prisoners would be adversely affected and quickly I'd be sunk. Association with head shrinkage is one of the surest ways on the wings to lose friends and not influence people. That is why when I work I doggedly stick to the practice. After all, that is why I am there.*[33]

Benevolent officialdom

The Barlinnie Special Unit was a benevolent regime, aimed at showing disruptive inmates that alternatives to violence exist and are possible. The regime assisted Jimmy Boyle to write his autobiography, with the encouragement of staff in the unit and of Scottish Office civil servant, Alex Stephen, who believed that prisoners should be able to publish their work. Stephen was helpful in guiding Boyle through the bureaucratic maze that faced him in publishing *A Sense of Freedom* while still serving a life sentence.

Parkhurst's Special Secure Unit in the early 1990s was no therapeutic community. Rather, it was a small prison-within-a-prison for top security prisoners and terrorists who, if they escaped, would pose a major risk to the public and/or an embarrassment to the government. Nevertheless, Valerio Viccei enjoyed a whole range of facilitating factors when he came to write his book *Knightsbridge* in the unit – a word processor in his cell, a tape recorder, stationery and, most helpful of all, a governor who was willing to let him get on with it. In the book Viccei expressed gratitude:

> *I never expected an English prison to be as good as this, and I'm saying so in all honesty. Parkhurst is a one-off and its governor John Marriott is a one-off as well. The man has earned my respect and my appreciation…I am also grateful to him for ensuring that this little unit, forgotten for years, had access to civil staff and teachers. I could hardly have managed to progress with this work were it not for the Education Department.*[34]

A chaplain's wife gave Erwin James the first inkling that he might have a talent for writing. She ran a voluntary class on the perils of alcohol and expressed enthusiasm for the style with which he had written his homework. James said later: "It was the first time since my life sentence began that anyone had suggested that I might possess a positive quality. Somehow, being alone in my cell that night didn't feel so bad."[35]

Much later on, after getting in contact with *The Guardian* about writing articles, he showed a teacher in the education department a letter from the editor, telling him his work was to be published. The teacher's response was "If I was you I'd pick another pastime" and an assistant governor he approached said "I could give you one big no or fifty small no's – but the answer would still be the same I'm afraid." Fortunately, the next echelon of officialdom took a positive view:

> *Prison service headquarters were more positive. When* The Guardian *explained what my contributions to the paper would entail and gave an assurance that prison rules governing prisoners' contact with newspapers would be rigorously adhered to, an official agreed to put the proposal to the prisons' minister. A few weeks later we got the good news: the minister was 'content for this to go ahead'.*[36]

The teenage Benjamin Zephaniah, into dub poetry but not yet writing, was encouraged in a different way. In prison he met a prison officer who shared his interest in kung-fu. When the officer was on the night-watch, he would let him out of his cell to spar:

> *One night after we finished we were talking and I gave him a bit of a*

> *performance and he said 'You've got to go out and do that, you've got to go out and let other people hear this.' He actually said 'Half the screws in this prison should sit down and listen to that'. And he came back weeks later and said 'You really got me thinking.' I'd got him thinking about his job and you know, to a little Handsworth boy who thought he was unimportant and everything, it makes you think these people recognise the talent that I've got, and it gives you hope.*[37]

As Benjamin Zephaniah found, help and support sometimes appear in unexpected forms. Mark Leech got the idea to write his book, *A Product of the System* following correspondence with the at-the-time outspoken judge, James Pickles, who contributed the foreword.

John McVicar did not need help in that area, but he did need someone to smuggle out the "densely covered, folded up pieces of foolscap" on which he had written the story of his escape from maximum security in Durham. Benevolence here came not from within the prison service, but his solicitor, who, according to McVicar, took the papers away with him after visits, on the pretext that they were notes for the defence.

The 'inside' press

In 1993, the Prison Reform Trust conducted a survey of prisons in England and Wales, with the aim of discovering how many produced their own magazine. Out of the hundred that responded, fifty-five said they had a magazine. Publishing their findings in a booklet, the PRT gave a short review of the magazines that they had been sent and highlighted some of the experiences that their survey had revealed. The aim was to encourage the prisons that did not have a magazine to set one up and to provide a forum for the sharing of ideas between those that already existed.

There is no doubt that prison magazines can assist communication channels between prison management and inmates. But as well as a means of exchanging information and opinions, they provide opportunities for prisoners who write to see their work in print. For the majority it will be the first time, maybe the only time. For others, a story or article in a magazine titled *Inside Out, Inside Story, Inside View, The Insider* – or maybe the slightly more imaginative *Behind The Door, Breakout* or *On Top* – has been the first step on the ladder that led to a writing career.

The origins of prison magazines lie in the weekly news 'lecture' as it was known, given each Saturday in convict prisons by the chaplain. He would select items which he considered to be of interest to the prisoners, avoiding any reports of crime or punishment and usually acknowledging only Tory politics. Sport was popular, but racing results were not given out.

By the 1930s, these oral bulletins, which had been introduced during the era of the rule of silence, had progressed to duplicated news sheets, initially synopses of world and national events compiled and typed out by a trusted prisoner and approved by the governor.[38] Soon cartoons, prison chess results, puzzles and quizzes were incorporated and a small number of prisons had their own newspaper or magazine.

Serving six years in Hull in the late 1960s, Tony Hoare applied to the governor to be allowed to start a magazine. His rationale was that other long-term prisons had them, why not Hull – although, as he said in Giles Brandreth's book *Created in Captivity*, the only one he was in any way impressed by was Parkhurst's *Outlet*.[39] His true motive for becoming involved was to obtain a typewriter on which he could type up the novel he had spent months writing, which he did by night. By day he edited what Brandreth considered at the time "one of the liveliest prison magazines ever to be produced in this country".

Sean Bourke, who edited the Wormwood Scrubs magazine *New Horizon* in 1966, did better than a typewriter - he had an office in D Hall, at the time home to the pseudonymous Zeno, who had already published a novel, and George Blake, serving forty-two years for espionage. Bourke's editorial duties were not onerous, amounting to around one day's work a month, but he claimed the perks made him "the most highly privileged prisoner in Wormwood Scrubs".[41] When, on 22 October 1966, the spy Blake escaped, never to return, Bourke played a major part in assisting him. By then, his editorship relinquished, he had been released.

Sorted, the magazine that Razor Smith founded and edited in High Down, ran for ten issues in the mid-1990s. Although he solicited contributors from other prisoners, much of the content was written by Smith himself. After years of fighting the system, he had found a niche and he threw himself headlong into the magazine. He wrote in his autobiography, "It is a great feeling to have created something from nothing and then hear so many people talking about it."[42]

High Down governor, Stephen Pryor, who saw the benefits of having a magazine, facilitated its production by providing a small amount of money for paper and printing. The result was a quirky magazine with articles about aspects of criminal and prison history, lively short stories by Razor Smith and others and interviews with anyone of note who visited the prison – on one occasion a former world boxing champion. After only four issues, *Sorted* won a Koestler Award, but when a new governor arrived at High Down the budget was withdrawn and the magazine came to an end.

In any prison, the governor's approval and support is crucial to the continuing existence of a magazine, particularly one run entirely by prisoners. When Peter Lewis, early in a fifteen year sentence, got himself transferred to Maidstone, a jail with a print shop, he found that the governor, Mike Conway, was as keen to have a magazine as Lewis was to start one. Lewis had some experience of such matters, having earlier edited an underground newspaper and a Welsh country music magazine.

The first issue of *Insider* appeared in 1999 and the print run soon reached 700 copies, half of them distributed outside HMP Maidstone to interested individuals throughout the criminal justice system and to others abroad. With its attractive layout, regular correspondents including lawyer Stanley Best, wildlife expert Bill Jordan and prisoners in California and New York, *Insider* was undoubtedly the most professionally produced magazine of its kind in Britain. In the summer of 2000, the *Insider* ran a national prison poetry competition, which led to the publication of a hundred of the best poems in *Bards Behind Bars*[43], raising over £1500 for a local children's hospice.

The magazine thrived until, in 2003, Peter Lewis was given two days notice that he was to be transferred to The Mount. By then, a new governor had replaced the supportive Mike Conway and the magazine, in the words of its erstwhile editor, was condemned to the annals of penal history. He wrote "I fear that the controversial content was often a source of embarrassment to the prison service which seems entrenched in Victorian attitudes… I feel as though I am now being made to pay the price for having the audacity to highlight the viewpoint of those incarcerated by the state." In his new location, Lewis received many letters of commiseration and support and soon set about planning future publishing projects.[44] A year later he was still in The Mount, where he revived *XMT*, a title that, like the *Insider* in Maidstone, had once thrived in The Mount, before falling into decline.

In *The Prisons Handbook 2005*, Martyn Cook and Rob Matthews, of the magazine *It's Wandsworth*, described the workings of an editorial team and listed twenty-eight magazines thought to be in existence at the time. Cook and

Matthews emphasised the benefits of having a forum within a prison to discuss concerns, saying "it has been useful and has led to increased confidence for men who live in an environment where paranoia and lack of self-esteem abound." [45]

The enterprising Peter Wayne would not fall into that category. While in Lindholme, he interviewed the governor, who thought he was going to be featured in the prison magazine *Rewired*. When he discovered that he was also about to appear in *Prospect* magazine, the interviewee was so annoyed that Wayne found himself transferred to a prison two hundred miles away. At least it provided him with more material. His next column in *Prospect* told how a "red-faced and liverish Governor Batt"– Wayne had been sufficiently courteous to change the name – accused him of "trying to flog an article about me in Fleet Street" and demanded a retraction.

Wayne's attempt at mollification by pointing out that *Prospect* was "not some tatty little tabloid ...Douglas Hurd is on the advisory board. You may have heard of him? Former foreign secretary?" failed miserably. The governor, he wrote, "was like Lear on the heath."[46] As it happened, Peter Wayne found his new location, Channings Wood in Devon, to his liking, commenting on the episode, "Such are the vicissitudes of a writer 'in residence'".

The newspaper

Published by New Bridge, a charity that creates links between offenders and the community, *Inside Time* has been essential reading for many prisoners in British jails since it began in 1991. In the early days and on occasion since, it has incurred the wrath of prison staff, who have not always been happy at their portrayal within the pages of the first and only national newspaper aimed at and largely written by prisoners in the UK. Initially the paper was published quarterly, but now appears monthly.

The first editor was Anna Reynolds, not long released following the quashing of her life sentence. When she moved on, another ex-prisoner, John Bowers, took over. *Inside Time* provides news and a forum for prisoners to exchange opinions. The 'Mailbag' pages have covered queries on every aspect of imprisonment – a typical issue, November 2004, had letters about the Freedom of Information Act, polygraph testing, justifiable discrimination, prison psychologists and certificates of posting. It is noticeable that many of the regular correspondents are serving long sentences – often life - and thus have a more vested interest in what is happening around them than inmates on short determinate sentences.

As well as keeping prisoners informed and helping to combat feelings of isolation, *Inside Time* encourages journalism, giving prison writers a platform within their own wider community. There are contributions from outside – the editorial team includes novelist Rachel Billington, the daughter of New Bridge founder Lord Longford – but it is the letters, articles, cartoons and poems of prisoners that make the paper unique.

The journal

Prison Writing, in its ten years existence, published prose, poetry and fiction by more than two hundred individual prisoners, many of whom were seeing their work in print for the first time. The journal, founded in Sheffield in 1992, appeared every six months for the next seven years, when it ground to a halt due to falling subscriptions. Two years later it re-appeared and two editions in book form were published by Waterside Press, after articles by John McVicar in *Punch* and Marcel Berlins in *The Guardian*, expressed regret at the journal's demise. A popular feature of *Prison Writing* was an extended interview in each issue with a subject prominently connected with prisons and books.

Hugh Collins, Howard Marks, Valerio Viccei, Anna Reynolds, Edward Bunker, Bruce Reynolds, John McVicar, Razor Smith and Carlo Gébler were among those interviewed, as well as writers with an interest in the milieu like Martin Amis, James Morton and Duncan Campbell. Most of the writing published came from the UK, but there were contributions from Death Row prisoners and others in the USA, from Australia and from Britons in European jails.

The first issue included an autobiographical account by Charles Bronson entitled 'Insanity Drove Me Mad', about his time in Broadmoor Hospital, and one by Tony Bashforth that began "There are 52 weeks in a year and in the year 1987 I was arrested 47 times. Not one of those arrests led to a conviction." Bashforth, a talented artist, provided an illustration for the cover and a later piece by him, about betting on a spider fight in Long Lartin, was printed in *Prison Writing 6*.

Two competitions, one sponsored by Yorkshire Arts and the second by the National Lottery, were successful in interesting new writers, including Matthew Williams who, like others who began in the journal, would see his work published and performed to a much bigger audience. The journal received acclaim from academics, members of the judiciary, prison service officials and the media but in the end it ceased to exist because it was not viable commercially, even with the subsidy and promotion of Waterside Press. Many prisoners and outside readers were sad to see the journal go. Razor Smith acknowledged the opportunities it gave him in his autobiography, *A Few Kind Words and a Loaded Gun*.[47]

Earlier, before the Waterside rescue attempt, he had written:

> Prison Writing *was more than just a platform for prison-based talent, it was a springboard to the outside world. It turned more cons onto poetry and prose than any number of glory-seeking writers in residence and budget-slashed education departments. Its demise means one more voice from the yards has had its vocal chords removed. Before* Prison Writing, *the only time I saw my name was on charge sheets and wanted posters. I feel as if I have lost a friend.*[48]

A lifer, John Wrigglesworth, wrote of the feeling of achievement he experienced when his work was accepted, saying "the money was always welcome but incidental. Seeing my work in print was such a great encouragement". The novelist Carlo Gébler, also writer in residence for many years at HMP Maghaberry in Northern Ireland, praised the interviews and the content. He said it was very useful for him to show putative writers in jail that there was "a professionally-produced magazine that might publish their work if the editor thought it was up to scratch" and commented on the satisfaction gained by prisoners when their work was accepted.[49]

The competitions

Arthur Koestler, who gave his name to the Koestler Awards Scheme, had first-hand experience of imprisonment. As a journalist sent to Spain in 1936 to cover the Civil War, he was arrested and sentenced to death for spying by the Fascists. Rescued by the British Foreign Office, even though he was Hungarian by birth, he went to Paris where he edited an anti-Soviet, anti-Nazi weekly. In 1939 he was arrested by the Germans and sent to Le Vernet Detention Camp, from where he managed to gain his release the following year. When he arrived in England he was once again arrested and spent six months in Pentonville for entering the country illegally.

Koestler became a highly successful author. In his most famous novel, *Darkness At Noon*, he drew on his own life to tell the story of a man living in an unnamed dictatorship who is arrested, imprisoned, tried and executed. The idea for the annual awards scheme came from his wish to provide prisoners with creative ways to use their time, to help alleviate the dehumanising effects of prison life. In 1962, with the support of the Prison Commission and the then Home Secretary, R.A.Butler, the first Koestler awards were made, for works of arts and crafts produced in prison. In 2005, the Koestler scheme attracted 4,000 entries in over fifty categories, including art, ceramics, music composition, matchstick modelling, furniture and dressmaking, hairdressing and engineering design.

The categories for writing included playwriting, prose, poetry and establishment magazines. About a quarter of the entries received awards, most between £20 and £60, with some special awards of £100 for exceptional work. Volunteer judges in the various categories, and a host of individual and corporate sponsors, together with charitable foundations and trusts, have helped the scheme become a unique and major arts project that has given hope and a sense of achievement to a huge number of prisoners over the years.

One of the early Koestler Award winners was the prisoner known as Zeno, with a collection of short stories in 1963. Tony Hoare had success with a novel, which he adapted into a television play. Almost every prison writer who has made any mark, large or small, has been encouraged by winning Koestler Awards. One frustration felt by some winners is that they do not receive personal credit; only the prison they are in is named.

For many years, while works of visual art were exhibited at an open show in London, the winning entries for writing were not published and remained mostly unread by anyone except the judges. This situation was rectified in the mid-1990s, when selections of the best prose and poetry works were produced in booklet form. Even then, the authors' names were not revealed.

Whether this is based on an over-protective attitude on behalf of the trustees, a perceived need to avoid notorious individuals receiving publicity at the scheme's expense, or a desire to emphasise prison education departments' part in participating, it denies writers their full sense of achievement and the wider credit to which they are entitled.

The other organisation to encourage prison writing through an annual competition is the Prison Reform Trust. An essay competition, open to prisoners and prison staff, ran for some years until 1997, when the Andrew Groves Short Story Competition was introduced. From 2000 the PRT has run an article competition on the subject of prison life, resettlement or criminal justice. Both competitions are open to prisoners from any country, as long as the work is in English. The themes entrants choose to write about are mostly predictable. Diana Ruthven, editor of the PRT's magazine *Prison Report* has been responsible for short-listing:

> *Many of the short stories must be autobiographical – about using smack or robbing cars, the whole experience of being sent down, graphic violence. You can't help thinking they're writing from personal experience. I know everyone writes from their own experience to a certain extent... Then there's the dream... 'When I woke up it was just a dream . . .' The most common one is the judge sending someone down, thinking he was going to get off and being sent to prison. The horror of it, looking out of the cell window and realising about the isolation – that's a most common one. And violence from other prisoners. We get a lot of suicide stories, people questioning the worth of their lives. I'm sure those are autobiographical. And a hell of a lot of looking back at childhood - abuse, care and alcoholism and all sorts of horrendous things... Heroin - I think I now know all the different ways of taking that. Dealing – the whole scene. There are a lot of prison themes - about friendship between prisoners - that comes out quite strongly. The whole culture and ethos, about you're mixing with people who are all bad in a way so it's a totally different set of morals from outside. The scam is a common one, too, and science fiction - even though the stories are supposed to be on the theme of crime and punishment.*[50]

In 2004 the PRT competition, sponsored by Barclays Bank, gave out six prizes. The winning article entries are published in *Prison Report*, but the short stories are rarely seen, beyond the PRT website. For most authors, getting their work into print is the real dream, but as the experience of *Prison Writing* shows so clearly, no matter how high the quality, there is a lot of interest in reading collections of prisoners' writing, but less inclination to purchase them in book or journal form.

One prison writer's view

Paul Lumsden's short stories have been published in *Prison Writing* and other literary magazines outside prison and he has won Koestler Awards. Much of his writing has been done in the Scottish system, notably Peterhead. Asked what he had found to be enabling or encouraging factors for a writer in prison, he replied:

> *There are no external ones in this prison, no writer in residence, zilch. Merely self-belief and motivation. There is a total lack of critical and knowledgeable feedback, so even rejection slips with helpful comments become a godsend. In a milieu of angst and despair, a pen can be a shrink without a couch, though pertinent questions can be missed.*[51]

To expand briefly on Lumsden's point, for writers in prison, whatever the facilities in any particular establishment, and assuming basic ability already exists, what is crucial is a high level of motivation and focus. Without a strong personal drive, facilities are of little consequence.

Time and Opportunity

6] Inhibitions

Space

In his book *Writers in Prison*, a study that concentrates mostly on political prisoners, Ioan Davies states, "To understand prison writing it is important to understand space and the reading of that space."[1] This may be so, although not all prison writing is about prison. What is more important is that, rather than a reader or academic being able to understand space, the prisoner who has produced the writing while incarcerated has come to terms with the limitations of space. If time is a facilitator to prison writing, space can be an inhibiting factor.

Prison is a microcosm of the criminal world. As such, the culture within is not generally conducive to conventional study, artistic appreciation or self-expression through literature. An inmate's living area stretches no further than cell, landing and exercise yard. The inescapable proximity of fellow prisoners is often oppressive, while the atmosphere can be depressing, volatile and violent, especially to a prisoner who wishes only to be able to sit down and write. Cells were not built to be used as workplaces and volumetric control, introduced in 1994,[2] requires that all the property in an inmate's possession, excluding a sound system and legal papers, must fit into two boxes. Any other property is sent out of the prison to a central storage location and is thus inaccessible.

Physically, prison space is no great distance from the outside world. But from the perspective of long-term inmates, that they could be a distant land. Unable to move around with free will, subject to stringent rules and regulations, they are required to be aware that the purpose and effect of imprisonment is to confine and constrain. This might inspire the imagination and motivation of some prisoners, but others find it overbearing and oppressive.

Matthew Williams is well qualified to comment on the effects of limited space on creativity. In 1989 he went from being a university student to a life-sentenced prisoner and, after escaping from Parkhurst in 1995, he was held for many years in Special Secure Units within the dispersal system. Despite the close confines of his surroundings, he has spent much of his time writing and painting:

> *Your average person has an invisible metal 'envelope' around them, which is their normal sphere of movement. It's a sort of psychological boundary they are used to - going to work, living in town, occasional holiday abroad etc. There are, however, natural 'ceilings' which are unreachable which set this boundary.*
>
> *For a prisoner, the 'ceilings' are much lower – in reality, for most of the time the 'envelope' is cell-shaped. When someone is first imprisoned, the 'ceiling' is bigger than your cell or prison and so it takes time to adapt your 'envelope' of movement to be the same size as your real environment. Until that happens, there will be a lot of tensions and pressure and extreme feelings of claustrophobia.*
>
> *Does this 'space' feeling inhibit creativity? I'm not sure. I think that feelings of tension and stress probably do inhibit creativity, and naturally 'flavour' any writing that does happen – hence reams of lonesome poetry by remand prisoners.*
>
> *One thing I have found is that prisoners, including myself, absorb themselves in fantasy worlds of the imagination. This can be passive, e.g. reading, or active – writing or painting. I think the purpose of it is to make some space in your own mind, or build things, even if only on a page. Perhaps prison writing is like a sort of mental hernia, where normal outlets for 'creating' which would otherwise go into family or work become squashed out into imaginary stories instead.*
>
> *At the extreme end, however, I think that people often get lost in their own mental wanderings, hence the number of lunatics produced by solitary confinement. Obviously, these views are generalisations, because some people will never be creative, whatever the circumstances, and some will always be mad.*
>
> *One of the main things prison gives, perhaps as a substitute for space, is time. Einstein would no doubt love the irony!* [3]

Time, too, reduces the tensions, stresses and feelings of claustrophobia, as the prisoner becomes more acclimatised to the environment. This could account for the great majority of dedicated prison writers, like Matthew Williams, being those serving long sentences; not until the claustrophobia begins to recede is a prisoner able to free his or her imagination. As a writer whose work is derived largely from imagination, Williams' motivation to write is to be creative in the strictest sense of the word.

His comment that prison writing is "a sort of mental hernia", squeezing out stories, expresses the ambivalence between limited space and ample time for writers like himself.

Suspicious words – censorship

It has often seemed that the authorities are fearful of prisoners publishing books or articles about imprisonment. The rule of silence for inmates and the days of staff being bound by the Official Secrets Act are long gone. The reporting of prison conditions has become a regular feature in the media. The Home Office has allowed prisoners and their surroundings to be filmed for television documentaries.

But prison rules, in the form of Standing Order 5B, 34 (9), remain a major obstacle to inmates who wish to write and send out their work for publication.

> Standing Order 5b,34(9) states:
> General correspondence may not contain material which is intended for publication or for use by radio or television (or which, if sent, would be likely to be published or broadcast) if it
>
> (a) is for publication in return for payment (unless the prisoner is unconvicted);
> (b) is likely to appear in a publication associated with a person or organisation to whom the prisoner may not write as a result of restriction in correspondence in paragraph 26;
> (c) is about the prisoner's own crime or past offences or those of others, except where it consists of serious representations about conviction or sentence or forms part of serious comment about crime, the process of justice or the penal system;
> (d) refers to individual prisoners or members of staff in such a way that they might be identified;
> (e) contravenes any of the other restrictions on content applying to letters

The announcement of the imminent publication of a book by the Moors Murderer, Ian Brady, met a hostile response in the British media, when it was reported in September 2001. Some years earlier, the story had emerged that he was writing his autobiography and there was an uneasy expectation that this would be it. Brady, a life sentenced prisoner on a whole-life tariff, who had been sectioned under the Mental Health Act, was a patient in Ashworth Special Hospital, Merseyside, where he had written *The Gates of Janus*. When the hospital authorities obtained an interim injunction, preventing the book's publication and distribution in the United Kingdom, Brady's solicitor commented that if it were not lifted his client could bring a complaint under the Human Rights Act for denial of free expression.

The hospital authority stated that they had sought the injunction to establish whether Brady had breached patients' confidentiality and whether publication of the book could affect the hospital's ability to carry out its statutory duties to maintain security, order and a therapeutic environment.[4] A fortnight later, having seen the book and found no breach of patient confidentiality, nor any reference to Brady's own crimes, the hospital authority asked the High Court to lift the injunction. Whether his solicitor's comment regarding a possible action under the Human Rights Act had influenced the hospital authority's decision is not possible to say.

As a lifer who had transferred from the custody of prison to that of the mental health system, Ian Brady was not of direct concern to the Home Office and was not subject to Standing Order 5b. Had he been, one can only speculate how far the prison authorities would have gone to try to prevent publication and distribution of his book.

Of the serial killers Brady wrote about, only two were British, Peter Sutcliffe and Graham Young, both of whom he had met in Broadmoor. He offered no insight into the crimes of another such murderer, Denis Nilsen, serving six whole-life tariffs. Nilsen, however, was quite able to state his own case and in late 2003 he brought an action in the high court against the governor of HMP Full Sutton, who had confiscated the manuscript of a prison memoir he had written in prison. The Home Secretary supported the decision and Nilsen, who sought the return of the manuscript in order to revise it, claimed that his right to freedom of expression had been breached under Article 10 of the European Convention on Human Rights.

The judgement in *Regina (Nilsen) v Governor of Full Sutton Prison and another*[5] struck a potentially serious blow against the publication of prisoners' writing, in that it affirmed the Secretary of State's right to ban any work that in his opinion might have a negative effect on any member of the public, including survivors and victims. In practice, the onus for action fell upon individual governors, with the likely result being widespread inconsistency.

The judgement ignored the recent 'ghosted' autobiographies published from prison by notorious criminals such as Reginald Kray, Charles Bronson and Archibald Hall, as well as the book that Valerio Viccei had been permitted to write and publish from the Special Secure Unit at Parkhurst. An ironic aspect to the judgement was that some years earlier in his sentence the prison authorities had allowed Nilsen to co-operate with a journalist, Brian Masters, who published a best-selling book on his life and crimes.

The Nilsen case highlighted some pertinent issues regarding prisoners publishing their written works. While the autobiography of a serial killer might not be to everyone's taste, should individuals not have the right to decide whether or not to buy or read such a book, assuming a publisher is willing to take it on? What criteria would be used for a governor or the Home Secretary to gauge the degree of public sensitivity?

For the judgement in the Nilsen case to cite the likely effect on the killer's victims – or their families - the question must be asked, why did the prison authorities allow the publications of other prisoners who had victims? Reginald Kray, via a ghost-writer, wrote in graphic detail of how he had murdered Jack 'The Hat' McVitie and did not accept that he should be expected to show remorse.[6] Such precedents suggest that, while prison rules should apply equally to all inmates, the judgement in the Nilsen case was influenced by the nature of his crimes.

In the aftermath of the case, there was no sign of any clamp-down by the prison authorities. Erwin James' columns continued in *The Guardian* and Razor Smith's autobiography was published by Penguin. Even though the prison service and Home Secretary had successfully defended the case brought by Denis Nilsen, it seemed that his controversial prison memoirs could still be published, for a number of copies of an unrevised version of the manuscript were reported to be in circulation, including one in the possession of a national newspaper.

Only one copy of a prison diary written by Ian Huntley is believed to be in existence. This document came to public notice in November 2005 when it was reported that the Prison Service were refusing to return the thirty pages of A4 on which Huntley, convicted in 2002 of the murder of two ten year old girls, had described his experiences in Woodhill Prison, including his feelings about the case against him and steps taken by him to commit suicide.[7] Soon after the last diary entry, Huntley took a large dose of anti-depressant tablets he had accumulated while held supposedly in conditions of close surveillance and his diary was confiscated by the prison authorities.

The news story broke when solicitors acting for Huntley demanded that the diary, said to be held in a safe at Prison Service Headquarters in London, be handed to his father. In what was described as "a secret" memorandum, an official claimed that if the diary was returned "the risk of publication in total or by extract is substantial. For this reason I recommend that we decline to allow the diary to be passed to the father or for the father to read the content." The official went on to say that the diary would have considerable monetary value should the content be disclosed, adding that the decision to refuse to give Huntley's father the diary could be challenged under human rights laws.

While legal battles relating to prisoners' writing are uncommon, many published prisoners have experienced over-zealous attitudes towards them by prison staff. In the 1960s, when Tony Hoare was doing the groundwork for what would be an illustrious career writing for television, even getting paper to write on could be an obstacle:

> *I knew a guy, he spent three years writing a novel – on toilet paper. You couldn't get paper to write on. One day a screw found it, says you're not allowed this and he threw it in the incinerator and the guy's charged with unauthorised possession. What's he gonna be like when he comes out? He's gonna say "Fuck you!" It might be different now, I don't know.*[8]

It is different in that paper to write on is not so hard to obtain, and censorship is, in the main, less arbitrary and immediate, but many prisoners have felt the wrath of staff who disagree with the notion of inmates writing. Razor Smith's autobiography, written in maximum security at Whitemoor, was a triumph after years of enterprising effort to get articles published. In his book he states that Belmarsh, where he spent months on remand, was the only prison that ever tried to seriously censor his writing, in particular the articles he wrote for Punch about fellow prisoner Jonathan Aitken.

Smith describes being threatened with solitary if he persisted in writing about prison. With his outgoing mail under scrutiny by the Belmarsh security department, he began dictating his copy over the telephone during association periods – only for his calls to be cut off. He states he was subject to more strip and cell searches than other Category A prisoners and after one search "I returned to my cell to find not only the standard wreckage but that one of the spiteful bastards had bent my radio aerial into a U-shape."[9]

Not only writing that is critical of the prison system has attracted such treatment. Tim Wickham, whose play script 'A Day in the Wrong Life' was published in *Prison Writing 16*:

> *After I sent the play out I was subjected to two weeks of endless strip searches, cell spins, withheld mail which they emphatically denied right up until the day thirteen letters arrived, dated over a two week period, and general other harassment based on suspicion of medication dealing. Most officers are sensible and not the twisted weirdoes the public often think but there are some utter bastards around and my play was an excellent basis for those who enjoy a good witch-hunt.*[10]

If prisoners' suspicions can appear to verge on the paranoid, they are no different to those of their keepers. In his autobiography, written in Scottish prisons, John Steele writes:

> *I've been told by those in authority that I shall be punished if I seek to have this book published; punished because I refused to let the Prison Department read it beforehand: it may set the prison system back many years, it wouldn't be fair to any governors wishing to write a book or thesis on the prison system …and I'll be punished should I cause the Secretary of State any further embarrassment.*[11]

Ruth Wyner, jailed in the Wintercomfort case that became a *cause celebré* for drug workers and the hostel sector, was encouraged by a publisher to write a book about homelessness. Called up by a governor, she was told there had been nine complaints about her writing and prisoners were afraid she was writing about them. He said the prison was concerned for her safety. When Wyner explained that she was writing about homelessness, the governor asked to see the work; when she handed it over he refused to return it.

To make the situation worse, Wyner admitted keeping a personal journal, which was also taken from her. When she complained she was told the prison was seeking advice as to whether any of the writing contravened Prison Service Standing Orders.[12] In her memoir, published after she was released, Wyner recalled the impact she had felt at the confiscation of her journal:

> *Without the writing I felt utterly bereft. My anger turned inwards, creating an empty depression. It was torment to think of prison officers going over the pages that contained my innermost thoughts.*[13]

During the time Clare Barstow has been serving her life sentence, she has met with most aspects of censorship, as well as the many other obstacles that inhibit writing in prison:

> *It's hard writing when you know that your work gets censored before it goes out. It's also hard when working on prison magazines, as often they don't get published because of censorship.*
>
> *Friends can be encouraging but they can also be jealous of success so you sometimes have to play down your achievements. And the limitations of space caused by volumetric control means much gets lost, thrown away or sent out. Cost can also be a problem in sending work out to publishers.*[14]

Clare Barstow's experience suggests that female prisoners who write face more obstacles than do most of their male counterparts. In one establishment she was removed to the punishment block when an article she had written about the way women are treated in prison was published in the left-wing newspaper *Fight Racism Fight Imperialism*. There were further problems when she wrote a letter to *The Guardian* about the treatment of women and the lack of support. She says: "I've had stuff refused – not sent out - room spins and security checks because of my writing." She finds the attitude of prison management and staff frustrating, "They're pleased when I win the Koestlers or get something performed outside because that's seen as glory for the prison, but they don't encourage it. Education are supportive but not governors or staff." Such is officialdom's ambivalence to prisoners' writing.

Wariness of people outside prison being able to read inmates' work has extended to prison magazines. The therapeutic community within the Barlinnie Special Unit began to produce a magazine, *The Key* in 1973-4, but despite the magazine enhancing the relationship between staff and inmates it ended after only three issues through censorship by the Prisons Department at the Scottish Office.[15]

Later, a survey published by the Prison Reform Trust highlighted the important part that magazines play in breaking down barriers between staff and inmates as well as helping prisoners to use their time constructively. It was suggested that there could also be a useful public relations role in informing the outside world that prisoners have interests and skills and are human. However, the returns to the survey found that "some prisons have actively discouraged the distribution of a prison magazine to the outside world, saying that people will 'get the wrong impression' and that it may have the perverse effect of exacerbating stigma."[16]

The sensitivities of prison staff

Inside Time, the monthly newspaper published by the charity New Bridge, serves a valuable function in providing a forum for prisoners to obtain and exchange information. Today, in the main, the paper is accepted throughout the UK system, but when it was founded in 1991, many prisoners who wanted to read *Inside Time* could not obtain a copy. Twenty thousand copies of each of the first two issues were printed and sent out, but many did not reach their destination.

According to editor Anna Reynolds, bundles were found in bins and others were sent back marked 'Not known at this address." By the time the third issue was ready to be distributed, the matter had come to the attention of *The Guardian* who reported that the co-operation of prison staff in making *Inside Time* available to inmates had been withdrawn because previous issues contained articles that criticised prison staff.

A spokesman for the Prison Officers Association told crime correspondent Duncan Campbell that although the paper was not officially banned, a decision had been taken at the P.O.A annual conference in May not to distribute it, as it "contained hostile and inaccurate material" that had caused some officers to be baited and taunted by prisoners.[17]

Distribution problems continued for some years. In 2002, Rachel Billington, a member of the editorial team said, "We've had and continue to have some governors who ban it. In a way it's a good sign if you're ruffling a few feathers. A lot of them wouldn't take it at first – they thought it was shocking to give a voice to prisoners."[18] A governor at Lincoln Prison was said to have banned *Inside Time*, while in Lindholme, according to Peter Wayne, a large pile of undelivered copies was found hidden away in the chaplain's office and another whole edition was left in the rain, stacked by the pig pens. He wrote in *The Observer*: "Try getting a copy to read yourself at night. *Playboy* had a better chance of getting through to the old Soviet Union."[19]

It was inevitable that Jeffrey Archer's *A Prison Diary*, written and published while the peer was still serving his four year sentence, would offend staff in Belmarsh, where the diary was set. His disparaging tone and comments caused prison officer David Hillier to condemn the peer's "breathtaking arrogance", saying: "For Archer to be so openly contemptuous of prison staff and their authority is a shameful disgrace."[20]

No earners

The last resort of the censor – or governor – who seeks to prevent a prisoner's work being sent out is sub-section (a) of Standing Order 5b 34 (9) - relating to correspondence "which, if sent, would be likely to be published or broadcast" in return for payment.

In 2002, while in Full Sutton, Matthew Williams attempted to post the script of a radio play to RTE, the Irish national broadcasting organisation. The same script had been entered in the Koestler Awards, where it won a £30 prize. The prison censor refused to let the script go out and the governor cited Standing Order 5b. Williams pointed out that the Koestler Awards, Prison Reform Trust and *Prison Writing*, among other organisations, paid prisoners for their work, but the governor stood firm.[21]

Williams was puzzled as to how he could enter a radio play in the Koestler Awards, with the approval of the governor, yet he was being denied the opportunity to have the play performed on the radio:

> *I delved further. It transpired that making money at all, outside of prison labour, was forbidden, for I would then be classed as 'running a business' and could face disciplinary charges. I fumed!*
>
> *Clearly, being part of the prison 'business enterprise' as party hat assembler didn't count – as a forced labourer on 45 pence an hour my 'business activity' was just peachy. Yet develop any notion of cash and a career through independent means and look out – lawbreaker!* [22]

He complained to the Directorate of High Security Prisons, who upheld the governor's decision. He then complained to the Prisons Ombudsman, making two main points:

1] that prisoners should be encouraged to earn a legitimate income from their skills, as a genuine, legal career would clearly aid rehabilitation.
2] as a tariff-expired discretionary lifer, the rule against "business activity" – enforced as part of prison punishment – should in his case be void, as in his case post-tariff imprisonment was due to the consideration of risk, not rehabilitation.[23]

The Ombudsman sent an investigator to Full Sutton. Williams told the investigator of the radio play he had submitted to the Irish radio station RTE and expressed his concern that if RTE were to pay him money for the play he would not receive it. He said that if he chose to sell his house while in prison, he would be allowed to keep the money from the sale, including any profit, and argued that there should be no difference between the sale of his physical and his intellectual property.[24] The investigator contacted Prison Service Headquarters about the rationale for the prohibition in Standing Order 5b on receiving payment. They advised that the rule on not conducting a business – quoted by Full Sutton in response to Matthew Williams' initial complaint that he could not post out his play – was not relevant. To make the situation more absurd, as the Ombudsman reports, " they were unable to say what the objection was to prisoners being paid for published writings."

Stephen Shaw, the Prisons Ombudsman, commented that Standing Order 5 was in urgent need of revision, that to prohibit fiction that did not draw on its author's criminal activity – such as Williams' play – was unreasonable. He wrote: "If prisoners can make a living from their artistic talents, this must be in the interests of their resettlement and rehabilitation, and hence of public safety. Access to these earnings while they are in prison could be properly restricted – like all private cash – under the incentives and earned privileges scheme."

He upheld Matthew Williams' complaint about not being able to receive payment and recommended that the prison service should urgently review and reconcile the contents of Standing Order 5b(34)9a and those of SO4 para51, "with a view to enabling prisoners to receive payment from whatever source for their works of art."

Some months after receiving this favourable response from the Prisons Ombudsman, Williams received a letter from the Director-General of the Prison Service, who, to his amazement, accepted the Ombudsman's recommendations in full. As Williams understood it, SO 5 was to be amended, at last allowing prisoners to write for publication. But when he tried to send out a copy of a fictional diary to *Prison Writing*, he found that the censor was not interested in promises made by the Director- General, or the findings of the Prisons Ombudsman. Once again he was told he could not send work out – as he might publish it for money. When he protested, he was told "Complain to the Ombudsman if you're not happy."

Williams wrote once again to the Ombudsman and to the Home Office for clarification, with no success. Worse was to come. In November 2003, he managed to send a short article to the Radio 3 programme *The Verb*, winning a book token. He was then told that when the token arrived it would be confiscated. Once again, he was confused by the Prison Service's double standard that had only a short while earlier allowed another inmate, Jeffrey Archer, to be paid a huge sum of money by a tabloid newspaper for extracts from his book, written in prison.

Once again, Williams wrote to those who held the power, but received no response. Then, his mother, to whom he had assigned copyright of his play script, entered it on his behalf in the P J. O'Connor Writing Competition at RTE in Ireland. The script, *Seascape*, was short-listed, to be produced in September 2004. Around the same time he heard that a painting he had entered in the Koestler Awards, via the Full Sutton education department, had been sold for £375. Who bought it? The Home Office, to decorate their work area.

On 27 September 2004, the day before his play was broadcast on Irish radio, Matthew Williams' attention was taken by a photograph of his painting in *The Sun* newspaper, illustrating an article that attacked the Home Office for wasting taxpayers' money and putting it in the pockets of convicted criminals by buying art works from the recent Koestler exhibition. The irony amused him, but still there was no sign of Standing Order 5b being amended, as the Director General appeared to have promised two years earlier. [25]

But had he promised? In the December 2005 issue of *Inside Time*, the Williams case was revisited. Rhian Evans, the deputy Ombudsman said, "We issued a report in August 2002 in which we recommended that the instruction be amended to allow payment. The Prison Service accepted the recommendation but, notwithstanding our requests for progress reports, the recommendation has not yet been implemented."

Nor does it seem as if it ever will be implemented, according to a Prison Service spokesman, who was quoted as saying: "The Prison Service has never agreed to amend Standing Order 5 to allow prisoners to receive payment for articles. We are currently looking at the rules around prisoners writing features and articles for publication." But what of novels, autobiographies and plays – such as the one written by Matthew Williams?[26]

Inconsistency

The threat of the censor's pen, a lethal instrument that at a stroke can kill an article, a play or a book that has taken years to write, has not always receded on a prison writer's release. Ten years before he made his mark in television, Jimmy O'Connor, at the time on life licence, submitted a playscript to the BBC. The play, *Beyond The Gate*, was accepted and broadcast – but with O'Connor's name removed from the credits. The explanation was that it was essential to the story for the BBC to film inside a prison and the Prison Service would not give permission if an ex-convict was seen to be involved.

The fact that so many prisoners have managed to publish their work while serving a sentence shows that there are people inside who are keen to encourage and assist literary expression, and that not all governors feel rigidly bound by Standing Order 5. What is critical to prison writing is how SO 5 is applied. Prison regimes are largely based on whatever management attitude prevails at a given time. As Jonathan Aitken says, "A lot of things are as long as the governor's foot." Even then, the different experiences at Whitemoor, where Denis Nilsen's manuscript was confiscated while Razor Smith's was allowed out to be published, show that the rules are not always applied consistently even within the same establishment.

Arbitrary – even erratic - use of the rules is, of course, not a new development. Back in the late 1960s, John McVicar was allowed to write up his escape from Durham and publish it first in a Sunday newspaper and afterwards as a book. He later wrote: "I threw up the smokescreen that I was preparing my own defence but I can't believe this washed with even prison warders."[27]

Writing this, McVicar believed that he was breaking prison rules, but when he wrote his escape account for the press he was not – Standing Order 5b applies only to convicted prisoners. The publication of *McVicar by Himself* in 1974 was an infringement, although nothing was done about it. He recalls, "No one said a word. It was never mentioned by any prison official or even warder. This was despite it being serialised in *The Sunday Times*. In fact, few of my fellow cons mentioned it either. I didn't shove it under anyone's nose."[28]

Jeffrey Archer had the highest profile of anyone who has ever published a book while an inmate of a British prison. The first volume of his prison diaries was published in 2002 on a wave of publicity and with many harsh words from the highest echelons of the Prison Service – even though his intentions had been no secret from the beginning of his sentence.

There were threats of injunctions and of Archer being punished – at one point it was even suggested, ludicrously, that he had prejudiced his parole - but no action. But when another Belmarsh inmate told the *Mail on Sunday* of his experiences sharing a cell with Archer, he was punished by four months in solitary confinement and left protesting that the incarcerated peer had received preferential treatment.[29]

Approval to write a column for *The Guardian* was given to Erwin James, once the authorities were satisfied that there would be no identification of other prisoners or reference to his crime. Such consideration is not available to all.

In 2002, Rosie Woodward, a journalist on the *Clerkenwell & Islington News*, had the idea that an inmate of one of the north London prisons could write a regular column for the paper. She saw prisoners as "a significant but silent part of the local community" and put some effort into trying to put the idea into practice: "Having spoken with a governor at Pentonville who was enthusiastic about the idea, I got a call from a very stern Prison Service press officer who emphatically refused any further discussion on the subject. She also mentioned that I was the twenty-eighth person to make such a request."[30]

Not all barriers to prison writing can be blamed on the prison authorities. When Razor Smith sent in his first contribution, the poem 'Old Lags', to *Prison Writing*, he said in an accompanying letter that he had been writing for some time but had not shown anything to his fellow prisoners. In his line of business as an armed robber, he said, writing was considered "rather effeminate."[31]

Ken Smith, who worked as a writer-in-residence in Wormwood Scrubs, said many inmates with whom he worked were inhibited on two levels about publishing their writing: "Some reflected that anything they wrote would be subject to the scrutiny and notice of the prison and the Home Office, and others declined the opportunity, for fear of being known as 'prison poets'."[32]

Limitations of space; difficulties in contacting publishers, producers or editors; censorship in its various guises, and peer group pressure - all inhibit prisoners who seek to write for publication or professional performance. There are other factors: prison education's focus on basic literacy has resulted in many creative writing classes being cut, while access to word processors is restricted to educational work.

But anyone who is inspired and motivated to write, wherever they are and whatever their situation, faces hurdles of some sort. Those who have sufficient commitment and talent succeed - and their work is often enhanced by the experience. Prison writers are no different.

Inhibitions

7] Effects

How much is credible?

When convicted criminals write about their experiences, in or out of prison, should we believe them? How credible is the word of someone who has committed an offence so serious as to warrant imprisonment? Is the word of a murderer less or more reliable than that of someone convicted of robbery, burglary, theft or other dishonesty?

Surely, the argument goes, prisoners are resentful towards the society that incarcerated them and thus their accounts of crime and punishment cannot be objective? Such considerations might rarely be asked of non-criminal autobiography or memoir, but in some quarters prisoners' writing has suffered from doubts about veracity, especially when the work criticised the prison system.

On occasion the doubters have been penal reformers. It was predictable that the Prison Officers' Association would denounce Joan Henry's *Who Lie In Gaol* when it was published in 1952; what was more surprising was the Howard League distancing itself from the controversy – and the book.[1] Both the Howard League and the Institute for the Study and Treatment of Delinquency supported the publication in 1961 of *The Struggle for Penal Reform* by Gordon Rose, an academic, who wrote that while "books written by ex-prisoners cannot be disregarded as possible sources of information, unfortunately, most of these are so obviously exaggerated that they are worthless."

Rose gave no examples of this alleged exaggeration, but went on to say that while such books were "occasionally" impressive in their attempts to be fair, or to give what seemed to be a rational account, by the time they were published they were usually out of date as changes were constantly taking place in the system. His argument was not enhanced by reference to certain books by ex-prisoners which he felt had "much that is useful" – including one from the previous century and three from the 1930s.[2] Rose did not explain how these testaments qualified on grounds of accuracy or contemporary relevance, where Jim Phelan, Walter Macartney and others had failed. Rod Caird considered Rose's disparagement of ex-prisoners' books in his own *A Good and Useful Life*, the result of twelve months spent in Wormwood Scrubs and Coldingley:

> *Comments like Rose's – and for parallels one need only look in the bibliographies of a few criminological works – presumably arise from the fear that the ex-prisoner's perception is so distorted by bitterness and antipathy that he is quite unable to give an 'objective' description of his own experiences.*[3]

A Home Office document of this period cautioned potential readers of books by ex-prisoners:

> *The testimony of those offenders who write books and articles about prisons is not necessarily representative, or even accurate, although it cannot be ignored merely because it is not in general flattering to authority.*[4]

Caird summarised the issues as they stood at the time:

> *These warnings are probably believed. After all, everyone knows that criminals (and ex-criminals) are a deceitful and unreliable lot, and ill-educated to boot – certainly not trained in the best standards of fair play. It is very easy to devalue the opinions of ex-prisoners, who appear to have a vested interest in attacking the institutions which have incarcerated them. Ex-prisoners must be among the least credible groups in society.*
>
> *However, leaving aside the implications of some authors' evident beliefs that the experience of imprisonment somehow disqualifies one from writing about it, it is true that the ex-prisoner who sits down to describe his time locked away has to be very careful.*
>
> *The greatest danger arises from the temptation to generalise about prison without sufficient grounds for doing so....*[5]

Sociologist, Stan Cohen, was aware that convicted criminals have little credibility. He pre-empted criticism of his protegé Walter Probyn in his introduction to the latter's autobiography, *Angel Face – the Making of a Criminal*. Cohen was aware of the difficulty of getting the convicted prisoner's account across to readers. He says the prisoner's world is one where there exists:

> *...what the sociologist Howard Becker nicely called a 'hierarchy of credibility'. There is a different distribution not just of property but also of the right to be*

> *heard and believed. Deviants have violated moral rules and are thus thought to have forfeited their right to be believed. They are at the bottom of a moral pyramid. The definitions of judges and police chiefs need not be checked out; those at the bottom have to be carefully scrutinised for 'bias'.*[6]

Cohen, writing in the 1970s when the public was perhaps less cynical about law enforcement than it is today, suggested the credibility of those at the top of the criminal justice system was beyond probity. But was - is - the word of those employed in the lower echelons? Not according to Joy Cameron, in her study of Scottish prisons from the Middle Ages to the early 1980s:

> *For further explanation of the failure of the system we have to look to the opinions expressed by two main groups, those who have studied or experienced prison and its consequences from 'the right side' of the bars (prison officers, probation officers, social workers, sociologists, etc) and those who have themselves been convicts. Neither group gives an entirely reliable account, the former because of prejudice, incomplete information, an over-developed taste for polemics and so on, the latter because of bitterness and resentment at real or imagined injustices and a desire to get their own back on the system...*[7]

She cites Alan Taylor, Peter Wildeblood, Zeno, John McVicar and Jimmy Boyle as worthy commentators, while cautioning against anyone who has gained first-hand experience of prison, as "their integrity is *ipso facto* suspect".[8]

It is questionable why, if Cameron believed everyone else, from prison officers to sociologists to be unreliable too, she thought a valid explanation of "the failure of the system" could be gained from either side.

To criminologist Shadd Maruna of the University of Belfast, the subjectivity of a prisoner's account is more important than the fact that he or she has a criminal record:

> *I'm not worried that they are written by 'convicted criminals'. I'd be more worried about written autobiography written by professional fictionalists. It turns out that fiction writers often can't break out of the fiction mode when writing autobiography. I remember being fascinated by Anthony Burgess's life story – much of which, I've since read, was pure fantasy.*
>
> *That said, it was great autobiography, nonetheless, and it conveyed subjective*

> *truths - it meant something to Burgess - even if not objective truths. I think offender autobiographies are similar. I don't expect them - or want them - to be perfect factual representations of history, I think they are interesting precisely because they are subjective accounts.*[9]

This view is shared by Carlo Gébler, who suggests that in lieu of a hierarchy of objectivity, where criminals would be placed at the bottom and politicians slightly above them, the debate has little merit:

> *No memoir is objective, that's why it's called a memoir: a memoir is an account of events as the writer recalls them and not as they necessarily were. Memoirs are partial, personal, which is why they're so attractive in the first place. Those who heap abuse on memoirs by ex-criminals should remember this. They should also remember that we, those who read, are not stupid. We can judge for ourselves and everyone – or almost everyone – has an in-built bullshit detection mechanism.*[10]

Judge Michael Murphy QC, one of several members of the judiciary to take an interest in *Prison Writing* during its ten years of publication, adds:

> *I suppose it goes through a filter process and you say to yourself, now is this far-fetched or not? I accept it and even the so-called far-fetched things troubled me. You'd look around maybe for corroboration at some of the things that are said, but I'm prepared to believe an awful lot about what happens in prisons.*[11]

Much depends on what and how the prisoner presents his or her story. Jonathan Aitken believes that on the whole, authenticity will in the end win out:

> *There's bound to be a certain amount of mistrust towards anyone in prison doing anything. That said, I think any account of what's going on in prison will come across on its own merits as either genuine or false and exaggerated. I'd be reasonably optimistic, even though a little mistrust may be around - but there's often a little mistrust about what journalists write when they've been inside a prison.*[12]

Professor Brian Williams of De Montfort University, Leicester, sees no reason to make credibility an issue:

> *In my view, the credibility of prison writing is not likely to be challenged merely on the grounds that it is written by offenders. To do so would involve rejecting the work of Victor Serge, Dostoevsky and Solzhenitsyn on specious grounds. Also, the range of material on prison life would be completely impoverished if one discounted autobiographical and fictional writing by prisoners themselves: we would be left with sociological and psychological studies, valuable in themselves but limited in their intentions, with autobiographical work by prison staff and with official accounts. Prisoners' writing immeasurably enriches these understandings of prison life.*[13]

The fulsome reviews and plaudits that Mark Leech received for his autobiography, *A Product of the System*, support Jonathan Aitken's assertion that in the end authenticity wins out. Judge James Pickles, who wrote the introduction to the book, described Leech as "a remarkable man" who had produced "a remarkable book". John Mortimer praised Leech's "vivid and excellently-written account of crime and punishment". Helena Kennedy QC admired his "honesty and insight". Brian Masters, in the *Sunday Telegraph*, said that Leech "writes like an angel"[14], although Masters' opinion could be counterbalanced by his description of Denis Nilsen as a "sensual romantic" in his own book on the serial killer.

Joy Cameron believed that neither prison staff nor inmates could be relied upon to provide objectivity. Gordon Rose considered most books by prisoners to be worthless. John McVicar, never a man to duck an issue, says, "The problem with prisoners' writings is they are invariably trying to get back at the system. It warps the narrative."[15] Jonathan Aitken refers to the mistrust of journalistic accounts but believes that in the end prisoners' work is inevitably judged on its authenticity.

Judge Michael Murphy QC speaks, as does Carlo Gébler, of a filter process in which the reader asks himself, is this far fetched or not? In an article in *The Howard Journal*, sociologist Steve Morgan proposes that a criminologist is "a gate-keeper to the truth which can be extracted from multiple and conflicting accounts." He too believes that Howard Becker's 'hierarchy of credibility', affects prison writers "in a closed world where speech and action are subject to restrictive codes and rules".[16]

As the praise for Mark Leech's autobiography shows, there does appear to be less scepticism around prisoners' writing today than existed when *The Struggle for Penal Reform* appeared in 1961. Then, few books had been published by ex-prisoners and none at all by a serving prisoner. As well as many more autobiographies and memoirs, the intervening years have brought prisons and prisoners onto the political agenda and into the public consciousness, through overcrowding, riots, drug abuse, suicides and even prosecutions of prison officers for acts of violence and corruption. The tabloid press may try to portray British prisons as holiday camps, but there is ample evidence to the contrary, as reputable journalists and, more pertinently, prisoners themselves have repeatedly shown.

A place in history

Penal history would be incomplete without prisoners' published writing. In the century between Oscar Wilde's *The Ballad of Reading Gaol*, Jabez Spencer Balfour's account of life in Parkhurst and Razor Smith's descriptions of Borstal, Belmarsh and the dispersal system, many changes occurred within the English and Scottish systems.

The anonymous B.2.15, who wrote *Among the Broad-Arrow Men* about his time in Leicester Gaol, the books by Jim Phelan and Wilfred Macartney, *McVicar by Himself*, Boyle's *A Sense of Freedom* and many others provide a framework for understanding the development of prison conditions and penal policies, and their effects on inmates, in a detail that is lacking in official reports. Peter Wayne recognised this when he described his motivation for writing about imprisonment as "what I have come to see as my life's task- the faithful and (if by necessity) subjective recording of an underworld shrouded in secrecy and paranoia." [17]

The value of journalism such as Wayne's tends to be topical and short-lived, but while the major contributions to the canon of prison literature have been mostly memoirs or autobiographies, other forms have made a lasting mark. The best example is Wilde's *Ballad*, in which, according to his biographer, he was so intent making a lament for prison conditions that he compromised his own art to achieve his aim.[18]

Another is Brendan Behan's *The Quare Fellow*, a stage play that critic Kenneth Tynan forecast would become part of theatrical history. The play's revival in 2004 was a reminder of how in the 1950s it had helped fuel the campaign to abolish capital punishment in Britain.

What does prisoners' writing tell us?

The experience of imprisonment

In his Foreword to *Parkhurst Tales*, a memoir by Norman Parker who had been released from a life sentence after serving twenty years, journalist Tom Mangold criticised the prison system. As a television documentary maker, Mangold was no stranger to prisons and prisoners, but he said of Parker's book:

> *Because, sociologically, Norman is not part of the famous criminal class, he has a detachment, awareness and objectivity that allow him the vision and insight to reflect not only with passion but also with sardonic understanding on those twenty years ... Norman's contribution to the debate is important. He has the credentials, and we should listen to him, for his is the authentic voice from inside, and it has something vital to tell us.*[19]

Another journalist, Ian Katz, contributing a Foreword to *A Life Inside*, the collected columns of lifer Erwin James from *The Guardian*, recalls reading the first of James's regular pieces:

At first glance it seemed preoccupied with a fairly obscure detail of prison life. But anyone who read it quickly sensed that a window into another world was opening. In just 800 words, Erwin gave Guardian *readers a powerful sense of the fragile equilibrium, the complex relationships, the simmering tensions and the paranoia that lie behind Britain's prison walls.*[20]

Writer and broadcaster Michael Palin, a judge in the 2001 Prison Reform Trust Short Story Competition, was impressed by the stories, however fictionalised, seen from a section of society whose views are rarely heard:

> *In a sense I learned more about prison life, the predicament of the offender and the problem of drugs in our society from these short stories than from any number of worthy official reports and unworthy acres of sensational newsprint. It seems of the greatest importance that we listen to all sides of an issue and an argument.*
>
> *If we close our ears, because the true picture is too uncomfortable and depressing, then we are only half alive. The strength of these stories is that*

they come directly from human experience, they are unfiltered and often unsophisticated, but all the more powerful for that. Their value is that they address feelings of alienation which are universal but often ignored.[21]

Stephen Shaw, the Prisons and Probation Ombudsman, believes that it is better that social problems be aired rather than ignored, and thus prisoners memoirs serve a useful purpose:

The reality of prison life of course is incredible boredom and routine. I think to some extent it's very difficult for anything that's going to be published to actually capture the mundane, predictable, grey, lack of choice, lack of stimulation, which is much closer to the day-to-day reality. Most prisoners have never been in a riot, most prisoners don't get nicked or go on an adjudication, most prisoners have never been near a segregation unit. Prisoners' accounts are valuable because it's better to be revealed than not revealed. They're valuable because otherwise it becomes middle class professionals like you and me describing experiences that we've never actually endured. Something first-hand always has a separate value but I do think that they can be distorted.[22]

Criticisms and allegations about the iniquities of the system are to be expected. For some, even the traditional belief that criminals can be reformed by imprisonment is a contentious issue. The sociologist Stan Cohen, in his introduction to Walter Probyn's autobiography, wrote of his protégé's "practical expertise at exposing the prison system's pretensions to 'reform'", adding, "These pretensions cannot be exposed too often."[23]

Cohen was writing in the 1970s, many years before the system's problems with overcrowding, drug abuse and suicide rates, long before the heavy emphasis on cognitive behavioural programmes. John McVicar, the beneficiary of Probyn's escape plan from maximum security in Durham in 1968, is in agreement. For him, the reality of prison is often obscured by propaganda put forward by those with a vested interest. By telling the escape part of his story he hoped to show what prisons and "certain types of prisoners" are really like: "In so doing I hope I also put the lie to the nonsense spouted about reform and rehabilitation".[24]

How prisoners cope

The "certain types of prisoners" that McVicar describes were some of the most notorious in England in the late 1960s and early '70s, those considered by the authorities to be so dangerous that they had to be held in maximum security. McVicar pens sharp portraits of ruthless gangsters, murderers and others who were too difficult for mainstream prisons to handle. His book was the first to tell how it felt for relatively young men with many years of imprisonment ahead of them.

While McVicar tells, in the second part of his book, how he decided to write and then study, Jimmy Boyle and Hugh Collins each fought the system and each of their books serves as a travelogue of the journey of redemption that led them from violence to art. Both credit the staff at the Barlinnie Special Unit and, like McVicar's, both men's stories provide a paradigm that could and should have been used by the prison authorities to inspire and divert young prisoners from crime. That, after all, was Boyle's stated objective in writing *A Sense of Freedom*.

Men and women from non-criminal backgrounds, those who go to prison for the first time, often find coping with the experience much harder than repeat offenders. First-timers' stories invariably tell of the shock of finding themselves behind bars and the struggle to come to terms with the actions that put them there, of difficulties in trying to find logic in the petty rules and regulations, of their fears and concerns and of meeting people whose behaviour and attitudes contrast with their own.

The novelist and former politician Jeffrey Archer appears to have coped well with the two years he spent inside. It might be said that the prison authorities had more problems dealing with him than he did with them. Reviewers, academics and even other inmates were divided on the merits of what he wrote about prison, but his three volumes of diaries sold well and must have enlightened readers who would have otherwise been unaware and uninterested in the reality of prison conditions.

When Zeno wrote about the life sentence from which he had been released, capital punishment had been abolished for only three years. The regime he described in Wormwood Scrubs was far more relaxed than it is in twenty-first century prisons holding lifers, giving the lie to those who believe that prison life has become softer. Had Judith Ward been convicted a decade earlier, the cries for her to be hanged would in all likelihood have been loud and long. But after more than fourteen years of despair and isolation, her conviction for killing twelve people was quashed. Her book, *Ambushed*, tells of the brutal reality of a miscarriage of justice.

Prisoners' memoirs show how humans interact in institutions. The former professional golfer John Hoskison's account of Wandsworth and Coldingley was widely reviewed in the national press and considered to have struck an accurate note about life in closed conditions in the 1990s. In the *Sunday Telegraph*, Theodore Dalrymple, opined that he knew from his own observations – as a former prison doctor - that everything in Hoskison's book was true.

He said:

> *His description of the casually inhumane nature of the prison bureaucracy – which imposes pettifogging rules while ignoring gross abuses - and of a way of life in which the most ruthless and psychopathic men rule the roost, is of far wider application: it is a precise description of how our unimprisoned underclass lives, where the Housing Department and the Department of Social Security are the prison warders. For our underclass, England is a vast HMP Coldingley.*[25]

The Guardian was no less forthcoming in assessing the lessons to be learned from Hoskison's book. The subject of the book, the author's three year sentence for killing a cyclist, is described as "more frightening than any thriller", the English prison "little better than a grim assembly line to manufacture criminals". Hoskison has learned how to break into cars, smuggle crack cocaine and 'chase the dragon' but when he is released he is unable to smile in public. The reviewer reiterates what has been learned from so many prison memoirs, that Hoskison's journal "belies the myth that English jails are 'holiday camps'."[26]

Beyond academia

Primary sources are invaluable to sociological and criminological research. For academics, extensive face-to-face interviews with prisoners and even with ex-prisoners can be logistically difficult. Many academics' experience of prison is limited to short, time-limited visits in the sanitised environment of an interview room or visits hall. Their work cannot therefore dig deep into the subject in the same way that the best memoir by a prisoner does. So, what can prisoners' writing tell us that academic research cannot? Shadd Maruna:

> *If you mean what can autobiography tell us that survey research and the study of official criminal records cannot, then the answer is: it can tell us about the person. Autobiographical research puts the human in human sciences. Consciousness, our ability to make sense of our lives, to turn our lives*

> *into stories, is central to what makes us human. It is impossible therefore, to understand humans through the study of human behaviour alone – as important as behaviour is.*[27]

Stan Cohen considered Walter Probyn's autobiography *Angel Face* to have:

> *...the dual characteristics of what for me has always constituted good sociology... The first characteristic is that demanded by the Chicago school of sociology of the nineteen twenties: that sociology should tell us what the civics textbooks leave out.. That is to say: we should be concerned with unmasking, debunking, reading between the lines...The other criterion... is the one articulated by the famous American sociologist C. Wright Mills many years ago: the ability to make the connection between private troubles and public issues.*[28]

Although Probyn's book has a greater sociological focus than most, if not all, other British prisoner autobiographies, his mentor's stance was unusual among academics. Steve Morgan, including Probyn in the sample that he wrote of in his *Howard League Journal of Criminal Justice* article, took a different view from Cohen, stating:

> *Prison autobiographies are not criminology in a formal sense as they do not adhere to any formal conventions of sociological method. They are, however, texts or documents of direct and critical understanding of the discourses and social practices of prison which can and should be analysed using formal methodology. They represent some of the most extended narratives and analyses of a particular social experience normally hidden from public view.*[29]

Professor Brian Williams, co-founder of *Prison Writing* in 1992, emphasises the uniqueness of the first-hand account:

> *Academic writing about prisons may be engaged, committed to change, and it may even take sides - but it cannot speak authoritatively about what people experience in prison. For example, lifers who serve many years protesting their innocence are difficult to understand unless you've met them or read their work.*[30]

For novelist Will Self, the real value lies in what we learn about the person:

> *I think they tell us the subjective truth of these situations: imprisonment, judgement, punishment – in a way that no other account possibly can. They make us aware of the living, breathing human who lies beneath the dead weight of society's judgement on malefactors. At their best they can even transcend the specific milieu they are concerned about to tackle larger questions about the human condition. Are we, like the prisoners in the cave in Plato's simile, all in some sense fettered?* [31]

Prisoner-turned-screenwriter Tony Hoare believes that the insights achieved by criminal and prisoner autobiographies must be conditional. Those who justify their criminal actions or rage against the system without reasoned argument often do more harm than good:

> *Jimmy Boyle and John McVicar are intelligent, observant men, articulate in their arguments who have actually spent years in prison. Like most of life's experiences only those who have direct first hand knowledge of the subject are going to get closer to the truth. There are others like them. One of the best I remember reading about the prison system, prisoners, etc, was a book called* Life, *written under the nom de plume of Zeno. He was a middle class guy doing life for murdering his wife, so not a professional villain, but that allowed him to have a balanced view. In other words he wasn't 'burdened' by the tendency of quite a few prisoners, who write, to overstate their case and lose the sympathy vote through bitterness, frustration or simple ignorance.* [32]

Benefits to teaching

There are no means of knowing whether prisoner/offender autobiographies have been widely used in the training of those professionally employed in the criminal justice system. Such anecdotal evidence as exists suggests very little use, or indeed interest.

Martin Davies, former probation officer and later Home Office researcher, was aware of the general doubts relating to credibility and bias, but he felt, "The weakness of these accounts for research purposes is not that they are necessarily untruthful or slanted, but that each represents only one person's view of a restricted range of prison establishments, and that, in sum, they represent the views of ex-prisoners who are especially literate or who have access to a ghost-writer of some kind." Nonetheless he believed that such works had much to commend them and recommended "a reading of say, twenty such books, gives a wider range of experience than might at first be anticipated."[33] Brian Williams, who has taught trainee probation officers and social workers at Sheffield, Keele and Leicester de Montfort Universities has used prisoners' writing to explain the purpose of prisons, how successfully that purpose is achieved and at what cost to prisoners and their families:

> *Trainee probation officers can certainly learn from this literature and it is regrettable, at least to me, that they are no longer required to undertake prison placements. Preparing students for these always gave me an opportunity to attack some of the myths about prison conditions, and encourage them to read about prisons before they went in, including prisoners' own accounts. This is no longer likely to happen on the BA/DipSw courses, where the curriculum is too crowded and there is insufficient time.*[34]

At the University of Birmingham, Mike Nellis used prisoner autobiographies to introduce students on the Diploma in Probation Studies course to criminology and, vicariously, to the world in which those with whom they were being trained to work, live. He wrote in *The Howard League Journal of Criminal Justice*:

> *I remain convinced that reading offender autobiographies can be both an intellectually rich and practically useful experience for would-be probation officers, firstly because they enable trainees 'to sway to and fro between life's specifics and theory's generalities'*[35] *and, secondly, because the best of them etch themselves so vividly in one's memory that they can be drawn on for insight and inspiration years after first encountering them.*[36]

As for what trainee probation officers learn from offender/prisoner autobiographies, Nellis detailed four main areas: insight into a different world – the criminal milieu; the complexity of change and desistance – how the criminals whose books are studied became rehabilitated; engaging with emotion and violence – the anger, detachment and graphic way in which criminals think (and write), and the variable reality of imprisonment – the first hand experience.

He concludes that "they are no substitute for a thorough, criminologicallyfocused, skill-based professional training, but they are a very valuable way of beginning that process." [37]

Views from the judiciary

The late Sir Stephen Tumim, who, on retirement as a judge, became an outspoken HM Chief Inspector of Prisons, was a tireless champion of prison arts. A man with a love of literature as well, and visual art, as chairman of the Koestler Awards Trust his underlying philosophy in the treatment of prisoners lay in Winston Churchill's words from 1910, "there is a treasure, if only you can find it, in the heart of every man".

As an inspector of prisons, Tumim was a true penal reformer and in his arts role he did much to continue the development of the Koestler scheme. In 1996 he wrote an introduction to *Invisible Crying Tree*, the collection of the correspondence between a lifer, Tom Shannon, and his farmer pen-pal, Christopher Morgan. In it Tumim said, "I commend this short book to anyone who does not know prison but wants to extend their knowledge of human nature" – a profound reference to what can be learned from prisoner's writing.[38]

In the opinion of Judge Michael Murphy Q.C., who sits on the North-Eastern circuit, what prisoners write should be of interest to anyone involved in the criminal justice system. Speaking of what he had read over the years in *Prison Writing*:

> *We really do need to understand the other side of it, we need to see the people on the other side. A lot of the people who sit in criminal work don't really understand what a prison is. We've all been on the trip, and we've all been around Armley or wherever and there are some who will go beyond that and do more. But even so, we don't actually see or hear what's in people's minds. And the only way you're going to get it is writing.*
>
> *They express something about their condition and where they are and what's going on in there, because unless we take the trouble to go to a prison, we don't see an awful lot of that. I try to go if I can once a year, or whenever, but you're given the anaesthetised version when you get there, I think – and this is very much not the anaesthetised version. You do get another angle on the people who are in the system, and there's no other way we're going to get it when you think of it. Even the stuff that isn't autobiographical, I think that tells you something about the person, the poems or prose pieces. It's an interesting insight into where they're coming from.*[39]

As if reinforcing Judge Murphy's point, Mr Justice Cooper told a journalist from *The Guardian* that in his six years on the High Court bench he had never visited a prison. He said he had "done" Feltham YOI and did intend to visit others. "I plead guilty," he said. He had, however, read *Inside* by John Hoskison, whom he understood to be attending training seminars for judges and telling them about his experiences in prison. Mr Justice Cooper said, "I sentenced the man - the book starts off with me sentencing him to prison. It's a very, very interesting book."[40]

But as Judge Simon Goldstein Q.C. discovered at the Old Bailey in January 2003, showing leniency on the basis of a defendant's supposed literary talent can have repercussions. The tabloid press had a field day when Goldstein gave a community sentence to a burglar, after being told he was trying to beat his drug habit and get his poems published. Mark Patterson, aged forty-one, had been caught with a machete, leaving a house in Deptford and had fifty previous convictions. Sentencing him to a drug treatment and testing order, the judge told him "The motivation for you to succeed under this order is not only what the specialists can do, but your absolute desire to try to make a success of your undoubted talent for writing poetry."

After the hearing, Patterson said "I explore all the big issues in my poetry. I've been given a gift and I want to share my wisdom with others." *The Sun* printed an example of his work, a crude, inartistic rhyme of the type that many prisoners write without any realistic hope of publication.[41] A police chief, the spokesman for a victims' pressure group and MPs from both main political parties criticised the judge's decision. Three months later, the lenient sentence was in the news again, when a warrant was issued for Patterson after he failed to co-operate with the drug treatment and testing order.

The dynamics of imprisonment and criminal values

Prison memoirs inform how humans interact in custodial institutions, how they react to the experience of being incarcerated, often for a large part of their lives. Many also show how the writers have dealt with the aftermath of the actions that put them in prison. They reveal the dynamics of prison life, where matters that would seem of little consequence outside can be of major importance to prisoners. When Home Secretary James Callaghan, on a tour of the maximum security wing at Durham in 1968, intervened in a dispute over shoes between John McVicar and the prison governor, McVicar won a moral victory on a matter that under normal circumstances would have been of little relevance.

Many autobiographies and memoirs give a sharp insight into criminal values, and in some cases the process of change and diversion from offending. Razor Smith writes:

> *Career criminals class the ordinary, law-abiding citizens as mugs and targets, too stupid, weak and cowardly to break out of the mould that society has set for them. The criminal is the hungry wolf, and straight-goers are the sheep providing a veritable smorgasbord of criminal opportunities. But contempt turns to envy when punishment for our rebelliousness is imminent. Suddenly we long to be part of straight society, wrapped in the cosy conventionality that straight-goers take for granted.*[42]

The unwritten 'criminal code', with its taboos, such as non-collusion with the police; hierarchies or 'pecking orders', and the way prison often creates environments that require enhanced masculinity in male prisons but lead to the suppression and diminishing of femininity in female prisons are phenomena that should be explored in sociological study. In such areas, criminal autobiographies and prison memoirs can be primary sources.

How do prison writers benefit?

The publication of books, journalism or poetry and the performance of plays on radio, television or stage is the culmination of a process that begins with inspiration and motivation to write. For prisoners, achieving recognition through writing can be an major factor in assisting change.

The post-prison lives of Brendan Behan, Jimmy O'Connor, John McVicar, Jimmy Boyle, Hugh Collins, Norman Parker, Tony Hoare and Mark Leech provide substantial evidence of how writing has served as a diversion from crime. But it is not only those who become well-known who benefit. Nor is that benefit always immediately apparent.

Jeremy Gavron, who spent two years as a writer in residence, later said, "Helping an inmate write or tell a story – not necessarily his own, but any narrative where one thing led to another, where cause could be seen to produce effect - I sometimes felt I was seeing a light slowly come on in his head for the first time."[43] Many prisoners go no further than that first light. If they persist, however, the effort is likely to be worthwhile. Carlo Gébler has been a writer all his working life. He says:

> *If you write consistently and steadily and for a long, long time, and you're lucky enough to find your voice, you discover you are not what you think you are. You discover that is nothing like the whole picture. You discover that in the personality, your personality, there are all sorts of things that you never knew were there.*[44]

The realisation of self

In *Borstal Boy* Brendan Behan reflects on how his attitude towards the British people changed during the time he spent at Hollesley Bay. Nearly two decades after his time in British custody, his skill as a writer enabled him to describe the process of that change, which had been brought about by a paternalistic regime that is not to be found in prison establishments today.

In between serving time in borstal and sitting down to write about it, Behan served several more prison sentences, including a four-month period in Strangeways, Manchester, for entering Britain using a false identity. While there, according to his biographer Michael O'Sullivan, he gave thought to the situation he was in, a vicious circle of "hope, political action, imprisonment and despair" that had hitherto prevented him realising his literary ambitions. With a mail-bag needle he scratched out a poem in his native Irish, entitled 'Repentance'. He began by stating his misdeeds were visible, "like packs of hounds" and told how his memory summoned them to howl at him.[45]

Many prisoners find satisfaction in artistic endeavour – as the popularity of the annual Koestler Awards Scheme shows. Some media, e.g. sculpture, pottery and painting are often said to provide a form of escape for the artist, but writing is often more of a confrontational experience. Working on his autobiography in Whitemoor brought home to Razor Smith the futility of his past life:

> *I am sick and tired of both crime and prison, and writing this book has been an emotional journey for me. I have had to go back to places that would have been best left in darkness and unvisited. But by shining a light in these places I can now see exactly where I went wrong. And that is a major step on the road to self-rehabilitation.*[46]

Jimmy Walker, a first-time offender:

> *I know writing is therapeutic and it can be a way of confronting the root of many problems either pre- or post-prison, but whether it's strong enough to drag you from the slippery slopes depends on the individual I suppose... The way I look at it is, prison is something I was almost destined to go through, hopefully to come out of the other side a better person, largely through my experiences in creative writing.*[47]

The extent to which writing played a part in diverting Benjamin Zephaniah from crime was brought home to him many years later on a visit to a prison. Opening the Koestler Awards exhibition in September 2004, he told the audience:

> *Recently I went to a poetry workshop in a prison and on my way in I was told by one of the officers that 'someone in here knows you'. When I arrived in the room, one slightly familiar face spoke up and said, 'Do you remember me? You took me on my first burglary.' Afterwards, we talked about our lives since then and I explained I had just come back from Papua New Guinea, the Caribbean and many other exotic places, giving poetry work- shops. Then he recited where he'd been since we met last and it was a list of prisons. Two paths, both journeys, but very different. We had started from the same place reciting rap poetry in the streets. Actually he was a better poet than me...*[48]

But for writing to help a prisoner turn his back on crime and find a better way to live, there needs to be some degree of success. The timing of that success can also be a major factor. Tony Hoare:

> *I think it's true to say, in retrospect, that if it hadn't been for the fact that I had my first script, a radio play, accepted and produced within a few weeks of being released from prison on parole, then received a commission from Granada TV to adapt my unpublished novel into a Sunday* Armchair Theatre *play shortly after, there was probably a chance that I would have drifted back into anti-social behaviour...It was only after I got my cheque for the Granada play I thought, well, this is better than being a working class wage slave or doing porridge. And indeed it was. And as I've been getting a reasonable crust*

out of it professionally for the past thirty years I guess it would be true, as lucky gamblers and successful villains say, that I had a right result.[49]

A sense of achievement

To any writer, the knowledge that someone considers his or her work worth publishing or broadcasting is a cause of satisfaction. If that writer is in prison, with all its restrictions and limitations, the feeling is likely to be even more uplifting. Matthew Williams describes hearing the performance of his first radio play:

> *On September 28th 2004 at 7.02 pm, RTE Radio 1 broadcast 'Seascape', giving me one of the strangest and most rewarding experiences I've ever had – that of actually hearing an imaginary world of mine made real, executed by a fantastic production team. It has encouraged me in my writing in a way nothing else has ever done.*[50]

Razor Smith recalls receiving a postal order for £15, token payment for two poems and an article in the second issue of *Prison Writing*. He also remembers the impact on him when he saw his work in print for the first time:

> *I was in a trance for six weeks! It took that long for it to sink in. I must have read it a thousand times and I showed it to everyone. The only thing that compared to it was being at the birth of my first son – it was such a buzz. Even at that stage I remember thinking that if I never had another word published I wouldn't mind because I had this.*
>
> *It was such a feeling of achievement, someone outside had paid me money and published my writing for everyone to read. It blew me away. I can still get the exact feeling when I open* PW2 *and see my name in the contents. My copy was literally worn out, my mum has got it at home somewhere, yellowed, frayed and held together with sellotape like an ancient holy relic.*[51]

A decade later and back in prison after a short-lived period on parole, Smith would enjoy the experience of holding a copy of his own autobiography – a feeling John McVicar was denied. The prison authorities might have turned a blind eye to him writing what became *by Himself*, but allowing to have a copy sent in was a different matter:

> *I never saw a copy of the book. I saw the* Sunday Times Mag *and was bowled over by seeing the shot of me as a kid on the cover. I remember watching the best sellers list and being disappointed that it never figured.*[52]

Valerio Viccei, the Italian who made headlines for robbing the Knightsbridge Safe Deposit Company of cash and property estimated at many millions of pounds, lived for thrills. His jet-set life of fast cars, glamorous women and high-value robberies led him to Parkhurst and a twenty-two year prison sentence, whereupon he wrote his one and only book, a boastful account of the crime that brought him the notoriety he clearly craved. Soon after publication he said:

> *Seeing my first ever book – written in a foreign language – in print, has been a great thing. It is an achievement difficult to match.*[53]

After his book was published, Viccei claimed to have been sent hundreds of letters of support. He certainly had letters of appreciation from both the trial judge and the police officer leading the case against him, to both of whom he had sent a copy.

In 1974, after some of Larry Winters' poetry was read at the Edinburgh Festival, he was contacted by a publishing company, interested in his work. Jimmy Boyle, his friend and fellow inmate in the Barlinnie Special Unit, later recalled:

> *Larry was asked what he felt and said he was interested so it was arranged that the publishers be brought in. This was a tremendous boost for Larry. He was making an effort to come off his drugs and the fact that he was gaining recognition as a writer came at the right time. All of this was bringing him to the point of trusting the people around him.*[54]

Unfortunately for Winters, time was running out. He died from a heroin overdose in the Special Unit in 1977. The short collection, *The Silent Scream and poems* was published posthumously.[55]

A means of communication with the outside world

Often, publication of a book while the writer is in prison brings new and welcome contacts with people outside the walls. Phillip Baker, interviewed by a journalist about his novel, published while he was in HMP The Mount, said:

> *For me, getting published isn't such a huge deal in itself, maybe because I'm still within these same four walls and I can't see it happening. I can't even go to the launch party. It's the feedback that's important. Since I wrote* Blood Posse *I've had people writing to me, people coming to see me, and that's what really keeps you going.*[56]

Janet Cresswell's play *The One-sided Wall*, performed on the London stage while she was a patient in Broadmoor, brought attention to her situation. From then on she was the subject of periodic features in the press, but not until 2002, fourteen years after the play, was she transferred from Broadmoor to a less secure mental hospital.

A sense of being able to engage with the outside world in a way he had never thought would be possible for a prisoner was what Erwin James got from seeing his columns about prison life in *The Guardian*. In his introduction to the second volume of his collected columns he says:

> *Writing for readers of a national newspaper was in itself a form of release. The column gave me all the motivation I needed to maintain a positive outlook. It was a chance to put my new abilities to real, practical use. Communicating with editors, negotiating with prison authorities to get their approval for the column to go ahead, knuckling down to produce copy that was good enough: this was a challenge like no other I'd ever encountered. It helped that I started to think of myself first not as a prisoner writing, but as a writer in prison. Suddenly, from being a powerless captive, I became an active observer; a chronicler of secret lives lived out in dark places.*[57]

In the first collection of his columns, James referred to how the opportunity to write for the newspaper about what he saw around him in prison had come at just the right time in his sentence and had given him a fresh sense of purpose.[58] He is one of the latest in a series of prisoners and ex-prisoners beginning with Jim Phelan in the 1940s, whose life has been enhanced by writing.

Does society benefit ?

When *The Guardian* appointed ex-prisoner Eric Allison to their newly created post of Prison Correspondent in 2003, the newspaper showed the importance of prison matters – written by someone with inside knowledge and experience - to the national news agenda. At the time, the editor emphasised that not enough is known about what happens in prisons. Although Allison was not recognised as a writer or prison commentator in the way that some other ex-prisoners are, the newspaper's management clearly believed that someone with a custodial history would have a wider view of the issues than a straightforward journalist.

To what extent society benefits from the publication of prisoners' and ex-prisoners' autobiographies and memoirs is difficult to ascertain. There are instances where projects have been set up on the proceeds of books, one being The Shannon Trust, established through the royalties of *Invisible Crying Tree*, the correspondence between Tom Shannon and Christopher Morgan.[59] The trust assists prisoners on release, thereby reducing the risk of them re-offending through lack of support.

The success of *A Sense of Freedom* enabled Jimmy Boyle to establish a fund for young people at Easterhouse in Glasgow, a housing estate beset by problems. Many of the residents had been moved there when the Gorbals were demolished and the area had quickly become a modern ghetto. Boyle wanted to get the message across to his readers that crime and violence lead only to personal destruction. His charity was intended to help towards alleviating the causes of that crime and violence, social deprivation and lack of positive opportunities for young people. Later, Boyle was involved with the Gateway Exchange, another Glasgow project with similar aims.

James Morton, author of numerous non-fiction crime books, including the *Gangland* series:

> *Prison memoirs show just how awful prison has been and in some places still is – the one-time brutality of warders and currently the medical treatment available or not available to prisoners, the lack of educational facilities, the quantities of drugs swilling around inside. Society may be able to say I don't believe it, but it will not be able to say I didn't know.*[60]

To anyone facing the prospect of imprisonment for the first time, memoirs can give some notice of what lies ahead. Former government minister Jonathan Aitken found himself in such a position:

> *I'd read a bit before I went in, once I knew I was going to prison. I'd read* Parkhurst Tales *by Norman Parker, I thought it was over the top. I read a*

> *book by John Hoskison - Inside. I was concerned by some of that stuff but not so concerned that I absolutely believed it. I thought it was a realistic picture, but a self-centred account. He obviously had a bad time. I was an optimist. I read others, can't remember the titles. I did my homework.*[61]

Society was denied the benefit of whatever insights Denis Nilsen might have offered in his autobiography, when the prison authorities confiscated his manuscript. In early 2004, two months after the High Court upheld the decision, the Government announced a major study of all serial and mass murderers, which would involve interviewing them in prison, to try to discover profiles and patterns that would assist future investigations. Only a few days after the announcement of the project, Nilsen was reported as telling a friend in a letter that he would never agree to co-operate because the Home Office had prevented him publishing his autobiography. He was quoted as saying, "I have spilled my guts out in three volumes and that is it."[62]

Ian Brady presumably felt that he too had made his contribution with his book on serial killers. He wrote from Ashworth Hospital, "Research conducted by the penal authorities is self-serving ... an exercise in pretension and time-serving by the tea and biscuit-munching professional drones."[63] Professor David Cantor of Liverpool University Centre for Investigative Psychology did not believe there to be any value in interviewing either Brady or Nilsen. He asked, "If they had any real insight, would they really have done these things?"[64]

Does it lead to change?

It has been said that Oscar Wilde gave more insight into prison conditions in *The Ballad of Reading Gaol* than either Charles Dickens and Charles Reade, both of whom he had previously criticised for their efforts to reform the penal system.[65] *The Ballad* is still quoted by prison poets and penal reformers more than a century after Wilde's death, but did it lead to any change at the time it was published, or in the immediate years that followed?

In the House of Commons on 28 March 1898, during the second reading of the Prison Bill, John Redmond M.P. bolstered his argument by quoting a stanza of *The Ballad*. A few years later, the criminologist George Ives cited Wilde's criticism of prison conditions and descriptions of the plight of inmates.[66] These were topical references, but within the criminal justice system of the day,

Wilde's poem led to no changes in law or penal policy. It evoked sympathy for the condemned man, but hanging remained in force until 1957 for murder of the type committed by the trooper in Wilde's poem.

The rule of silence continued until the early 1920s and for many years afterwards prisoners were not allowed to speak to each other while at labour. Although Wilde had been so keen for his poem to bring attention to prison conditions, nothing changed. Leicester Prison, as described in *Among The Broad Arrow Men*, published in 1924,[67] is little different from Reading when Wilde was there, twenty-six years earlier.

Since Wilde, a multitude of prisoners and former prisoners have criticised conditions, staff attitudes, government policies, the law relating to imprisonment, the lack of opportunities to live a responsible life on release, and other facets of imprisonment. Many of their books have been brought to wider attention by the media and the points they have made have been shown to have some validity. But have they led to penal reform? Have they influenced the politicians and civil servants who are responsible for the development of prison policy? In short, does society benefit from prison writing?

Of Hugh Collins' *Autobiography of a Murderer*, Allan Massie of the *Daily Telegraph*, suggested that the home secretary and the secretary of state for Scotland should read the book, "and ponder its lessons".[68] Although the Koestler Awards Scheme would never have got off the ground without the support of R.A.Butler, and while Jack Straw gave the opening speech at the Koestler exhibition in 1998, there is no evidence that any other home secretary has ever read an autobiography or memoir by any prisoner, let alone recognised lessons to be learned therein. Former Tory minister Jonathan Aitken believes that prisoners' writing has value, but, given his personal experience, his is perhaps an untypical view:

> In the great free market of ideas about penal reform and law and order policy, I think contributions by prisoners can be rather valuable. Is a home secretary likely to be influenced? Well that depends on who the home secretary is. I think that if a home secretary reads about life in prison in a newspaper he is quite likely to be influenced by that. For example, Leon Brittan and Michael Howard, two friends of mine who've held that job, Douglas Hurd, too. All of them would have been capable of being interested in and responding to, although they probably wouldn't have done it publicly, something interesting written by prisoners.[69]

The issue here is one of credibility – not only of the prisoner's story, but also the politician's reputation with the electorate if he accepted the story. Many years after he left the Home Office, Sir Douglas Hurd said he could not recall any specific examples of being influenced as home secretary by prisoners' writing. He added that in his later role as chairman of the Prison Reform Trust he had become more conscious of how prisoners' writing helped to stimulate public interest in prisons.[70]

Jimmy Walker, *Prison Writing* competition winner, thinks change can certainly be achieved:

> *Campaigns against penal injustice can begin from a con's pencil. It's so important that a voice is heard from the inside.*[71]

Novelist and journalist Will Self:

> *It's the business of an open society to examine its most closed portions. It's the business of responsible lawmakers to look at the consequences of their policies. I think that prisoners' writing has influenced policy and formed part of the ongoing discourse that society holds with itself about the nature of crime and punishment.*[72]

Judge Michael Murphy QC:

> *I don't think it brings about rapid changes overnight, but it must to some extent. The change may not be on a grandiose scale, but you think of Solzenitsyn. Would we have known anything about what was going on inside the Gulag without someone like him? I don't think we would.*[73]

Penal reform is rarely achieved swiftly. It is not surprising that there are no obvious examples of improvements brought about by anything a prisoner or ex-prisoner has published; prison systems do not work like that. It took vast media coverage of the Strangeways riots in 1990, and the resultant Woolf Inquiry and Report, to bring about improvements that had been decades overdue in the old Victorian jails. The Home Office and prison service could not ignore Strangeways; they can easily ignore prisoners' writing, no matter how well-received it is by the media, the public, academia or anyone else. If memoirs and journalism do contribute towards changes in policy it is only by their contribution to an ongoing debate.[74]

Effects

For some writers, an autobiography is only the beginning. *A Sense of Freedom* established Jimmy Boyle as a commentator on penal matters, a role in which he had obvious credibility. Boyle campaigned for reform and worked hard on his Scottish projects to give young people alternatives to crime and wasted lives.

In the years following the publication of the book, Stephen Shaw, later to be Prisons Ombudsman, knew Boyle. Asked whether the book, with its graphic descriptions of violence within the Scottish prisons, achieved any positive change, Shaw says:

> *I don't know whether you can separate Boyle the book from Boyle the man. I think Boyle the man has continued to change some essentially middle class attitudes towards offenders and offending. That book should still mean something to any reader, even though it's of its time. There's a raw honesty about that, and his other one.*[75]

No book by an inmate of a British prison has caused as much of a stir as Jeffrey Archer's *A Prison Diary* did on its publication in 2002. Among reviewers there was almost unanimous agreement that this was a book that would bring about change in Britain's decrepit prisons. In the *Independent on Sunday*, Clive Anderson said:

> *Any accurate story of life behind bars in Britain today is likely to shock, but especially one written by a prisoner who comes to the penal system late in life. ... After all, the prison system is a disgrace and the more we hear about it the more likely we are to do something to make it better ... a high profile account of life on the inside is to be welcomed. And one can scarcely think of a better man than Jeffrey Archer to provide it.*[76]

Anthony Howard in *The Sunday Times*:

> *He has contrived to write a surprisingly effective book, that for once lines him up firmly on the side of light. A Prison Diary might not be Oscar Wilde's The Ballad of Reading Gaol but, with luck, it could have very much the same effect.*[77]

A leader in *The Guardian* declared:

> *Two new and surprising voices joined the penal reform debate yesterday:*

> *Lord Archer and the* Daily Mail. *Both should be welcomed. The wider the church the better… We want more memoirs, not fewer. Sunshine is the best disinfectant the hell holes can receive."* [78]

Even the academic *Howard League Journal* joined in the acclaim, saying "for perhaps the first time in his life, Jeffrey Archer has performed a genuine public service." The book was worth reading, stated the reviewer, because it yet again highlighted this country's obsession with jail.[79]

With vast coverage in the national and regional press, Archer's book sold over 4,000 copies in the first week, while he languished at North Sea Camp open prison in Lincolnshire. The director-general of the Prison Service was not happy with the situation, but Juliet Lyons, director of the Prison Reform Trust, said, "If publication of these diaries alerts the public to the poor conditions in our overcrowded jails, they may prove a force for change."[80]

In the event, they did not, which should have been no surprise to anyone. In previous years, the annual reports of successive HMP Chief Inspectors of Prisons had repeatedly criticised conditions. If the government and the prison authorities did not listen to Sir Stephen Tumim and Sir David Ramsbotham, they were unlikely to take notice of a convicted perjurer.

Effects

8] Those who oppose

The issue of whether convicted criminals should be allowed to write for publication extends beyond any prison rule, indeed beyond prison itself. In essence it is a moral debate that focuses on the effects on victims and on the matter of prisoners profiting from their criminal activities. Often the media inflame the issue, pandering to the likely reaction of some sections of the public, while at the same time publicising the object of their criticism and creating more upset for victims. Bemoaning the passing of a bygone era when doing time meant breaking rocks or sewing mailbags, they can appear resentful of the means by which once-notorious criminals have rehabilitated themselves. As journalist Allan Brown wrote in a *Sunday Times* article headed "Knee-capping too good for literary villains":

> *Here we have Jimmy Boyle and Hugh Collins, writers, raconteurs and pundits to a man. Few such fellows displayed much interest in the state of the modern novel or the lively arts of rhetoric when they were carving people up…there is a rising tide of criminal quasi-literature - fiction and non-fiction - a genre in itself, characterised mainly by the strenuous moral contortions undertaken by the authors as they attempt to deodorise their consciences.*[1]

The genre to which Brown refers is popular. Books sell and authors receive payment. In any other form of literature that would be accepted without comment, but the autobiographies and memoirs of prisoners and ex-prisoners are different.

They are written by people who have committed very serious offences and their publication in some quarters meets with great disapproval. The writers themselves argue that they have repaid their debt to society by being imprisoned and deprived of their liberty. But that argument does not appease their critics.

Rubbing salt in wounds

Of all the books by murderers, gangsters and other criminals, none has aroused the same degree of opposition as Ian Brady's study of serial killers, *The Gates of Janus*.² Thirty-five years had elapsed since the Moors Murders but Brady's notoriety, along with that of his accomplice, Myra Hindley, had not faded. Even though the book was not autobiographical and, as his solicitor was keen to emphasise, Brady would receive no money, the families of his victims were incensed that he had been allowed to publish it.

Urging the public and shops to boycott the book, Danny Kilbride, whose 12-year-old brother John was murdered by Brady and Hindley, said "It's wrong. Anyone who has committed crimes such as he has committed should not be allowed to do this in the first place."³ The mother of another victim, twelve year-old Keith Bennett, said the book should not be published. She told a reporter, "I think it's absolutely disgusting that a publisher is willing to accept this book from this man."⁴

The announcement that Brady would not benefit financially as his share of the royalties would go towards the care of his mother, in her nineties, did nothing to curb the outrage, with the front page headline of one tabloid declaring: "FURY OVER BRADY'S £12,000 BOOK DEAL",⁵ while Phil Gallie MSP, the Scottish Conservatives' home affairs spokesman, said:

> *It is deeply disturbing to think of Brady getting access to material about the crimes of others and writing to other killers about his crimes. There must be greater scrutiny over such patients and prisoners. Nor is it right that Brady's mother will profit from the crimes of her son. If anyone is to profit it should be the families of his victims."* ⁶

Victims' organisations spoke out. Norman Brennan, director of the Victims of Crime Trust, urged bookshops in Britain not to sell the book, as Dee Warner, of the campaign group, Mothers Against Manslaughter Murder and Aggression, criticised Brady for profiting from his crimes. She said:

> *It is disgusting that criminals are allowed to make money from their crimes and I am sickened that the book is getting the go-ahead. If Brady wasn't a killer nobody would buy this book. It is just his name that is being used to make money. People seem to forget that the families of the victims are still grief-stricken and publishing this book only reminds them of the horrendous murders. I can understand books being published for academic purpose, but Brady is just satisfying morbid fascination.*⁷

If the families of Brady's victims took any crumb of comfort from press reports that his book did not refer to his own crimes, they would have been horrified to read reports that, as well as his study of serial killers, he had written an autobiography, with instructions for it to be published after his death.[8]

The news that Hugh Collins was to publish his first volume of autobiography brought a strong reaction from the family of William Mooney, the man he killed. Prior to their fatal confrontation, the two men had been associates in Glasgow gangs. The victim's son, James Mooney, was outraged about the book, and a BBC documentary film planned to coincide with it. He told the *Sunday Mail*, "He had my dad's blood on his hands. What he is doing is evil." He said he was physically sick when he heard about the book and film: "I did not even know how my father died until I read about this man's sick boasting. Collins seems to think nothing about the effect on the family of his victim...Collins has no qualms about wanting to make money. It's as if he wants to twist the knife into my family." A spokeswoman for Macmillan Books was quoted as saying Collins was not trying to make money from his crimes.[9] Later, Collins said:

> World In Action *did a programme and a researcher went to the family. There's a son and he had no knowledge of who his father was. I can try and understand his anger. I can understand it... I made the suggestion that I would be quite willing to face the family and take the flack off them. But the* Sunday Mail *and a couple of the tabloids got onto it and tried to arrange it. They were talking about a publicity stunt so I backed off. I don't think that would be helpful to anybody.*[10]

The Mooney family were not the only people to complain about Hugh Collins' book. Others were unhappy with him naming them, not least his own father, who tried to put an injunction on Collins' literary debut. Prisoners he had mentioned by name were angry about the way he had portrayed them, a situation that he defended:

> *I've took a risk, just in being honest about people. I've had death threats ... I suppose in a way I've sort of provoked guys like that, but I'm trying to expose myself, I'm not going to try and dress up anybody else or make apologies for them. I'm trying to describe that world, where everybody's arse-holes. It's not a case of he's ok, he doesn't rape guys . . .everybody in that world are arse-holes.*[11]

In the Scottish media, not only autobiography raises the ire of protesters. There was outrage in December 1995 when it was reported that a play written by a prisoner in Peterhead Prison, William Thomson, was to be performed at the Lemon Tree theatre in Aberdeen. The play, titled *'Screw The Nut'*, was said to be based on Thomson's experiences of incarceration and had been co-written by a prison tutor. The production was cancelled after protests following the news that the play's publicity named Thomson, a lifer who had killed a two-year old child when he was fifteen.[12]

The antipathy towards a child killer could be understood. Less anticipated was the reaction to an advertisement in a bookshop in East Kilbride for a forthcoming appearance by Jimmy Boyle, to sign copies of his first novel, *Hero of the Underworld*. Boyle had been out of prison almost twenty years, his two volumes of autobiography had been very successful and he was widely respected for his work in diverting young people away from crime. This did not impress the residents of East Kilbride, who threatened to smash up the bookshop. The shop manager told the *Daily Mail*, "I really underestimated the depth of feeling."[13]

The profits of crime

The opinion that prisoners and ex-prisoners should not profit from writing about crime is not restricted to victims and victims' groups. When the National Lottery agreed to fund a *Prison Writing* competition with categories for non-fiction, short stories and poetry, it was with the condition that none of the money provided should be used for prizes – even though the proposal for the competition included nominal cash prizes for winning entries. The rationale – although it was not clarified – was presumably concern that prisoners should not be seen to receive direct benefit from the Lottery.

In the past, some publishers have been deterred from taking on books by former prisoners. Cape was in this situation after commissioning Rosie Johnston to write a prison memoir. The contract was said to be worth £35,000. Johnston had been convicted of supplying the drugs that led to the death of her friend at an Oxford University party in 1986. After mutterings about making payments to criminals, Cape took fright and the contract was withdrawn. Johnston found another company to publish *Inside Out*, but the deal was worth only £5,000.[14]

When the pseudonymous Erwin James was recruited to write his 'A life inside' column for *The Guardian*, criticism was pre-empted by a statement at the foot of each column: "Erwin James is serving a life sentence. The fee for this article will be paid to charity." When James moved to an open prison and was eligible to work and earn money, the statement ceased to appear.

John McVicar, asked if he ever faced criticism that his book *McVicar by Himself*, or the film based on it, glamorised the criminal lifestyle replied, "The main resentment is making money from one's crimes, not glamorisation."[15]

That resentment was a key factor in the controversy over the publication of Jeffrey Archer's *A Prison Diary*. Colin Moses, chairman of the Prison Officers' Association said:

> Prison is not supposed to be a place where someone convicted of perjury can continue to make money. .. It seems to us by his recent actions that prison has not had any rehabilitating effect on him at all.[16]

The Sun declared:

> It's preposterous that a convicted man can make hundreds of thousands of pounds from his jail memoirs. Archer has made the penal system look stupid. It's up to the public to hit back where it will really hurt him – his pride. Don't buy the book."[17]

Archer received widespread criticism over the money he was said to be making from the royalties on his book. The *Daily Mail* was reported as having paid the fee for serialisation rights to prisoner and drug charities and there were calls for Archer to do the same. But not only the jailed peer was the object of criticism.

In the *Mirror*, Tony Parsons supported Archer for publishing his book, while lambasting the *Mail* for serialising it. He railed:

> It is not Archer who is the two-faced, snivelling hypocrite today. It is the Daily Mail, *the money-grabbing serialiser of his prison diary…The* Daily Mail *is a holier-than-thou newspaper that spends its days peeping at a deteriorating country and tutting loudly from behind its net curtains. And here they are getting caught with their fingers in the till.*
>
> *How can these Tory law-and-order lovers ever justify buying a book from a crook? How can the* Daily Mail *bang on about the decline of moral standards when they hope to profit from a convicted liar? How can Middle England sleep*

> safe in its beds when the Daily Mail *rushes to sign up a felon who is still doing time?How can the* Daily Mail *wring its hands in horror at crime statistics when prisoner FF8282 is on their list of contributors?*
>
> *The* Daily Mail *turns out to be soft on crime, and soft on criminals who are peddling their memoirs. It is not Archer who is the villain of the piece. He is doing what any writer does - using his personal experience to fill those hundreds of empty white pages, to try and make some sense of his life and - hopefully - pay the rent at the same time.*[18]

Archer's conviction for perjury left no personal victims. The opposition to him receiving payment for writing about prison was based on his celebrity, existing wealth and his reputation as a prominent Tory at a time when the party took a tough line on criminal justice issues.

Peter Wayne and Razor Smith, old-fashioned criminals both, had no such baggage when they began to write for money while still in prison and neither received criticism from within the media. Norman Parker, whose prison-based books were published after his release on life licence, felt that he had been unduly criticised, according to an interview conducted over a lunch with *Financial Times* journalist, Kate Kellaway:

> *Taking courage, I asked if murderers should be able to become rich and famous on the basis of what they have done. 'Yeah, yeah,' he interrupted. 'For my first book I stood for that. I was Norman the Murderer who happened to have written a book. But it sold 20,000 in hardback. OK, now I've got my second book published. It's a full-length book. By all means criticise my book. But I feel I've served my time; I did 24 years for killing a criminal with his own gun after he attacked me.'*
>
> *Evidently I had touched a raw nerve. I tried to interrupt the flow, but without success. 'Every man and his dog has an opinion about prisons but it's an extremely unfounded opinion. So if nothing else I am informing the debate. But you would have thought I was committing a series of crimes the way some people have reacted.'*[19]

The prevention of payment campaign

In July 1998, the Press Complaints Commission considered the matter of newspapers paying convicted criminals for their stories. Extracts from a book by the author Gitta Sereny about Mary Bell, who, at the age of eleven, was convicted of murdering two younger children, had been published in *The Times* and the news that Bell, on life licence, had been paid £50,000 for her co-operation with the author aroused great criticism. However, the Press Complaints Commission's involvement was not relevant to the arrangement between author and subject, as its jurisdiction extends only to newspapers and their editors' code of conduct, which prohibits payment to convicted criminals unless justified in the public interest.

The PCC upheld the right of *The Times* to serialise the book, and, in separate complaints, the rights of three other papers, one of which had serialised a book by an IRA informer and two who had paid for interviews with two nurses convicted of murdering a colleague in Saudi Arabia. The PCC's adjudication stated that while it is wrong to glorify crime, it is not necessarily wrong to write about it and there are occasions on which the public has a right to know about events relating to a crime or criminals:

> *However, there was one further and general matter the Commission wished to address. Like many members of the public - and like many editors - the Commission believes that while payments may in some cases be necessary, they may at the same time be extremely offensive. However, that is a moral and subjective judgement which goes beyond the scope of the Commission and an objective Code at the heart of which is the public interest and the public's right to know. It is a matter of broader public policy for Government and Parliament.*[20]

The PCC also noted that, although the Proceeds of Crime Act 1995 and the Criminal Justice Act 1988 included provisions to prevent convicted criminals in certain circumstances from profiting from crime, there was a time limit of six years after conviction. The following day, it was reported that that Jack Straw, the Home Secretary, was considering ways to extend the period in which the proceeds of a criminal's autobiography could be confiscated, although it was recognised that the Human Rights Bill, at the time going through Parliament, was likely to make this difficult.

Five years later the PCC came under criticism after censuring *The Guardian* for paying £720 to John Williams, a prisoner in Hollesley Bay, who wrote a right of reply to Jeffrey Archer's *Prison Diary*, then being serialised in the *Daily Mail*. Although it had been reported that Archer was being paid for his work, it was now said that he had not been. The PCC, rejecting the public interest defence put forward by *The Guardian*, said Williams should not have been paid.

When *The Guardian* published a robust criticism of the PCC, who had exonerated the *News of the World* for paying £10,000 to a convicted criminal who arranged a fake plot to kidnap a celebrity, the Commission demanded information about payments made to Erwin James for his weekly column in the paper.

The Guardian assured its readers that it would continue to write about prisons and penal policy, saying "Among the voices who deserve to be heard in this debate are prisoner and former prisoners. Where it seems to us appropriate that they should be paid for their work, we will pay them."[21]

There the issue of paying prisoners rested until early 2005 when, in the run-up to the general election, the Conservatives announced they would ban convicted criminals from publishing books about their experiences in prison. A Labour MP, Peter Bradley, asked "Who have they got in mind", reminding the Tories that two much publicised books had been published by their own Messrs Archer and Aitken. It was not revealed how the law might be implemented, or changed, to enforce the ban, given that the Proceeds of Crime Act was usually applied to assets directly related to the crime, such as a house bought with the proceeds of drug dealing. The Conservatives did not win the election and no more was heard of the idea.

No simple solution

The prison service might not like it, nor the media, victims and others, but if a prisoner gets his work to a willing publisher or producer, there is nothing that can be done to stop the work being used for commercial gain. Whether he or she receives payment whilst still in prison is another matter, but most inmates have someone – a mother, wife or friend to help them get round that particular difficulty.

As for ex-prisoners, the reality is there are no restrictions, beyond those that any writer has to observe. Whatever distress they may cause by describing their crimes, it seems that the Human Rights Act has dispelled any notion of new legislation to curb their pens or typewriters.

Stephen Shaw, Prisons Ombudsman, supports the principle that a serving prisoner who can earn money from writing should be allowed to do so:

> *I have no problem with prisoners publishing while serving their sentences. I think they should have the right. Is it proportionate to prevent somebody from exercising their right to publish? I don't believe it is. The second point is, we are all very interested in the re-settlement agenda and if somebody has actually got some writing talent, they should be allowed to exercise that. They could put the money aside for when they are released and it may be a way they can actually make a lawful living.*[22]

The novelist and journalist Will Self, who helped find a publisher for Razor Smith's autobiography, says each case should be judged on its merits:

> *There is a wealth of difference between a prisoner sincerely examining their offending through writing, with a view to effecting their own rehabilitation, and providing another career for themselves, and a prisoner who seeks to sensationalise criminal activities with a view to profiting from them. The current position on prisoners writing for profit is extremely grey, but I see no reason why an assessment of the validity of a prisoner's writing shouldn't form an aspect of their parole and sentencing reviewing.*[23]

Professor Brian Williams takes a similar view, while recognising the difficulties of exercising any selection process:

> *The question of whether prisoners should be allowed to profit from their writings depends very much on the circumstances in individual cases. I wouldn't want to see unscrupulous white-collar offenders making huge sums of money out of poor but sensationalised prison writing, and I wouldn't want ruthless murderers to profit from writing about their crimes in ways which re-victimised the families of their victims. However, it's a slippery slope preventing one type of offenders and not another.*[24]

Carlo Gébler has no problem, whatever media prisoners choose to work in. He believes that if someone is willing to pay for anyone's writing they should be entitled to the money. Accepting that his view is not widely popular he says:

> *These are my reasons: Liars and cheats, fakes and politicians, and all sorts of other grubby individuals, get money by writing about their sordid lives. So if they do why shouldn't criminals? I can't bring myself to believe that because*

a man's been in jail he must automatically be debarred from profiting from a literary account of jail or what got him to jail, while other malfeasants aren't debarred. A man's punishment if he does wrong is jail.

When we prohibit criminals or ex-criminals from benefiting from their published accounts we're adding something to their tariff which wasn't there originally.[25]

Causing distress to victims, the morality of prisoners earning money and, more generally, convicted criminals profiting from their crimes are the main factors cited by opponents of prison writing. Those who believe that the purpose of imprisonment is solely to punish are never likely to see the benefit of prisoners examining their pasts through writing, nor of them earning money that will help re-settlement on release. The victim issue is of course much more complicated.

One possible attempt at a solution could be for victims or victims' groups to receive a significant part of the proceeds of prisoners' literary earnings through the amendment of Prison Standing Orders. Stephen Shaw, in his response to Matthew Williams' complaint regarding receiving payment for his radio play suggested the need for change in SO5(b), albeit not along these lines. The introduction of such a proposal would undoubtedly pose difficulties and it may be that victims or their support groups would not consider it appropriate.

A greater discretion and sensitivity on the part of publishers would be something that many victims might see as helpful. The Press Complaints Commission which has jurisdiction over newspapers and magazines, is often criticised as being toothless, but its existence has prevented some sensationalised accounts ostensibly written by convicted criminals from appearing in newspapers. The Publishers Association, a trade body that represents the industry to Government and the European Commission, could consider whether it has similar responsibilities with regard to books, although it is likely that its membership does not include some of the smaller presses whose titles can still grab headlines for the wrong reasons.

Amidst the confusion, inconsistency, anger and distress, only one thing is clear: there is no simple solution.

9] Epilogue

"Prison isolates. People are held mute, anonymous, incommunicado. Art communicates a sense of self and society," said art critic, Caroline Tisdall. A supporter of the Barlinnie Special Unit experiment, she believed that through inmates' sculpture, painting and poetry it was possible "to trace the passages of men from cages to communication."[1]

Oscar Wilde wrote to explain and to seek redemption in the eyes of his former lover. By expunging his pride and arrogance in the writing of *De Profundis*, he produced a work of much greater emotional depth than the stage plays that had made him famous. In penury after his release from prison, he wrote *The Ballad of Reading Gaol* as a means of earning money.

Wilde was a professional writer but a man broken by his trial and sentence. For him, as for many others since, inspiration and motivation came together and some inner force stirred him to write in prison. In Cell 3.3 at Reading, Wilde found his prison muse. The result, *De Profundis*, was a major influence on John McVicar seventy years later, when he, on remand in Brixton Prison in altogether different circumstances from Wilde's, sat down to write his story.

Jimmy Boyle, Larry Winters, Hugh Collins and others found their muse in the Barlinnie Special Unit. Dartmoor provided material as well as that inner force for Jim Phelan and Jimmy O'Connor. In Hull, Tony Hoare contemplated his life in crime and wrote a novel. The therapeutic prison Grendon Underwood was the setting for Mark Leech to write a radio play and later his autobiography. An exercise yard conversation between two old Cockney villains was the trigger for Razor Smith to write his poem 'Old Lags' and begin his journey from confirmed criminal to dedicated writer. There are many more. But besides inspiration and motivation, anyone who is to write with success must have some basic ability.

Not all prison writers can change, even when they achieve success. Larry Winters, mentally unwell and with access to illicit drugs, died before his talent could be fully realised, but Walter Probyn, who saw his personal critique of the criminal justice system acclaimed by academics, still returned to prison. The support of editors and a publishing contract was not enough to keep Peter Wayne from re-offending. Valerio Viccei was killed in a shoot-out with police after being deported to his native Italy. But the lives of many prisoners have been improved through writing, and not only those who turned it into a career. Publication has given them positive self-esteem, often for the first time in their lives. They have found a new way of expressing themselves, in words rather than crime, and they have found that the written word can be more effective than disruptive behaviour when dealing with authority, in or out of prison.

There is evidence that there are benefits for society from prisoners' writing. As to whether autobiographies and memoirs bring about change by influencing policy and conditions, there is no hard evidence that they do. Within the prison system there remains a great deal of ambivalence as to whether writing for publication should be allowed.

It may have been proven to be a genuine route to rehabilitation and one of the few ways that prison can help to equip inmates for work, but when a recommendation by the Ombudsman to amend Standing Order 5 goes unheeded, as it did in Matthew Williams' case, it seems that even in the twenty-first century, the prison authorities are not willing to lift the stone-clad veil of secrecy that has so long pervaded their institutions. They will support the Koestler Scheme and welcome writers in residence into the prisons, but are nervous about being seen to encourage inmates to follow the positive examples of men like John McVicar and Jimmy Boyle.

Maybe they fear that to remove the ban on publishing would create a British Jack Henry Abbott. Supported by the Pulitzer Prize-winning novelist Norman Mailer, Abbott published a polemic against society, *In the Belly of the Beast*, while serving life for murder in the USA. The book gained massive publicity and was instrumental in gaining Abbott's release, which would not have occurred otherwise. Soon afterwards, Abbott murdered again. There has been no case to compare in any way with Jack Henry Abbott in Britain, but the media's coverage of prisoners' work often seems designed to raise the suspicion among readers that the author is somehow trying to 'write' his or her way out of jail.

While ever Standing Order 5 remains, there will be inconsistency in the way it is applied. Some prison governors will allow manuscripts to leave their establishments, others will not. The differing experiences of Denis Nilsen and Razor Smith in Whitemoor show that inmates in the same prison are not dealt with by the same standard. If the prison service had carried out their reported threat to seek an injunction to prevent the publication of the first volume of Jeffrey Archer's diaries, the situation might have been clarified. In the event they did not – probably on advice that such an application would have failed. Maybe the prison service, and more so the government, prefers that the position remains unclear. Perhaps it is preferable that an occasional prisoner is able to tell his story apparently by default, than for all to be given the unrestricted opportunity, a situation not likely to win votes for politicians.

But if there were no restrictions, how easy is it for a prisoner to get work published or broadcast? In particular, how easy is it for one lacking in notoriety and thus unknown to the market? The novelist Will Self believes that the prisoner/writer will always labour at a disadvantage against many of his peers who are at liberty. He says, "The stigma of being a serving prisoner vastly outweighs whatever cachet may attach to his gritty portrayal of crime and incarceration."[2] However, the experience of his protégé Razor Smith, who was unknown outside his south London criminal circle and the prison system, shows that if the book is good enough, a publisher – Penguin in Smith's case - will be interested.

Rather than being at a disadvantage, the prisoner or ex-prisoner has an identity that publishers and press can exploit. Tony Hoare:

> *I think any criminal that's got a good story to tell that's quite well done will have more chance than the guy that's sitting at home trying to get off the ground. It's all focussed on him and the press like that. Whenever I got press coverage it was always about my past, never about my work. They talk about your work, you think, Oh this about my work, but it's not, it always turned out that they were fixated on the fact that you were a criminal and what did you do and how many years did you get – not about the work. It's a journalist's thing – what's the sensational angle here?*[3]

Most authors of the autobiographies and prison memoirs that have remained in public or academic consciousness were already recognisable names, through their crimes or their behaviour in prison. Many of the others had only one story to tell, one book to write. Often, this was relevant to an event or short period of time that quickly passed. After brief attention the authors then faded away – some reluctantly, some back to prison, some, having had their say, happy to put it all behind them. For the latter group, writing was often a catharsis that publication served only to confuse.

The worst side of the tabloid press's attitude to the publication of prisoners' writing is perhaps exemplified by a news story in the Scottish edition of *News of the World*.[4] Under the headline "Banged to Writes", readers were introduced to two of the contributors to *Prison Writing 15* with the news, "A shocking book has gone on sale in Scotland showcasing writing by two of the country's most notorious criminals." A psychologist, Professor Hannah Steinberg, "who builds profiles of people from what they have written" was called upon for her critical assessment of poems by Robert Mone and a short story by Paul Agutter. She was reported to be "amazed at her own accuracy", saying "both texts got me down. But in some ways they are quite brilliant too."

In the ten-year lifespan of *Prison Writing*, no one had ever before reported being shocked or even "got down" by the journal's content. For the first such complaint to come from the *News of the World* was considered quite an achievement.

Autobiography has long been the preferred medium for the majority of prison writers, although a wealth of other literary works have been published and performed over the past fifty years or so. There have been successful film and television scripts and plays for the theatre, but no novel has made a critical or commercial impact. Hugh Collins's two fictional works novels dealt with the Glasgow crime world, Jimmy Boyle's debut novel drew on dark experience, but they were not set in prison. The dynamics of prison wings and exercise yards brim with human interaction and everyday dramas, but in modern times no inmate or ex-inmate has captured that in a novel.

Neither writers, academics, prisoners nor anyone else interviewed during the research for this book could shed any light on the situation. John McVicar, who wrote the script for the movie based on his life story, did suggest that fiction requires more writing skills than autobiography or memoir and, apart from Jeffrey Archer, prisoners are unlikely to have had the necessary "apprenticeship" [5] – but this does not explain the success that Edward Bunker and Chester Himes enjoyed with novels set in American prisons.

The much-publicised iniquities of the British prison system in the early twenty-first century show no sign of easing. Alongside overcrowding, drug abuse, suicide, lack of preparation for release, high re-offending rates and all other ills that the authorities must struggle to cope with, the issue of whether prisoners should be allowed to write for publication might appear unimportant.

But prisoners write about these problems from the inside. They write of what they experience in cells and punishment blocks, on landings and prison yards. The best of them, the ones that tend to endure, write personal accounts that give insight into the causes of offending, the ability to cope with long periods of imprisonment and the transformation from criminal to responsible citizen. From them our knowledge can be enhanced. Prison writers should not be hindered or ignored.

Epilogue

Bibliography

Aitken J., **Porridge and Passion**, Continuum, 2005

Amis M., **Experience**, Jonathan Cape, 2000

Arrowsmith P., **Somewhere Like This**, Panther 1971

B.2.15, **Among the Broad-arrow Men – a Plain Account of English Prison**, A.C. Black, 1924

Baker P., **Blood Posse**, Picador, 1994

Balfour J. B., **My Prison Life**, Chapman and Hall, 1907

Behan B., **Borstal Boy**, Hutchinson, 1958

Behan B., **Hold Your Hour and Have Another**, Hutchinson, 1963

Behan B., **The Complete Plays**, Methuen, 1978

Bourke S. **The Springing of George Blake**, Cassell, 1970

Boyle J., **A Sense of Freedom**, Canongate, 1977

Boyle J., **The Pain of Confinement – Prison Diaries**, Canongate, 1984

Boyle J., **Hero of the Underworld**, Serpent's Tail, 1999

Brady I., **The Gates of Janus - Serial Killing and its Analysis**, Feral House, 2001

Brandreth G., **Created in Captivity**, Hodder & Stoughton, 1972

Bunker E., **Mr Blue – Memoirs of a Renegade**, No Exit, 1999

Caird R., **A Good and Useful Life**, Hart-Davis- McGibbon, 1974

Cameron J., **Prisons and Punishment in Scotland**, Canongate, 1983

Carr R., **Brixton Bwoy**, Fourth Estate, 1998

Carrell C. & Lang J. (eds), **The Special Unit, Barlinnie Prison – its evolution through its art**, Third Eye, 1982

Chessman C., **Cell 2455 Death Row**, Prentice Hall, 1954

Bibliography

Collins H., **Autobiography of a Murderer**, Macmillan, 1997

Collins H., **Walking Away**, Canongate, 2000

Collins H., **No Smoke**, Canongate Crime, 2001

Collins H., **The Licensee**, Canongate Crime, 2002

Davies I., **Writers in Prison**, Blackwell, 1990

Davies M., **Prisoners of Society: Attitudes and Aftercare**, Routledge & Kegan Paul, 1974

Dendrickson G., & Thomas F., **The Truth About Dartmoor**, Gollancz, 1954

Ellman, R., **Oscar Wilde**, Hamish Hamilton, 1987

FF 8282, **A Prison Diary – Belmarsh: Hell**, Macmillan, 2002

Hart-Davis, R (ed), **Selected Letters of Oscar Wilde**, Oxford University Press, 1979

Henry J., **Who Lie In Gaol**, Gollancz, 1952

Henry J., **Yield to the Night**, Gollancz, 1954

Hercules T., **Labelled a Black Villain**, Fourth Estate, 1989

Hoskison J., **Inside – One Man's Experience of Prison**, Murray, 1998

Ives G., **A History of Penal Methods**, Stanley Paul, 1914

James E., **A Life Inside – a Prisoner's Notebook**, Atlantic, 2003

Jameson N. & Allison E., **Strangeways 1990 – a Serious Disturbance**, Larkin, 1995

Johnston R., **Inside Out**, Michael Joseph, 1989

Krishnamma, S., **The Ballad of the Lazy L**, Rani Press, 1994

Leech M., **A Product of the System**, Gollancz, 1992

Lewis P. (ed) **Bards Behind Bars**, HMP Maidstone, 2000

Macartney W., **Walls Have Mouths**, Gollancz, 1936

McVicar J., **McVicar by Himself**, Hutchinson, 1974

McVicar J., **McVicar by Himself**, Artnik, 2002

McVicar J., **Dead on Time**, Blake 2002

Norman F., **Bang to Rights**, Secker & Warburg, 1958

O'Connor J., **The Eleventh Commandment**, Seagull, 1976

O'Connor U., **Brendan Behan**, Hamish Hamilton, 1970

O'Sullivan M., **Brendan Behan**, Blackwater Press, 1997

Parker N., **Parkhurst Tales**, Smith Gryphon, 1994

Parker N., **Parkhurst Tales 2**, Blake, 1997

Pearce J., **The Unmasking of Oscar Wilde**, Harper Collins, 2001

Peckham A., **A Woman in Custody**, Fontana, 1985

Phelan J., **Jail Journey**, Secker & Warburg, 1940

Piper R., **Take Him Away**, Queenspark Books, 1995

Plimpton G. (ed) **The Writer's Chapbook**, Penguin, 1992

Probyn W., **Angel Face – The Making of a Criminal**, Allen & Unwin, 1977

Reynolds A., **Tightrope – a Matter of Life and Death**, Sidgwick and Jackson, 1991

Reynolds A., **Insanity**, Fourth Estate, 1996

Reynolds B., **Autobiography of a Thief**, Bantam, 1995

Roby P., **Oscar Wilde**, Cambridge University Press, 1988

Rose G., **The Struggle for Penal Reform**, Stevens and Sons, 1961

Shannon T. & Morgan C., **Invisible Crying Tree**, Doubleday, 1996

Smith K., **Inside Time**, Harrap, 1989

Smith R., **A Few Kind Words and a Loaded Gun**, Viking, 2004

Steele J., **The Bird that Never Flew**, Sinclair-Stevenson, 1992

Taki, **Nothing to Declare – Prison Memoirs**, Viking, 1991

Viccei V., **Knightsbridge – the Robbery of the Century**, Blake, 1992

Ward J., **Ambushed – My Story**, Vermilion, 1993

Wilde O., **De Profundis and Other Writings** (including The Ballad of Reading Gaol), Penguin Classics, 1986

Willets, P., **Invisible Bars**, Epworth Press, 1965

Wilson B., **Nor Iron Bars a Cage**, Kimber, 1964

Wilson, H., **Angels of Death**, Argyll, 1994

Winters L., **The Silent Scream and poems**, EUSPB, 1979

Wyner R., **From the Inside – Dispatches from a Prison**, Aurum Press, 2003

Zeno, **Life**, Macmillan, 1968

Other sources:

Arts Council of Great Britain, Writers in Prisons information pack, 1993

Howard League Journal of Criminal Justice, Vol. 38 No.3, 1999

Howard League Journal of Criminal Justice , Vol 41, No. 5, 2002

Howard League Journal of Criminal Justice , Vol 2, No. 2, 2003

Prison Magazines – a Survey and Guide, Prison Reform Trust, 1994

Prison Poetry, Burnbake Trust, 1991

Prison Statistics England and Wales 2002, H.O. Cm5996

Prison Poets, Hampshire Probation Service, 1987

Prison Writing Vols. 1-14, Sheffield, 1992- 1999

Prison Writing Vols. 15-16, Waterside Press, 2001 & 2002

Raw Edge 5, 1997

Footnote Reference

] Foreword

[1] *The Independent*, 12 February, 1994.

[2] Interview with the author, published in **Prison Writing 8**, 1996.

[3] See *Bunker, No Beast So Fierce* (1973), *The Animal Factory* (1977), *Little Boy Blue* (1981) and *Dog Eat Dog* (1996); *Himes, Cast The First Stone* (1952).

[4] McVicar and Boyle's non-fiction will be discussed later. In 1999 Jimmy Boyle published his first novel, **Hero of the Underworld**.

[5] Ion Davies. **Writers in Prison**, Blackwell, 1990.

1] The Governor was strong upon the Regulations Act

[1] Richard Ellman. **Oscar Wilde**, Hamish Hamilton 1987.

[2] Extracts from *De Profundis* taken from Penguin Classics Edition, **De Profundis and Other Writings**, 1986.

[3] Rupert Hart-Davis (Ed). **Selected Letters of Oscar Wilde**, Oxford University Press 1979.

[4] See *The Guardian* 28 November 1997.

[5] Wilde, **Ibid.**

[6] Joseph Pearce, **The Unmasking of Oscar Wilde**, Harper Collins 2001.

[7] Wilde, **Ibid.**

[8] **Ibid.**

[9] **Ibid.**

[10] **Ibid.**

[11] Ellman.

[12] Wilde, **Ibid.**

[13] Hart-Davis.

[14] When the book was printed for the seventh time, in June 1899, Wilde agreed that his name should appear as author, beside "C.3.3".

[15] The Ballad of Reading Gaol was dedicated to "C.T.W. Sometime Trooper of the Royal Horse Guards, obiit H.M.Prison, Reading, Berkshire. July 7, 1896".

[16] **Wilde**, Penguin Classics Edition, 1986.

[17] Wilde, **Ibid.** The governor of Reading at the time of the execution was Colonel J. Isaacson, a severe disciplinarian and predecessor of Major Nelson who allowed Wilde the materials to write *De Profundis*.

[18] **Ibid**

[19] *Daily Chronicle*, 28 May 1897 under the heading: "The Case Of Warder Martin, Some Cruelties Of Prison Life". Reprinted in *Letters*.

[20] Wilde, **Ibid.**

[21] "Most expressed reservations but recognised that a literary event of importance had occurred." Ellmann.

[22] *The Sunday Times*, 5 July, 1992. The books reviewed were **A Product of The System** by Mark Leech and **The Bird That Never Flew** by John Steele.

[23] Jabez Spencer Balfour, **My Prison Life**, Chapman and Hall, 1907.

[24] **Ibid.**

[25] **Ibid.**

[26] B.2.15, A.C. Black, 1924. The title is a reference to prisoners' uniforms, which were marked with broad arrows.

[27] **Ibid.**

[28] **Ibid.**

[29] **Ibid.**

[30] Victor Gollancz, 1954.

[31] W.F.R. Macartney, **Walls Have Mouths,** Gollancz, 1936.

[32] **Ibid.**

[33] **Ibid.**

[34] **Ibid.**

[35] **Ibid.**

[36] **Ibid.**

[37] Jim Phelan, **Jail Journey**, Secker & Warburg, 1940.

[38] **Ibid.**

[39] For background information on Jim Phelan I am grateful to Mike Nelliss, whose article 'Gypsies, Tramps and Thieves – the Storytelling of Jim Phelan' was published in **Prison Writing 5**, 1994.

40 Phelan, **Ibid.**

41 **Ibid.**

42 Frank Norman, **Bang To Rights**, Secker & Warburg, 1958.

43 Brendan Behan, **Borstal Boy**, Hutchinson, 1958.

44 Christopher Logue in *The New Statesman and Nation.* Date unknown, cited in **Brendan Behan**, O'Connor U., Hamish Hamilton, 1970.

45 **Ibid.**

46 *The Times*, 10 August 1948.

2] Life stories

1 *The Times*, Law Report, 2 January 2004. Nilsen was granted leave to appeal in May, 2004.

2 **McVicar by Himself**, John McVicar. Hutchinson, 1974.

3 John Pearson, Weidenfeld & Nicholson, 1972 – generally considered to be the definitive book on the Krays.

4 *McVicar*, released in 1980, starred Roger Daltrey of The Who rock group as John McVicar.

5 **A Sense of Freedom**, Jimmy Boyle. Canongate, 1977.

6 **Ibid.**

7 Jimmy Boyle, **The Pain of Confinement, Prison Diaries**, Canongate, 1984.

8 Jimmy Boyle, **Hero of the Underworld**, Serpent's Tail, 1999.

[9] **Boyle**, 1984.

[10] **McVicar by Himself**, Artnik, 2002.

[11] John Steele, **The Bird That Never Flew**, Sinclair-Stevenson, 1992. Revised and re-published by Mainstream, 2002.

[12] See Skelton D. & Brownlie L. Frightener – **The Glasgow Ice Cream Wars**, Mainstream, 1992. Also, T.C. Campbell and Reg McKay, **The Wilderness Years**. Canongate, 2002.

[13] Opened in 1973, the Special Unit at HMP Barlinnie, Glasgow, was in existence for twenty-one years.

[14] Hugh Collins, **Autobiography of a Murderer**, Macmillan, 1997.

[15] **Ibid.**

[16] Hugh Collins, **Walking Away**, Canongate, 2000.

[17] **Canongate Crime**, 2001.

[18] **Canongate Crime**, 2002.

[19] Valerio Viccei, **Knightsbridge, the Robbery of the Century**, Blake, 1992.

[20] This was the official estimate in the case. The sub-title of Viccei's book is **How I escaped with £60 million from the Safe Deposit Centre**, but there is no reference to such an amount in the text.

[21] *The Guardian*, 20 April, 2000 – 'Wolf's last stand'.

[22] Letter to author, 1991.

[23] Interview with the author, HMP Parkhurst, 1992, published in **Prison Writing 2**, 1993.

[24] Mark Leech, **A Product of the System**, Gollancz,1992.

[25] Published originally (1995) by Oxford University Press as **The Prisoners' Handbook**; later by Waterside Press as **The Prisons Handbook**. Most recently published by MLA Press.

[26] FF 8282, **A Prison Diary**, sub-titled **Belmarsh: Hell**, Macmillan, 2002.

[27] *Daily Mail*, 5 October, 2002.

[28] *The Observer*, 6 October, 2002

[29] FF 8282.

[30] **Ibid.**

[31] **Ibid.**

[32] *Independent on Sunday*, 13 October 2002.

[33] 'Old Lags' and 'Lucky Bastard', **Prison Writing 2**, 1992. See later pages for Razor Smith's poetry, fiction and journalism.

[34] Correspondence with the author, 2005.

[35] **Ibid.**

[36] Razor Smith, **A Few Kind Words and a Loaded Gun – the Autobiography of a Career Criminal**, Viking, 2004

[37] **Ibid.**

[38] **Ibid.**

[39] **Ibid.**

[40] Robert McCrum, reviewing **A Prison Diary, Volume Two**, Jeffery Archer. *Observer*, 27 July, 2003.

[41] Zeno's real identity remains unknown, despite considerable efforts to discover it by the author.

[42] Zeno, **Life**, Macmillan, 1968.

[43] **Ibid.**

[44] **Ibid.**

[45] **Ibid.**

[46] **Ibid.**

[47] Research indicated that after ten years in custody, a prisoner's psychological health was prone to deteriorate, thus most lifers were released within this period.

[48] Rod Caird, **A Good and Useful Life**, Hart-Davis, McGibbon, 1974.

[49] **The Prison Rules, Statutory Instrument 388**, 1964. The 'rules' to which Caird refers were apparently in each cell, printed on cards. These were supplementary to the Prison Rules 1952.

[50] Caird.

[51] John Hoskison, **Inside – One Man's Experience of Prison**, John Murray, 1998.

[52] *The Guardian* 29 January, 2001.

[53] Jonathan Aitken, **Porridge and Passion**, Continuum, 2005.

[54] S.R. Krishnamma, **The Ballad of the Lazy L**, Rani Press, 1994.

[55] **Ibid.**

[56] **Ibid.**

[57] 'Alarm Watches: an Opinion', and 'Charly's Brother', **Prison Writing 4 & 5**, 1994.

[58] Quoted in publicity material.

[59] Taki, **Nothing To Declare: Prison Memoirs**, Viking, 1991.

[60] **Ibid.**

[61] Norman Parker, **Parkhurst Tales**, Smith Gryphon, 1994.

[62] See Mike Nellis, **The Howard League Journal of Criminal Justice,** Vol 41, No 5, December 2002.

[63] Parker, **Ibid.**

[64] Norman Parker, **Parkhurst Tales 2**, Blake, 1997.

[65] Walter Probyn, **Angel Face – The Making of a Criminal**, Allen & Unwin, 1977.

[66] **Prison Statistics England and Wales**, 2002, H.O. Cm5996.

[67] Trevor Hercules, **Labelled a Black Villain**, Fourth Estate, 1989.

[68] Joan Henry, **Who Lie In Gaol**, Victor Gollancz, 1952. The film on which it was based was titled *The Weak and the Wicked.*

[69] Joan Henry, **Yield to the Night**, Gollancz, 1954. Filmed with the same title, starring Diana Dors.

[70] Gordon Rose, **The Struggle for Penal Reform**, Stevens and Sons, London, 1961.

[71] Henry, 1952.

[72] See Mike Nellis, Remembering Joan Henry in **Prison Writing 3**, 1993.

[73] See obituary *Daily Telegraph*, 1 January, 2001.

[74] Various women associated with the Suffragettes, not included here as they were politically, rather than criminally motivated.

[75] Audrey Peckham, **A Woman in Custody**, Fontana, 1985.

[76] Wendy Woods, *The Guardian*, 31 July, 1985.

[77] Rosie Johnston, **Inside Out**, Michael Joseph, 1989.

[78] *The Observer*, 13 January 1991.

[79] Anna Reynolds, **Tightrope – a Matter of Life and Death**, Sidgwick and Jackson, 1991.

[80] **Ibid.**

[81] *The Times*, 26 January, 1991.

[82] Interview with the author, published in **Prison Writing 6**, 1995.

[83] Ruth Wyner, 'The Festive Season in Prison', in **Prison Writing 15**, 2001.

[84] Ruth Wyner, **From the Inside, Dispatches from a Women's Prison**, Aurum Press, 2003.

[85] **Ibid.**

[86] **Ibid.**

[87] Phoebe Willetts, **Invisible Bars**, Epworth Press, 1965.

[88] Pat Arrowsmith, **Somewhere Like This**, Panther, 1971.

[89] Judith Ward, **Ambushed – My Story**, Vermilion, 1993.

[90] **Ibid.**

[91] **Ibid.**

3] Facts, Fictions, Poems & Plays

[1] Jimmy O'Connor, **The Eleventh Commandment**, Seagull, 1976.

[2] *The Independent*, 13 September, 1997.

[3] Interview with the author, **Prison Writing 1**, 1992.

[4] John McVicar, **Dead On Time**, Blake Publishing, 2002.

[5] Brendan Behan's columns in the Irish Press were published as a collection, *Hold Your Hour and Have Another*, Hutchinson, 1963.

[6] Deputy Governor of Parkhurst Prison, *ex parte* Leech [1988] 1 All ER 485.

[7] *The Guardian*, 9 May, 1990.

[8] 'Locked into a Fight for Survival', *The Guardian*, 17 October, 1990.

[9] Leech.

[10] Letter to author, 16 January, 1996.

[11] 'The Prisoner', **Prospect**, June 1997.

[12] **Ibid**, December 1996

[13] **Ibid**, April, 1997

[14] *The Times*, 3 June, 1998. Interviewed by Jason Cowley

[15] **Prospect**, December 1998, extracted in *The Times*, 22 November 1998

[16] Smith, 2004, See also Razor Smith's comments on the **Punch** articles in an interview with the author, published in **Prison Writing 15**, 2001.

[17] The article was later published in John McVicar's **Dead On Time**, 2002.

[18] Erwin James, **A Life Inside – a prisoner's notebook**. Atlantic Books, 2003.

[19] *Guardian Society*, 14 January, 1998. 'Time of grief, Diary of a prison inmate'.

[20] *The Guardian*,'Real Lives', 3 January, 2000.

[21] The final 'A life inside' column appeared on 12 August, 2004 and described Erwin James's release after serving twenty years. He continued writing for *The Guardian*, his column titled 'A life outside'.

[22] *The Guardian*, 'A Life Inside', 15 November, 2001.

[23] **Ibid** 8 August, 2002.

[24] **Ibid** 29 January, 2001.

[25] **Ibid** 26 November, 2002.

[26] **Ibid** 10 May, 2001.

[27] **Ibid** 9 October, 2002.

[28] *The Guardian*, 2 June, 2003.

[29] Nicki Jameson and Eric Allison, **Strangeways 1990 – A Serious Disturbance**, Larkin Publications, 1995.

[30] Interview with the author, published in **Prison Writing 8**, 1996.

[31] Jimmy Boyle, **Hero of the Underworld**, Serpent's Tail, 1999. The characters

had been a long time in gestation. Photographs of two sculptures by Boyle, titled 'Hero of the Underworld' and 'Lockjaw' appeared in **The Special Unit. Barlinnie Prison – its evolution through its art**, edited by Christopher Carrell and Joyce Laing (Third Eye Centre, 1982). In the book, Boyle stated he was writing a play, of which Hero was the central character. He said that as he developed the main characters he sculpted them. The work had to be curtailed when he was transferred from Barlinnie to Saughton Prison in Edinburgh, shortly before he was released.

[32] Howard Wilson, **Angels of Death**, Argyll, 1994.

[33] Anna Reynolds, **Insanity**, Fourth Estate, 1996.

[34] The *Daily Telegraph*, 5 March 1994.

[35] *The Observer*, 20 February 1994.

[36] **Prison Writing 3**, 1993.

[37] **Vengeance – A Passport Anthology**, Passport/ Serpent's Tail, 1993.

[38] **Prison Writing 16**, Waterside Press, 2002.

[39] **Ibid.**

[40] **Prison Writing 12**, 1998.

[41] **Prison Writing 10**, 1997.

[42] **Ibid.**

[43] **Prison Writing 16**, 2002.

[44] **Prison Writing 4**, 1995.

[45] **Prison Writing 16**, 2002.

[46] **Ibid.**

[47] **Ibid.**

[48] **Prison Writing 13**, 1998.

[49] Ken Smith, **Inside Time**, Harrap, 1989.

[50] John Fuller and P.J. Kavangh, Ruth Padel, Jo Shapcott and Matthew Sweeney in Koestler Award Scheme report, 2002, published by The Koestler Award Trust.

[51] Another indication of prisoners' preference for poetry compared to other forms of writing was seen in a **Prison Writing** competition in 1995. Entries numbered 36 works of non-fiction, 74 of fiction and 406 individual poems.

[52] Ellman.

[53] Larry Winters, **The Silent Scream and poems**, EUSPB, Edinburgh, 1979.

[54] **Ibid.**

[55] In **The Pain of Confinement**, Jimmy Boyle, writes: "Larry and I discussed the 'silent scream' – that moment when one is alone in the locked cell facing the full horror of confinement. Those of us who have experienced long periods of confinement immediately recognise the tortuous 'silent scream', but rarely talk about it." (Diary entry for 2 November, 1974).

[56] Winters, **Ibid**.

[57] **Ibid**.

[58] **Ibid**.

[59] **Ibid**.

[60] Larry Winters' life and work was later celebrated in a film, also titled *The Silent Scream*.

[61] **Prison Poetry**, Burnbake Trust, Southampton, 1991.

[62] See Alex Alexandrowicz and David Wilson, **The Longest Injustice**, Waterside, 1999.

[63] **Prison Poets**, Hampshire Probation Service, Winchester, 1987.

[64] **Prison Writing 2**, 1992. Reproduced here in full, copyright Razor Smith.

[65] *The Independent*, 7 December, 1993.

[66] **Prison Writing 5**, 1994.

[67] Bruce Reynolds, **Autobiography of a Thief**, Bantam, 1995.

[68] Interview with the author, 2002.

[69] O'Connor, 1976.

[70] *The Independent*, 13 September 1997.

[71] Interview with the author in London, 2002.

[72] *The Guardian*, 25 November, 1987.

[73] *The Times*, 9 August 1986.

[74] *The Times*, 23 April, 1989.

[75] *The Sunday Times*, 1 March, 1989.

[76] *The Independent*, 3 May, 1989.

[76] Interview with the author, published in **Prison Writing 6**, 1995.

[78] See **Prison Writing 4**, 1994.

⁷⁹ Tom Shannon and Christopher Morgan, **Invisible Crying Tree**, Doubleday, 1996.

⁸⁰ Brian Wilson, **Nor Iron Bars a Cage**, William Kimber, 1964.

⁸¹ Ian Brady, **The Gates of Janus**, Feral House, Los Angeles, USA, 2001.

⁸² **Ibid.**

⁸³ **Ibid**.

⁸⁴ **Ibid**.

⁸⁵ *The Independent*, 14 January, 2004.

4] Inner forces

¹ He was released after serving four years.

² O'Sullivan.

³ Edward Bunker, **Mr Blue –Memoirs of a Renegade**, No Exit Press, 1999.

⁴ Interview with author, published in **Prison Writing 11**, 1997.

⁵ Boyle, 1984.

⁶ Phelan, 1940.

⁷ **Ibid.**

⁸ *The Observer*, 22 November 1998.

⁹ Interview with author, 2002.

10 Letter to author, 18 September 2002.

11 Letter to author, November 2004.

12 **Ibid.**

13 Interview with author, **Prison Writing 15**, 2001.

14 Interview with author, 2002.

15 *The Mirror*, 7 October, 2002.

16 Taki, **Ibid**, 1991.

17 For details of the books Wilde received in prison, see Hart-Davis.

18 Quoted by Joseph Pearce in **The Unmasking of Oscar Wilde**, Harper Collins, 2000.

19 Peter Roby, **Oscar Wilde**, Cambridge University Press, 1988.

20 John McVicar, **McVicar by Himself**, 2002

21 Tom Wolfe and E.W. Johnson, (Eds) **The New Journalism**, Picador, 1975

22 Interview with author, published in **Prison Writing 1**, 1992

23 Interview with author, **Prison Writing 11**, 1997

24 Phelan.

25 Henry, 1952.

26 See: O'Sullivan.

27 Macartney.

[28] **Ibid.**

[29] O'Connor, 1975.

[30] *The Times*, 3 June, 1998.

[31] Interview with author, published in **Prison Writing 15**, Waterside Press, 2001.

[32] Interview with author, 2002.

[33] Interview with author, 2002.

[34] Interview with author, published in **Prison Writing 6**, 1995.

[35] Interview with author, 2002.

[36] Hercules.

[37] **Raw Edge 5**, 1997. In black culture, especially American, a toaster is one who tells a narrative story told in rhyme or song.

[38] Leech.

[39] *The Guardian*, 7 December, 2002.

[40] Brendan Behan, 1958.

[41] **Ibid.**

[42] Phelan. "A few words about the convict categories for warders may help to an understanding of the various official types. A warder was, progressing downward, a bleed'n gent, bleed'n good, thumbs up, all right, not bad, a bit crooked, wicked, a basterd, a bitches basterd, and bleed'n murder. In the categories at either end of the list there were only one or two people."

[43] Bruce Reynolds, 1995.

[44] **Prison Writing** 7, 1995.

[45] Quotations taken from **The Writer's Chapbook**, edited interviews from the *Paris Review*, Penguin, 1992.

[46] Cohen in Probyn.

[47] **Ibid.**

[48] Boyle, 1977.

[49] Entry for 30 May, 1977 in Boyle, 1984.

[50] Henry, 1952.

[51] Hoskison.

[52] Steele.

[53] Reg Wilson, 'Hope it Rains Again', **Prison Writing 16**, Waterside Press, 2002.

[54] Letter to author, March 2002.

[55] Smith, 2004.

[56] Hercules.

[57] Martin Amis, **Experience**, Jonathan Cape, 2000.

[58] Interview with author, published in **Prison Writing 2**, 1993.

[59] Ian Brady, **The Gates of Janus** – Serial Killing and its Analysis, Feral House, Los Angeles, USA, 2001.

[60] *Sunday Telegraph*, 2 December, 2001.

[61] *The Times*, 25 September 2001.

[62] Both Boyle quotes are from his introduction to Carrell and Laing, (eds) 1981.

[63] McVicar, 1974.

[64] Interview with author, published in **Prison Writing 15**, 2001.

[65] *The Guardian*, 21 April, 2003.

[66] Letter to author, 2003.

[67] Interview with author, 2002.

[68] Interview with author, published in **Prison Writing 11**, 1996

[69] *The Times*, 13 August, 1994

[70] Wilde, O. *De Profundis*, first published 1905.

[71] 1 October, 1897, in Hart-Davis, OUP 1979.

[72] **McVicar by Himself**, revised and re-published, 2002.

[73] See **Prison Writing 2**, 1993 *Remembering Joan Henry*, Mike Nellis.

[74] *The Guardian*, 7 January, 1999.

5] Time and Opportunity

[1] In the case Becker v Home Office in 1972, Lord Denning, then head of the Court of Appeal (Civil Division), ruled that the Prison Rules did not give prisoners any rights at all.

[2] Smith, 1989.

[3] Paul Ruddock, 'Why Write?' **Prison Writing 6**, 1995.

[4] Letter to author, 2002.

[5] Published by Continuum in 2004 and 2005.

[6] Interview with author, 2002.

[7] See **Raw Edge 5**, 1997.

[8] McVicar, 2002.

[9] Hoskison.

[10] Zeno, **Ibid**, 1968.

[11] Quoted by Giles Brandreth in **Created in Captivity**, Hodder & Stoughton, 1972.

[12] Reynolds, 1991.

[13] *The Times*, 3 June, 1998, 'Born to be bad' by Jason Cowley.

[14] Phelan.

[15] *Sunday Express*, 14 August, 1994

[16] *Daily Telegraph*, 5 March, 1994.

[17] O'Connor, 1976.

[18] Interview with author, published in **Prison Writing 15**, 2001

[19] Ward.

[20] Interview with author, published in **Prison Writing 2**, 1993.

[21] *Sunday Times*, 25 November 2001.

[22] Arts Council of Great Britain, **Writers in Prisons** information pack, 1993.

[23] *The Guardian*, 19 October, 1994.

[24] Letter to author, 2003.

[25] Interview with the author, published in **Prison Writing 6**, 1995.

[26] *The Guardian*, 7 January, 1999.

[27] Ron Piper, **Take Him Away**. Queenspark Books, Brighton, 1995.

[28] *The Guardian*, 7 January, 1999.

[29] **Ibid.**

[30] Author's discussion with inmates at HMP Maghaberry, 14 March, 2001. Also, questionnaires completed by inmates.

[31] Interview with author, published in **Prison Writing 16**, Waterside Press, 2002.

[32] Letter to author, 2004.

[33] Talk on working in prison for Northern Ireland Voluntary Trust, Belfast, 2001.

[34] Viccei. John Marriott, Governor of HMP Parkhurst, was made a scapegoat by politicians following an escape from the prison in 1995. He had for a long time urged the Home Office to improve security at the prison. A popular man who had the respect of prisoners, he resigned. He died in 1998.

35 *The Guardian* 21 April, 2003.

36 **Ibid.**

37 **Raw Edge 5**, 1997.

38 See W Macartney, on *Parkhurst News*, 1933-35.

39 Brandreth.

40 **Ibid.**

41 Sean Bourke, **The Springing of George Blake**, Cassell, 1970.

42 Smith, 2004.

43 **Bards Behind Bars**, ed. Peter J.Lewis, HMP Maidstone, 2000.

44 Letter to the author, November 2003.

45 **The Prisons Handbook**, ed. Mark Leech, MLA Press, 2005 The article first appeared in the 2002 edition, thus the figure of twenty-eight may not be accurate for 2005.

46 **Prospect**, March 1997

47 Smith, 2004.

48 **Prison Writing 14**, 1999.

49 **Ibid.**

50 Interview with author, 2002.

51 Letter to author, 2002.

6] Inhibitions

[1] Ioan Davies, **Writers in Prison**, Blackwell, 1990.

[2] See the Woodcock Report into prison security, following the escape of prisoners from HMP Whitemoor in 1994.

[3] Letter to author, 15 November 2004.

[4] *The Guardian*, 11 September, 2001.

[5] *The Times*, 2 January, 2004.

[6] Reginald Kray, **Born Fighter**, Century, 1990.

[7] *Daily Mirror*, 28 November, 2005.

[8] Interview with author, 2002.

[9] Razor Smith, 2004.

[10] Letter to author, 2002.

[11] Steele.

[12] Wyner.

[13] **Ibid.**

[14] Interview with author, 2002.

[15] Carrell & Laing.

[16] **Prison Magazines – a Survey and Guide**, published by Prison Reform Trust, 1994.

[17] *The Guardian* 23 August 1991.

[18] Interview with author, 2002.

[19] *The Observer Review*, 21 December, 1977.

[20] *Daily Express*, 12 October, 2002.

[21] Standing Order 4 (51) states that prisoners may enter "public competitions" and may submit art work or work of literary merit for sale or publication for profit through any charitable organisation (e.g. the Koestler Trust), with the approval of the governor. Money prizes or income may be credited to private cash.

[22] Correspondence with the author, 2004.

[23] Ibid.

[24] Prison Ombudsman's response, dated 1 August 2002, to Matthew Williams' complaint. Case 10920/02.

[25] In an interview with the author in December 2002, the Prisons and Probation Ombudsman, Stephen Shaw emphasised his belief that inmates should be able to publish, and be paid. He said, "I have no problem with prisoners publishing while serving their sentences. I think they should have the right. Is it proportionate to prevent somebody from exercising their right to publish? I don't believe it is. The second point is, we are all very interested in the re-settlement agenda and if somebody has actually got some writing talent, they should be allowed to exercise that. They could put the money aside for when they are released and it may be a way they can actually make a lawful living."

[26] *Inside Time*, December 2005.

[27] McVicar, 2002.

[28] Interview with the author, 2002.

[29] Terry Fossett in *Mail on Sunday*, 13 October, 2002.

[30] Correspondence with the author, 2002.

[31] Letter to author, 1992.

[32] Arts Council of United Kingdom Information Pack, 1993.

7] Effects

[1] See Mike Nelliss, **Prison Writing 3**, 1993.

[2] Rose.

[3] Caird.

[4] Home Office, **People in Prison**, 1969.

[5] Caird.

[6] Stan Cohen in Walter Probyn, **Angel Face, the Making of a Criminal**, Allen & Unwin, 1977.

[7] Joy Cameron, **Prisons and Punishment in Scotland**. Canongate, 1983.

[8] Alan Taylor was a journalist who had started life in the slums of Glasgow and been a prisoner in Dartmoor. His autobiography **From A Glasgow Slum to Fleet Street**, was published in 1949. Peter Wildeblood was imprisoned for homosexuality. His book **Against the Law**, played a part in the campaign that eventually brought about a reform of the law.

[9] Correspondence with author, 2004.

[10] Correspondence with author, 2004.

[11] Interview with author, 2002.

[12] Interview with author, 2002.

[13] Correspondence with author, 2005.

[14] *The Independent*, 23 April, 1995.

[15] Interview with author, 2002.

[16] Steve Morgan, 'Prisoner Lives: Critical Issues in Reading Prisoner Autobiography', **The Howard Journal of Criminal Justice**, Vol 38 No.3. August 1999.

[17] *Observer* 6 December 1998, 'Inside Wayne's World', by Anthony Andrew.

[18] Ellman, - "the length of the *Ballad* was necessary to shake confidence in the penal system; he knew that it must fall between poetry but he was prepared to face some artistic imperfection for the sake of changing what was intolerable."

[19] Foreword to Parker, 1994.

[20] James, 2003.

[21] **Prison Report**, 2002.

[22] Interview with author, 2002.

[23] Cohen in Probyn.

[24] McVicar, 2002.

[25] *Sunday Telegraph*, 21 June, 1998.

[26] *The Guardian*, 2 October, 1999.

[27] Correspondence with the author, January 2004.

[28] Cohen in Probyn.

[29] Morgan.

[30] Correspondence with author, 2005.

[31] Correspondence with the author, 2005.

[32] Interview with author, 2002.

[33] Martin Davies. **Prisoners of Society: Attitudes and Aftercare**, Routledge &Kegan Paul, 1974.

[34] Correspondence with author, 2005.

[35] Quoting from K.Plummer, **Documents of Life: An Introduction to the Problems and Literature of a Humanistic Method**. Unwin Hyam, London, 1983.

[36] Mike Nellis, **The Howard Journal of Criminal Justice**, Vol 41, No 5, December 2002.

[37] **Ibid.**

[38] Shannon & Morgan.

[39] Interview with author, 2002.

[40] *The Guardian*, 29 January, 2001.

[41] *The Sun*, 4 January, 2003.

[42] Razor Smith, 2004.

[43] *The Guardian*, 7 January, 1999.

[44] Carlo Gebler, talk to Northern Ireland Voluntary Trust, 8 November, 2001.

[45] O'Sullivan.

[46] Razor Smith, 2004.

[47] Interview with the author, 2002.

[48] Koestler Awards opening ceremony, London. 23 September, 2004.

[49] Interview with author, 2002.

[50] Letter to author, 2004.

[51] Interview with author, 2001, published in **PW15.**

[52] Interview with author, 2002.

[53] Interview with author, Parkhurst 1992, published in **PW2**, 1992.

[54] Boyle, 1984.

[55] **EUSPB**, Edinburgh, 1979.

[56] *Daily Telegraph*, 5 March, 1994.

[57] *The Guardian* 8 April, 2005.

[58] James, 2003.

[59] Doubleday, 1996.

[60] Interview with author, 2005.

[61] Interview with author, 2002.

[62] *The Guardian* 27 February, 2004.

[63] **Ibid.**

[64] **Ibid.**

[65] See Pearce.

[66] George Ives, **A History of Penal Methods**, Stanley Paul, 1914.

[67] B.2.15.

[68] Quoted in the publicity material for Collins' first novel, **No Smoke**, 2001.

[69] Interview with author, 2002.

[70] Correspondence with author, letter dated 18 December, 2002. Sir Douglas Hurd was home secretary 1985-89.

[71] Correspondence with author, 2002.

[72] Correspondence with author, 2005.

[73] Interview with author, 2002.

[74] In the 1950s Brendan Behan's play *The Quare Fellow* coincided with the campaign to abolish capital punishment, as did Jimmy O'Connor's television play *Three Clear Sundays* in 1963. Both were acknowledged as playing a part in the campaign. Peter Wildeblood's autobiography **Against the Law**, published following his conviction and imprisonment in the Montagu case of 1954, helped to change attitudes towards homosexuality.

[75] Interview with author, 2002.

[76] *Independent on Sunday*, 13 October, 2002.

[77] *The Sunday Times*, 6 October, 2002.

[78] *The Guardian,* 20 October, 2002.

[79] **Howard League Journal of Criminal Justice**, Vol 2, No.2, May 2003.

[80] *Daily Mail,* 7 October, 2002.

8] Those who oppose

[1] *The Sunday Times*, 31 March, 2002.

[2] Brady.

[3] *Sunday Herald*, 11 November, 2001.

[4] *Daily Mail*, 18 August 2001.

[5] Ibid.

[6] *Sunday Record*, 11 November, 2001.

[7] *Daily Express*, 25 September 2001.

[8] *Daily Record*, 30 November 2001.

[9] *Sunday Mail*, 26 January,1997.

[10] Interview with author, published in **Prison Writing 11**, 1997.

[11] **Ibid.**

[12] *Sunday Mail*, 28 April, 2001.

[13] *Daily Mail*, 11 February 1999.

[14] *The Times*, 8 October, 1989.

[15] Interview with author, 2002.

[16] *The Sunday Times*, 6 October, 2002.

[17] *The Sun*, 7 October, 2002.

[18] *Mirror*, 7 October, 2002.

[19] *Financial Times*, 5 November, 1996.

[20] Press Complaints Commission, 22 July, 1998.

[21] *The Guardian*, 11 July, 2003.

[22] Interview with author, 2002.

[23] Correspondence with the author, 2005.

[24] Correspondence with author, 2005.

[25] Correspondence with author, 2005.

9] Epilogue

[1] Carrel & Laing.

[2] Correspondence with author, 2005.

[3] Interview with the author, 2002.

[4] *News of the World*, 26 August, 2001.

[5] Interview with author, 2002.

Index

A Few Kind Words and a Loaded Gun 33-4, 67, 83, 131
A Good and Useful Life 37, 152
A Life Inside 60-1, 158
A Prison Diary 29-32, 145, 177, 184
A Product of the System 29, 57, 156
A Sense of Freedom 23-5, 87, 103, 110, 124, 157, 160, 173, 177
A Woman in Custody 47
Abbott, Jack Henry iv, 192
Agutter, Paul 70-1, 194
Aitken, Jonathan 38-9, 59, 114, 148, 155-6, 173-5, 187
Alba 80
Alexandrowicz, Alex 74
Allison, Eric 62, 172-3
Ambushed – My Story 119, 160
Amis, Martin 105, 130
Among The Broad-Arrow Men 9-10, 157, 175
Anderson, Clive 177
Anderson, Freddie 26
Angel Face – the Making of a Criminal 43-4, 102, 153, 162
Angels of Death 65
Archer, Jeffrey 29-32, 38, 41, 52, 61, 91, 98, 111, 145, 147, 149, 160, 177-8, 184-7, 192, 194
Arrowsmith, Pat 50
Autobiography of a Murderer 26-7, 175
Autobiography of a Thief 90, 100-1
Avenues 78

B.2.15 (nom-de-plume) 9, 10, 15, 18, 157
Baker, Phillip 66, 117, 171-2
Balfour, Jabez Spencer 8, 9, 15, 18, 52, 157
Bang To Rights 16, 93

Index

Bards Behind Bars 128
Barstow, Clare 70, 80, 89, 117, 143
Bart, Lionel 16
Bashforth, Tony 130
Beat Poets 72
Becker, Howard 153, 156
Behan, Brendan iii, 17, 18, 52, 56, 80-1, 86, 94, 98-9, 157, 167-8
Bell, Mary 186
Berlins, Marcel 130
Berry, Prof. Francis 74
Best, Stanley 128
Big Youth 97
Biggs, Ronnie 61
Billington, Rachel 130, 144
Birnberg, Benedict 106
Blake, George 36, 127
Blood Posse 66-7
Boethus ii
Borges, Jorge Luis 102
Borstal Boy 17-8, 52, 98-9, 168
Boswell, James 74
Bourke, Sean 127
Boyle, Jimmy iii, 23-4, 26-7, 52-3, 63-5, 72, 83, 87, 91, 103, 107, 110, 124, 154, 157, 160, 163, 167, 171, 173, 177, 180, 183, 191-2, 194
Bradley, Alfred 77
Bradley, Peter, MP 187
Brady, Ian 22, 82-3, 106, 120, 138-9, 174, 180
Brain, Billy 12
Brandreth, Giles 127
Brennan, Norman 181
Brittan, Leon 175
Brixton Bwoy 66-7, 122
Bronson, Charles 29, 130, 140
Brooke, Daphne 72, 96
Brown, Allan 180

Brown, Rap 97
Bunker, Edward ii, iii, 62-4, 86-7, 95, 130, 194
Bunyan, John ii, 19, 30
Burnbake Trust 74
Butler, R.A. 132

C.3.3 – see Wilde, Oscar 5, 9
Caird, Rod 36-7, 152-3
Callaghan, James 166
Cameron, Joy 154, 156
Campbell, Duncan 130, 144
Cantor, Prof. David 174
Carr, Rocky 66, 122
Cell 2455, Death Row 86-7
Cervantes iii
Channon, Olivia 47
Chessman, Caryl ii, 86
Clean Break 78
Cleaver, Eldridge 97
Clemmer, Donald 15
Cohen, Stan 43, 102, 119, 153-4, 159, 162
Collins, Hugh 26-7, 52-3, 63-5, 83, 87, 93, 107-8, 110, 130, 160, 167, 175, 180, 182, 191, 194
Coming Out Party 76
Conway, Mike 128
Cook, Martyn 128
Cooper, Mr Justice 166
Created in Captivity 127
Cresswell, Janet 78-9, 172
Curtis Brown, Spencer 110

Dalrymple, Theodore 161
Dante 91-2
Darkness at Noon 132
Davies, Angela 44, 97

Index

Davies, Ioan iv, 136
Davies, Martin 163-4
De Consolatione Philosophiae ii
De Profundis 1-8, 18-9, 35, 52, 85, 92-3, 191
de Sade, Marquis iii
Dead On Time 56
Defoe, Daniel iii
Dendrickson, George 11
Dickens, Charles iii, 98, 174
Divina Commedia 91-2
Dog Eat Dog 62
Don Quixote iii, 9
Dostoevsky iii, iv, 94-6, 120, 156
Douglas, Lord Alfred 1-3,
Dreyfus, Alfred 30
Dylan, Bob 96

Ede, James Chuter 19
Ellman, Richard 4
Ellroy, James 62
Ellsworth-Jones, Will 55
Evans, Rhian 147

FF 8282 – see Archer, Jeffrey 29-32
Fielding, Henry iii
Fings Ain't Wot They Used To Be 16
Fishman, Jack 55
Foreman, Freddie 41
Fraser, Frankie 41
From the Inside, Dispatches from a Women's Prison 49-50
Frost, Robert 102
Fyfe, Sir David Maxwell 45

Gallie, Phil, MSP 181
Garvey, Marcus 44, 97

Gavron, Jeremy 66, 111, 121-2, 167
Gébler, Carlo 122-4, 130-1, 155-6, 167-8, 188-9
Genet, Jean iii, 94-5
George, Barry 59
Glazer, Daphne 68
Glidewell, Lord Justice 50
Goldstein, Judge Simon, QC 166
Grace Abounding to the Chief of Sinners iii
Grass, Gunter 96
Green Volcano 14
Gunn, Thom 96

Hadaway, Tom 119-20
Haig, Earl 19
Haldane, Robert Burdon, MP 1-2, 92
Hall, Archibald 29, 140
Harris, Jane 121
Hattersley, Albert 101
Hayes, George 114
Hendry, Noeleen 121
Henry O 94-5
Henry, Joan 45-7, 50, 93, 103, 110-1, 152
Hercules, Trevor 44-5, 97, 105
Hero of the Underworld 24, 63-5, 183
Hesse, Hermann 96
Hillier, David 145
Himes, Chester iii, iv, 32, 194
Hoare, Tony 77-8, 96-7, 115-6, 120, 127, 132, 141, 163, 167, 169-70, 191, 193
Hobson, Harold 17
Holborough, Jacqueline 78
Hood, Thomas 92
Hooper, Mr Justice 38
Hoskison, John 37-8, 103-4, 110, 115, 160-1, 166
How To Write Radio Drama 98

Index

Howard League for Penal Reform 46, 152
Howard League Journal of Criminal Justice 156, 162, 164, 178
Howard, Anthony 177
Howard, Michael 59, 175
Hudson, Christopher 40
Huntley, Ian 140-1
Hurd, Sir Douglas 129, 175-6

In the Belly of the Beast 192
Insanity 65
Inside Out 47, 126
Inside Time (Ken Smith) 71, 120
Inside Time (newspaper) 49, 81, 129-30, 144, 147
Insider 128
Invisible Crying Tree 81, 165, 173
It Must Be Better Than Doing Porridge 77
It's Wandsworth 128
Ives, George 174

Jackman, Eileen 118
Jackson, George 44
Jail Journal 14
Jail Journey 14-15
James, Erwin 59-61, 108, 125, 140, 149, 158, 172, 184, 187
Johnson, Samuel 74, 102, 109
Johnston, Rosie 47, 183
Jordan 79
Jordan, Bill 128

Kafka 96
Katz, Ian 158
Kay, Mr Justice Maurice 21
Keeling, Mr 19
Kellaway, Kate 185
Kennedy, Helena, QC 156

Kentzer, Ian 108, 121
Kerouac, Jack 96
Kilbride, Danny 181
Killing For Company 21
King, Geordie 69-70
Kirwan, Bernard 86
Knightsbridge – the Robbery of the Century 27-8, 124-5
Koestler Award Scheme iv, 29, 35-6, 39, 61, 71, 85, 115, 117, 119, 128, 131-3, 145, 165, 168-9, 175, 192
Koestler, Arthur 131-2
Kray brothers 22, 26, 29, 41, 140
Krishnamma, S.R. 39-40, 110
Kropotkin 5

Labelled a Black Villain 44-5, 97, 105
Law and Order iii
Lawless, Mark D. 75-6
Lawson, Dominic 57
Leech, Mark 29, 56-7, 98, 156-7, 167
Lewis, Peter 128
Life 35-6, 93, 115
Lifer 14
London's Burning 78
Looking Towards a New Horizon 80
Lorca, Frederico Garcia 80
Lumsden, Paul 133-4
Lykiard, Alexis 121
Lyons, Juliet 178

Macartney, W.F.R. 11-13, 15, 18, 52, 93-5, 118, 152, 157
Mackenzie, Compton 11, 13
Mailer, Norman 97, 192
Malory, Sir Thomas ii
Mandela, Nelson ii
Mangold, Tom 158

Index

Mannhein, Hermann 15
Marks, Howard 130
Marriott, John 28
Martin, David 42
Maruna, Shadd 154-5, 161-2
Massie, Allan 175
Masters, Brian 21, 140, 156
Matthews, Rob 128
Mawdsley, Robert 42
McVicar by Himself 22-3, 92-3, 157, 184
McVicar, John iii, 7, 21, 23-5, 32, 40, 43, 51-3, 55-6, 59, 83, 92-3, 107, 109-10, 114-5, 126, 130, 148, 154, 156, 159-60, 163, 166-7, 170-1, 184, 191-2, 194
Mein Kampf 19
Minder 78, 97
Mitchell, John 14
Mone, Robert 194
Mooney, James 182
Mooney, William 27, 182
Morgan, Christopher 81, 165
Morgan, Steve 156, 162
Morte D'Arthur ii
Mortimer, John 156
Morton, James 130, 173
Moses, Colin 184
Mr Blue 62, 86
Murphy, Judge Michael, QC 155-6, 165-6, 176
My Prison Life 8-9

Nabakov, Vladimir 102
Narey, Martin 30-1
Nellis, Mike 15-16, 110, 164-5
Nelson, Major J.O. 2, 8
New Horizon 127
Newman, G.F. iii, 95

Nicholson, James 119
Nietzche 96
Nilsen, Denis 21, 32-3, 140, 148, 156, 174, 192
No Beast So Fierce 62
No Smoke 27, 64
Nor Iron Bars a Cage 81-2
Norman, Frank 16-17, 52, 93
Northcliffe, Lord 8
Nothing To Declare: Prison Memoirs 41, 91

O'Connor, Jimmy 55-6, 76-7, 83, 94-5, 118, 148, 167, 191
O'Sullivan, Michael 86, 168
Out of the Wood 121
Outlet 127

Page, Tim 121
Paines Plough 79
Palin, Michael 158-9
Paradise 79
Parker, Norman 41-2, 158, 167, 173, 185
Parkhurst Tales 41-2, 158, 173
Parris, Matthew 57
Parsons, Tony 91, 184-5
Patterson, Mark 166
Peckham, Audrey 47, 50
Phelan, Jim 13-16, 18, 35, 52, 56, 88, 93, 99-101, 116, 152, 157, 172, 191
Picasso, Pablo 34
Pickles, Judge James 29, 156
Pierrepoint, Albert 17
Piper, Ron 122
Plater, Alan 77, 120
Plummer, Lieut. Col. 8
Plymouth, Earl of 58
Poe, Edgar Allen 96
Porridge 16

Porridge and Passion 38-9
Prayers for People Under Pressure 114
Press Complaints Commission 185-7
Prison Poets 74
Prison Reform Trust iv, 81, 126, 132-3, 143-5, 158, 176, 178
Prison Writers 120
Prison Writing iv, v, 32, 40, 48-9, 52, 67-71, 75, 80, 89, 101, 104, 108, 113, 123, 130-1, 133- 4,142, 147, 149, 155, 162, 165, 170, 176, 183, 193-4
Probyn, Walter 'Angel Face' 22, 43-4, 52, 102, 119, 153-4, 159, 162, 191
Pryor, Stephen 118
Psalms for People Under Pressure 114
Pulp Fiction 62

Ramsbotham, Sir David 178
Rankin, Ian 83
Reade, Charles 174
Red 79
Redmond, John, MP 174
Regina (Nilsen) v Governor of Full Sutton Prison, 2004, 139-40
Rewired 129
Reynolds, Anna 47-9, 53, 63, 65, 79, 83, 96, 109, 116, 121, 129-30, 144
Reynolds, Bruce 76, 90, 100-1, 130
Reynolds, Reginald 15
Richardson, Charles 22, 41
Rogers, Lord Richard 58
Rooney, Babs 23
Rose, Gordon 152, 156
Ross, Robert 2, 5
Ruddock, Paul 113
Runyon, Damon 32, 95
Rusbridger, Alan 62
Russell, Bertrand 46
Ruthven, Diana 133
Screw The Nut 183

Seale, Bobby 97
Seascape 89, 147, 170
Seize the Time 97
Self, Will 32, 67, 93, 163, 176, 188, 193
Sereny, Gitta 186
Serge, Victor 156
Sewell, George 76-7
Shannon, Tom 81,165
Shaw, George Bernard 102
Shaw, Stephen 146, 159, 177, 187-9
Sherrin, Tom 117
Silverman, Sidney MP 17
Smith, Henry 12
Smith, Ken 71, 113, 120, 149
Smith, Noel 'Razor' 32-4, 59, 67, 74-5, 83, 90, 93, 95, 104-5, 107, 110-1, 118-9, 128, 130-1, 140-1, 148-9, 157, 167-8, 170, 185, 188, 191-3
Solzhenitsyn, Alexander iii, iv, 96, 156, 176
Sorted 127-8
Soyinka, Woyle iv
Sparks, Ruby 12
Standing Order 5b, 34-9, 138-9, 145-8, 189, 192
Steele, John 25-6, 52, 104
Steinbeck, John 95
Steinberg, Prof. Hannah 194
Stephen, Alex 124
Stone, Michael 58
Straffen, John 22
Straw, Jack 175
Styron, William 62
Sutcliffe, Peter 82
Sutherland, Prof. John 98

Take Him Away 122
Taki 40-1, 52, 91
Tap on the Shoulder 76

Index

Taylor, Alan 154
Taylor, George 12
Ten-a-Penny People 14
The Ballad of Reading Gaol 1, 5-8, 18, 72, 74, 85, 92-3, 95, 109, 157, 174-5, 177, 191
The Ballad of the Lazy L 39-40
The Bible 38, 91
The Bird That Never Flew 25-6, 104
The Cauldron 35
The Dream of Eugene Aram 92
The Eleventh Commandment 83, 94
The Facts Speak for Themselves 98
The Garden Girls 78
The Gates of Janus – Serial Killing and its Analysis 81-2, 106, 120, 139, 180-1
The Hostage 17-18
The House of Bernard Alba 80
The Key 143
The Killing Fields 40
The Licensee 27, 64
The New Journalism 93
The One-sided Wall 78, 172
The Pain of Confinement 24, 87, 103
The Pilgrim's Progress iii, 1, 9, 19
The Prisoner's Tale iii
The Prisons Handbook 29, 128-9
The Profession of Violence 22
The Profile of a Gentleman 76
The Quare Fellow 17, 52, 80, 86, 157
The Rime of the Ancient Mariner 92
The Silent Scream and Other Poems 72-4, 96 171
The Struggle for Penal Reform 152, 157
The Sweeney 77-8, 97
The Thief's Journal 94-5
The Truth About Dartmoor 11
The Verb 147

The Villain's Tale 95
The Weak and the Wicked 45
Thomas, Dylan 76
Thompson, Hunter 93
Thompson, J. Lee 46
Thomson, William 183
Three Clear Sundays 76, 118
Thus Spake Zarathustra 96
Tightrope - a Matter of Life and Death 47-8, 96, 116
Tisdall, Caroline 191
Tolkein, J.R.R. 96
Tumim, Sir Stephen 165, 178
Turner, Jimmy 12
Tynan, Kenneth 17, 157

Underworld 40

Verlaine, Paul iii, 5
Viccei, Valerio 27-9, 52, 105-7, 117-9, 124-5, 130, 140, 171, 191
Voltaire iii

Walker, Jimmy 68, 108, 176
Walking Away 27
Wall, Bruce 80
Wallace, Edgar 95
Walls Have Mouths 11-3, 94
Ward, Judith 50-2, 119, 160
Warner, Dee 181
Watson, Ian 68, 89
Waugh, Auberon 57
Wayne, Peter 57-9, 88, 95, 116, 129, 144, 157, 185, 191
Who Lie In Gaol 45-6, 93, 110, 152
Wickham, Tim 142
Wild Things 79

Index

Wilde, Oscar iv, 1-3, 7, 13,18, 19, 30, 35, 41, 52, 72, 76, 81, 85, 91-5, 103, 109, 157, 174-5, 191
Wildeblood, Peter 154
Willetts, Phoebe
Williams, John 186-7
Williams, Matthew 68-9, 89-90, 96, 130, 136-8, 145-8, 162, 170, 189, 192
Williams, Prof. Brian 81-2, 155-6, 164, 188
Wilson, Colin 82, 106, 120-1
Wilson, Howard 65, 72
Wilson, Reg 104
Winters, Larry 52, 72-4, 96, 171, 191
Within These Walls 57
Wolfe, Tom 93
Woodward, Rosie 149
Woolridge, Charles Thomas 5
Words from Within 121
Wrigglesworth, John 67, 131
Wright, Kit 121
Writers in Prison iv, 136
Wyner, Ruth 49-50, 142-3

X, Malcolm 97
X, Michael 97

Yield to the Night 45-6
Young, Graham 82

Zeno 35-6, 93, 110, 113-6, 127, 154, 160, 163
Zephaniah, Benjamin 97-8, 114, 125-6, 169

www.ingramcontent.com/pod-product-compliance
Lightning Source LLC
Chambersburg PA
CBHW050629300426
44112CB00012B/1722